MIXING IT UP

Book Seven, Louann Atkins Temple Women and Culture Series

Multiracial

Subjects

MIXING
IT UP

Edited by SanSan Kwan
and Kenneth Speirs

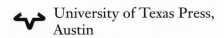 University of Texas Press,
Austin

Requests for permission to reproduce material from this work
should be sent to Permissions, University of Texas Press,
P.O. Box 7819, Austin, TX 78713-7819.

⊛ The paper used in this book meets the minimum requirements of
ANSI/NISO Z39.48-1992 (R1997) (Permanence of Paper).

Library of Congress Cataloging-in-Publication Data

Mixing it up : multiracial subjects / edited by SanSan Kwan and Kenneth Speirs.
      p.   cm. — (Louann Atkins Temple women & culture series ; bk. 7)
    Includes bibliographical references.
    ISBN 0-292-70585-9 ((cl.) : alk. paper) — ISBN 0-292-74345-9 ((pbk.) : alk. paper)
    1. Racially mixed people—Race identity—United States.   2. Racially mixed people—
United States—Intellectual life.   3. Racially mixed people—United States—Biography.
4. United States—Race relations.   5. Pluralism (Social sciences)—United States.   6. Performing arts—Social aspects—United States.   7. Racially mixed people in literature.
8. Ethnicity in literature.   9. Popular culture—United States.   I. Kwan, SanSan.
II. Speirs, Kenneth.   III. Series.
E184.A1M569   2004
305.8'0092'273—dc22

                                                                                    2004002874

For Kai

CONTENTS

PREFACE

Naomi Zack

Overall, the contributors to this anthology write themselves, and I think that they do so in a way that makes it possible for readers to read themselves in these pages. How is that possible when out of a population close to 300 million, only 7 million self-identified by checking more than one box for race on the 2000 United States Census? While I agree with Stefanie Dunning that contemporary portrayals of multiracial Americans as saviors and redeemers of this country's problems with race are premature, if not naïve and false, I want to suggest that there is something about the discomfort of being more than one race in the United States which speaks to a universal aspect of the human condition. This discomfort does not stem from the fact that everyone is racially mixed. Not everyone is racially mixed, and neither are they racially pure. Since its inception during the age of discovery, the modern biological idea of race has always posited a taxonomy of human races that was supposed to have a basis in the science of biology. Over the twentieth century, the biological sciences retreated from supporting such a taxonomy, first by separating the inheritance of culture from the inheritance of biological race, and second by concluding that physical variation among humans is too continuous to support anything like what society posits as racial divisions. To be sure, children resemble their parents if their parents resemble each other, but the heritability of physical traits deemed racial in society is not enough to support a biological taxonomy of race. And even though human groups are believed to have spent different amounts of time in distinctive geographical areas, we are a migratory species, and there is no way to determine how much ancestral time in a given place is enough to define racial membership in any scientific sense. Since there are no races in current biological understanding, there can be no mixed races. That is why it is not the case that we are all mixed.

The universal dimension of the essays herein relates to their moments of truth about the unreality of race, which is something that applies to all human beings. To the extent that social race rests on false biological beliefs—and I think that is a large extent—race is fictive. This is not to say that people do not act as though race is real, and it is not to say that a simple cognitive apprehension of the falsity of race is sufficient to do away with racism. Humankind has held all sorts of harmful and hateful superstitions that have deformed the lives of groups and individuals. You do not have to stand in the truth in order to hurt someone. But if you do stand in the truth, or stumble onto it, or find yourself forced into it, then you may be in a position to do yourself, and those who listen to you, some good.

The fiction of race has been a totalizing fiction. People are not supposed to be Black or White or Asian in the same way that they are tall or selfish or old. Rather, people are supposed to belong to certain races in a way that characterizes them as whole persons. The taxonomy of race has divided humankind into fictive subspecies. The result is that one is Black or White or Asian in the same way that one is *Homo sapiens* or that other living beings are dogs or tigers or bears. The whole person is supposed to be defined by her racial label, and one is not usually allowed to make up such labels to fit one's individuality. Therefore, when none of the available labels fits, a person is driven to question her identity, to reinvent an identity, to reinvent a self. If the multiracial person does so on the grounds of race, by writing a new racial identity for herself, as, for instance, Carole DeSouza suggests that Cherríe Moraga has done in *Loving in the War Years*, well, in that case she is still working within the grand paradigm of race.

Nonetheless, I think that the soul-searching and extremely situated and personal nature of multiracial theory, which is what this collection substantially presents, is an existential moment in academic letters. I agree with SanSan Kwan and Kenneth Speirs that Raquel Scherr Salgado properly identifies mixed-race theory as many theories stemming from first-person narratives. One questions the grounds of one's particular existence because one's situation forces one to do that or else lose the vitality of conscious presence. In questioning those grounds, one ends up questioning the grounds of everyone's existence, which are normally taken for granted. That is, it is not a question of whether I am specifically Black or White or Asian, but whether I have a race at all, something that everyone is supposed to have. The result of questioning such as this is unsettling, but strangely revitalizing and regrounding. So, when Adrian Carton, the paternal son of Anglo-Indians and the maternal son of

Britishers, emigrates from the United Kingdom to Australia, his only peers are other dislocated multinationals. But when he visits the ancestral homeland of his longing—India—his failure to see anything familiar there, anything which he has not already experienced in previous displacements, turns him into a skeptic about the whole notion of home. Or, when Richard Guzman nostalgically idealizes the state of California as a comfortable place for interracial couples, he also realizes that it is the California in his mind which he is envisioning as the world in which his multiracial children will one day live, a world that their very existence might help to create.

There is nothing easy about mixed-race identity, despite its apparent privileges and despite the middle-class status of most of these writers. Membership in the middle class is psychically costly because it imposes exacting social disciplines, especially in academia. There had to be middle-class multiracial Americans before such a thing as multiraciality could even have a voice on a printed page, but the price is that typically their complaints are of middle-class accountability, complaints about constantly having to say what one is, about having one's feelings hurt for not being what others want, about the injuries caused by social judgments—and stares. Mixed-race middle-class people offend the sensibilities of those who live in the fictive taxonomy of three or four races, and those offended lash out. They think they have a right to do this. They do not, but one has to contend with them anyway. Orathai Northern and Alice White separately narrate such strategies of surviving in the middle class, expressing forms of resistance that attest to the courage required to overcome everyone's Aunt Grace's expectations—about anything. But Aunt Grace has two forms really: women and the media. It is not accidental that most who write about mixed race are women and that most of the mixed-race symbols in the mass media are women. Women are the main players in the politics of the family. Women have traditionally enforced the racial identities and purities of American families, and women, now financially independent and politically and intellectually empowered, can revise such strictures. I do not think it is accidental that the multiracial performers who enact issues of American ethnicity, as discussed by Cathy Irwin and Sean Metzger, are women. And, Tiger Woods notwithstanding, the same can be said about the mass media icons of mixed race, whom Evelyn Alsultany considers. The fact that women continue to be responsible for disproportionate amounts of compassion and communication in their roles as daughters, sisters, aunts, cousins, grandmothers, and friends, as well as wives and mothers, means that we are in many ways on the front lines of the negotiation of racial identities and perhaps, eventually, of all fictive racial taxonomies.

I want to thank SanSan Kwan and Kenneth Speirs for inviting me to write this preface. As a philosopher, I am usually in the company of those who cultivate personally removed words, and it is a pleasure to assist in introducing the writing of thinkers who are part of what their words represent.

Naomi Zack
Eugene, Oregon
August 30, 2002

ACKNOWLEDGMENTS

It is a pleasure to acknowledge our many debts to friends and colleagues. We would like to thank, first and foremost, the authors whose work is collected here. We are grateful to the anonymous readers from the University of Texas Press for their incisive comments and helpful suggestions. We feel greatly indebted to Theresa May, editor-in-chief at the University of Texas Press, for her patience and support, as well as her early interest in this project. Thanks also to Leslie Doyle Tingle, assistant managing editor at the University of Texas Press. A fellowship from the City University of New York enabled Kenneth Speirs to devote more time and energy to this book. And our gratitude to the sustaining presence of our families.

MIXING IT UP

INTRODUCTION

SanSan Kwan and Kenneth Speirs

We are always in negotiation, not with a single set of oppositions that place us always in the same relation to others, but with a series of different positionalities. Each has for us its point of profound subjective identification. And that is the most difficult thing.

—Stuart Hall, "What Is This 'Black' in Black Popular Culture?"

We began with the future. The origins of this collection are rooted in our imaginings of the future for people of mixed race. We are a newly married couple. We are also an interracial couple. When our thoughts occasionally, and excitedly, roam toward future events and experiences, we find ourselves wondering about our children. How will they live? How will they understand what it means to be both "Asian" and "White"? How will they choose to identify themselves? How will they be identified by others? How will these identifications influence their lives?

From these personal considerations of the future, we were moved to know more about the experiences of other mixed-race individuals. *Mixing It Up: Multiracial Subjects* is the result of our inquiry. We gather here ten autobiographical essays that narrate, from a personal perspective, the very diverse experiences of multiraciality. These wonderful essays were chosen based on our belief that the individual life offers the best response to both historical and contemporary erasures and misrecognitions of multiraciality. Writing their own lives now, these writers, we hope, inscribe multiraciality onto the future.

Historically, multiraciality in the United States has been a mark of shame and ignominy. The need to establish and sustain firm categories of race as a way to maintain White dominance in America left no place for the multiracial. Thus the mixed blood, who threatened these categories, was either monoracialized or represented as "deviant" and "pathological." As Michael Omi notes in the foreword to a recent collection on mixed-heritage Asian Americans, "The rigidity of the 'one-drop rule' of race, long-standing eugenic fears of racial pollution, and the persistence (until the 1967 Supreme Court decision in *Loving v. Virginia*) of antimiscegenation laws demonstrate how the color line historically has been policed in the United States" (xii).

In more recent years, we find thankfully that multiraciality has become a more visible and accepted feature of our cultural landscape. The phenomena of mixed-race marriages, multiracial families, interracial relationships, and cross-race adoption are on the rise. While some of our contributors take issue with the ways in which the United States Census 2000 recognizes and thus reifies racial categories—and also fails to recognize multiraciality as a category in itself—the Census is groundbreaking in that it now allows respondents to check more than one box for race, and it provides no less than thirty separate racial categories from which to choose, plus eleven different subcategories under "Hispanic ethnicity" and four additional write-in lines (Bureau of the Census). In the year 2000 there were more than 1.3 million mixed-race marriages in the United States (Campo-Flores et al. 40). As our contributor Richard Guzman notes, the reality of the mixed-race experience fuels a growing multiracial movement in America that boasts college clubs (Prism at Harvard and Spectrum at Stanford), magazines *(Interrace, New People, Mavin)*, and a growing body of impressive research and writing.[1] Multiracial figures in popular culture, we also notice, are enjoying increased visibility. Several of the essays in our collection explore the questions the new visibility of mixed-race stars such as Tiger Woods and Mariah Carey raise.

This is not, of course, to deny the persistence of acts of discrimination and violence toward interracial couples, as well as the very specific forms of prejudice that multiracial people experience, such as exclusion from "stable" racial categories, the enduring "What are you?" question, continual misrecognition, accusations of passing, and so forth.[2] The multiraciality confronts a culture dependent on visibility in order to name and to classify. The visual provides the context through which our limited categories of race are most often read and designated. We see, we label. Despite the well-known fact that race is a biological fiction, our fetishistic attachment to skin, hair, and body enables essentializing determinations. For many, the mixing of races poses a substantial threat to the ideal of racial purity.[3] The multiracial image upsets the existing visual cartography. As a result, a multiracial individual is often forced into a cartography that cannot ever fully accommodate her; parts of her must disappear.

Nevertheless, in contrast to the history of oppression and elision of mixed-race people, the current rise in multiraciality signals, for some, a utopian progression toward racelessness. According to this logic, the ideal is for all of us to eventually become one brown race. The possibility of a color-blind society provides an attractive solution to the pervasive challenges of our racialized world. Michael Omi provides us with several examples of this "solution." For instance, he observes that a 1996 *New York Times Magazine* article by Stanley Crouch declares in its title that "Race Is Over: Black, White, Red, Yellow—Same Difference" (xii). Speculating on the next one hundred years, Crouch argues that race will cease to be an important identity marker. Carrying this optimism further, Senator Bulworth, in Warren Beatty's 1998 film *Bulworth*, promotes intermarriage as the most effective way to end racism. To do away with race through mixed-race marriages, Bulworth reasons, is to do away with racism. "All we need," he raps, "is a voluntary, free-spirited, open-ended program of procreative racial deconstruction" (quoted in Omi, xii). Mixed-race marriages and children, according to this line of thinking, accelerate the movement away from racial identification and politics and toward a raceless society. With such a trend, claims a recent article in *Newsweek*, "the color line is fraying around us. . . . [and] with the rudest reminders of racism washed away, it will be a lot easier to tell ourselves that we finally have overcome" (quoted in Williams-León and Nakashima, 4). The vision of a color-blind society that has finally "overcome," that attaches no special meaning, and certainly no special rights or privileges, to an individual's race, resonates with American society's long-held valuing of abstractions such as "fair play" and "equal access and opportunity." In fact, for many the melting-pot ideals of equality and equal opportunity are central to American democracy.

While the historic representation of the mixed-race individual as tragic, pathological, or threatening is unsustainable, this collection argues that the seemingly egalitarian multicultural paradigm is similarly problematic. This melting-pot ideal avoids the challenges of race in favor of a kind of "brown washing." To embrace a "brown" or raceless society and to dispense with concepts of race are to deny the beauty there is in difference, a beauty that each of our unique essays reveals in its own way. Brown washing hopes to erase the ugly patterns of racism and in one grand gesture homogenize us all. This collection, on the contrary, is built on the desire to acknowledge these patterns and at the same time celebrate our differences. Such a celebration of differences is central to our imaginings of our children's lives, the genesis of this project. Our celebration, however, precisely acknowledges that not all mixes are the same. Each is a product of specific historical influences, racial hierarchies, and power relations that are not always in harmonious balance. In other words, the confluence of more than one so-called racial category into a single body clearly does not end racism. The varying histories of power and oppression are carried within the mixed-race body, and it is important to recognize these tensions. The challenge, we suggest, is for our children to understand themselves as not simply "brown," but as, for example, Chinese-English-Scottish-German-American all at once—with the various unequal histories that these identities carry.

But how do we do this? In an era preoccupied with racial classifications, how do we find a place that honors the multiplicity, as well as the particular histories, of mixed-race experiences without simply creating another encompassing box? The great diversities of individual mixed-race genealogies are difficult to subsume under one politically efficacious category. What's more, even to talk about a concept of mixed race is itself to reify racial categories, with mixed race being simply a combination of various separable, but stable, classifications. The concept of mixed race, we must recognize, carries the danger of reinscribing monoracial paradigms.

This collection of autobiographical essays is based on the belief that, by virtue of its place outside of established racial and ethnic designations, multiraciality is not generalizable. Abstract discourses on race, which attempt to define and to fix, cannot fully apprehend multiraciality. Thus, we propose that the personal is the best avenue to understanding that which is necessarily unclassifiable. It is only through the individual lived experiences of mixed-race people that we can understand the plural nature of multiraciali*ties*.

Mixing It Up: Multiracial Subjects opens with essays from two leading scholars in the field of mixed-race studies. These articles identify major issues in the field and thus provide some necessary context for the essays that follow. In "American Mixed Race: The United States 2000 Census and Related Issues," Naomi Zack explores the treatment of mixed race in the most recent United States census. In her estimation this treatment reflects long-held misunderstandings about race and racial identification in America, particularly erroneous ideas about the biological basis of race. These misunderstandings, supported by notions of racial purity, have been accompanied by a general denial of mixed-race identity. Zack considers education and activism as ways of achieving mixed-race identity recognition—on the heuristic grounds that such recognition will ultimately disabuse Americans of their false beliefs in the biological reality of race.

Raquel Scherr Salgado's "Misceg-narrations" outlines the overarching argument for our collection. Surveying the recent history of racial theory in the United States, Salgado argues that in the late 1960s and early 1970s the politics of identity, reacting against the hegemony of White and Eurocentric discourse, necessarily essentialized ethnic difference, thereby subsuming other histories, languages, cultures, and experiences that did not quite fit. This strategic essentializing has more recently been replaced by poststructuralist theories of conditionality and contingency. The problem with this new shift, Salgado observes, is that politics or theory that slips and slides cannot be very efficacious. Theories necessarily stand outside the contingencies of experience, working instead to define, categorize, and classify. This means, however, that theory cannot fully account for the complexity of an experiential moment, which is both emotional *and* intellectual. Thus, Salgado asks, where does that leave those of us who are of mixed race, who hover on the margins of one and another ethnicity, who incorporate paradox and contradiction, and who depend on nuanced language to translate experience? Can we have a theory?

Her highly compelling answer to this crucial question, in fact, provides the framework for this project, a collection of personal essays that "theorize" the experience of multiraciality. Salgado argues that any development of multiracial theory will be difficult unless it grows out of personal narrative. Increasingly, postmodern theorists have used the self as a referent and relied on autobiography and memoir as a genre, acknowledging in the act the need to make theory performative and, at the same time, concrete. Any theory addressing mixed race, of necessity, will resurrect both author and work to central positions precisely because the mixed-race experience is so individualized it needs the universalizing resources of literature to communicate itself. That is, if theories of multiraciality are to be written, if they are to do the work of inscribing the multiracial into U.S. society, they must be written in ways that are personal, experiential, contingent, performative, and yet still insistent. In particular, the essay represents an ideal model because it combines theory and personal reflection. A multiracial theory, inspired by the personal essay, can make an individual story universal, because only such a theory can show us that we are, and are not, so different.

Zack's and Salgado's essays lay the foundation for exploring the multiracial subjects narrated in the personal essays that follow. It should be noted that our collection is unique not only in its combination of the personal and the theoretical, but also in its expansion beyond the traditional Black/White discourse of multiraciality in the United States.[4] The writers included in *Mixing It Up* narrate a wide variety of multiracial heritages, including: Anglo-Indian, Iraqi-Cuban, Eurasian, Mexican-Jewish, Korean-German-Irish adopted by White American parents, and Asian adopted by Black American parents. In addition, our essays move in and out of the United States and other locales, recognizing the always already transnational nature of multiraciality.

The first essay in our collection, Adrian Carton's "A Passionate Occupant of the Transnational Transit Lounge," dramatizes the dynamics of likeness and difference that are central to the mixed-race experience. As the title of his intriguing essay suggests, Carton, who is of mixed European and South Asian origin, takes us on a global journey, from his early childhood in 1970s Britain to his migration to Australia in the 1980s, and through numerous transit lounges in Los Angeles, Bangkok, and other places along the way. As he moves, he narrates his struggles with his sense of belonging, of home, feeling always and everywhere that his home is elsewhere. Thus India as a mythic home occupies an increasingly urgent place in Carton's imagination; finally he "returns" to India, only to recognize that here, too, his sense of self is fraught with uncertainty and complication, as is India itself. The piece explores the multiplicity of his South Asian Eurasian experience, as categories of hybrid racial description change within spaces of national context and transnational traveling. On a more theoretical level, Carton discusses the ways in which the nation-state narrates itself by configuring citizenship—and thereby identity—through a process of inclusion and exclusion. Each nation's process differs, but in his experience they all give the Eurasian no home at all except the home of the imagination, the home of the transnational transit lounge.

As with Carton's imaginings of India as a mythic home, Richard Guzman in "Miscegenation and Me" explores the greater freedom and possibility California offers mixed-race couples. Weaving together history, theory, and personal narrative, Guzman's essay surveys the history of interracial love in the United States. Contrasting the experiences of interracial couples in California with those in other parts of the United States, he sees California as a space of racial turbulence, and paradoxically perhaps as the racial "paradise" toward which the whole country may be moving. Noting the growing acceptance of interracial marriage, Guzman's essay points with hope to a future in which multiracial children might reconfigure the way we view (mixed) race.

Orathai Northern's beautiful essay, "'What Is She Anyway?'— Rearranging Bodily Mythologies," continues the exploration of geographies—actual and ideal—and multiracial subjectivity. The essay blends narratives of family, travel, kinship, and birth across distant and disparate spaces, connected through exchanges of (mis)identification and (mis)identifying gazes. In a personal meditation about traveling to and through spaces where her body signifies in familiar and unfamiliar registers, Northern (re)considers how visual economies of race shift and permutate depending on the landscape she inhabits and who is (mis)reading whom. Traveling within the Southern United States and South and Southeast Asia, Northern investigates the ways in which she maps race onto others and race is mapped onto her. She hopes to make legible her own vexed investments in racial codes, codes that she uneasily relies upon at times, and challenges at others, recognizing them as mutable social constructs that often perpetuate biologism and essentialism.

Alice White's "Resemblance" similarly explores the situational, shifting nature of multiracial identity. Her essay employs the notion of resemblance, or physical likeness, to present the problem of identity formation and self-knowledge from the point of view of a mixed-race woman. Employing a fragmented personal voice and sometimes decontextualized depictions of momentary images, White's work is more like a prose poem than an expository essay. In its very form, then, it exemplifies the kinetic experience of multiraciality. White offers a series of anecdotes to gradually build a picture of an increasingly complex biracial identity. The stream of questioning voices and contradictory images eventuate in the author's ultimate sense of confusion and placelessness. Contributing to this sense, White, an American-born adoptee of Korean and German-Irish origin raised by a White family, does not see her likeness among her adoptive parents and siblings, her classmates, or her neighbors. She strives to recognize her image reflected in the mirror and in photographs, but the contradictions she finds only contribute to her doubt. This inability to find resemblance—to recognize herself and be recognized—impacts her sense of identity in complex and profound ways.

Further exploring the challenges of locating a multiracial self, Stefanie Dunning, in "'Brown Like Me': Explorations of a Shifting Self," interrogates several assumptions found in typical representations of mixed-race people. For example, she dismantles the notion that biracial people are "raceless," that they "combine the best of both races," and thereby transcend the racial divide. Dunning turns her attention to an investigation of the traditional literary characterization of the multi- or biracial subject as "the tragic mulatto," who must disavow some part of herself or narratively die in order that the identificatory conflict be solved. Resisting these notions of multiraciality, Dunning chooses in her own life to embrace the contradictions and complications of both discussing and representing multiraciality.

Evelyn Alsultany, in "Toward a Multiethnic Cartography: Multiethnic Identity, Monoracial Cultural Logic, and Popular Culture," similarly works to interrogate and reconceptualize existing notions of multiraciality. Using her personal experiences of misrecognition in social interactions as a starting point, Alsultany demonstrates that the current operating cartography of ethnic identity is too narrow to account for multiethnic identity. In seeking out ways to make our ethnic cartography more inclusive of multiethnic identity, Alsultany, whose father is Iraqi and whose mother is Cuban, considers the role of the media and examines representations of multiethnic celebrities in popular culture. Through her examination of various representations of Mariah Carey and Paula Abdul, she tracks the ways that their multiethnic identities are reinscribed as monoracial. In contrast, Alsultany examines the experiences of Tiger Woods and Melissa Howard and argues that their challenges to a monoracial cultural logic present at least the possibility of a shift in our conceptual mapping of ethnic identities.

In the co-authored "Keeping Up Appearances: Ethnic Alien-Nation in Female Solo Performance," Cathy Irwin and Sean Metzger enact a critical dialogue on the limits of autobiographical solo performance by examining the cases of two female multiracial performers in Los Angeles. Focusing on the personal in these performances, in addition to drawing on their own multiracial experiences, their essay raises and explores a number of intriguing questions: How does the multiracial body, narrating her personal history through the medium of live performance, negotiate an identity among dominant racial and ethnic minority communities? What is the specific role of the multiracial female body in the reproduction of ethnicity and American-ness? In what ways do different constituencies (theatrical venues, ethnic communities, and performers) invest in these performances, and what are the consequences of such commitments? This lively essay addresses these questions by looking at both Sandra Tsing Loh's *Aliens in America* and Paula Westin Solano's *Appearances*.

The tensions that Irwin and Metzger uncover in these performances are further examined in Carole DeSouza's "Against Erasure: The Multiracial Voice in Cherríe Moraga's *Loving in the War Years*." DeSouza contextualizes her argument by outlining the ways that the United States has institutionalized monoraciality as compulsory, rather than granting some individuals the right to exist as "both" of their parental races. DeSouza shows the ways in which we are socialized to accept the criterion of one race per person. For an individual to claim two or three races is to risk appearing schizophrenic or compromised. This essay then demonstrates how the tragic mulatto/a exemplifies social and political investments in racial disharmony and works to create fear in multiracials, who are cast as naturally inferior, pathological, and doomed. In search of a racially multiplicit voice of her own, DeSouza looks to an example of contemporary American literature that deconstructs American conceptualizations of "race." In DeSouza's keen analysis, Cherríe Moraga's *Loving in the War Years* proves a complex discursive site against historical erasure and the traditional negative literary interpretation of the multiracial. Moraga's recounting of her childhood monoracial socialization, her reinterpretation of blood as a measure of similarity, and her multilingual narrative, all culminate in a multiracial voice that challenges the "either/or" binary based on racial purity.

As Stuart Hall reminds us, "[w]e are always in negotiation." *Mixing It Up: Multiracial Subjects* lives in this fluid site of negotiation. These personal narratives, each reflecting different positionalities, demonstrate the various ways mixed race disrupts efforts to fix and to categorize. The lives written here struggle to overturn both past crimes and present discriminatory practices, while working to create new multiracial subjectivities. This is the most difficult thing, as Hall reminds us; this we believe is the most necessary thing.

Notes

1. In the area of critical studies see, for example, David Parker and Miri Song, eds., *Rethinking "Mixed Race"* (London: Pluto Press, 2001); William S. Penn, ed., *As We Are Now: Mixblood Essays on Race and Identity* (Berkeley and Los Angeles: University of California Press, 1998); Maria Root, ed., *Racially Mixed People in America* (Newbury Park, Calif.: Sage, 1992); Maria Root, ed., *The Multiracial Experience* (Newbury Park, Calif.: Sage, 1996); Werner Sollors, *Neither Black nor White Yet Both* (New York: Oxford University Press, 1997); Teresa Williams-León and Cynthia L. Nakashima, eds., *The Sum of Our Parts* (Philadelphia: Temple University Press, 2001); Naomi Zack, *Race and Mixed Race* (Philadelphia: Temple University Press, 1993); Naomi Zack, ed., *American Mixed Race: The Culture of Microdiversity* (Lanham, Md.: Rowman and Littlefield, 1995). In the area of memoir see, for example, James McBride, *The Color of Water: A Black Man's Tribute to His White Mother* (New York: Riverhead Books, 1996); Rebecca Walker, *Black, White, and Jewish: Autobiography of a Shifting Self* (New York: Riverhead Books, 2001); Gregory Williams, *Life on the Color Line: The True Story of a White Boy Who Discovered He Was Black* (New York: Penguin, 1996).

2. See Parker and Song, 3–4.

3. For example, Bob Jones University, until 2000, had a policy against interracial dating.

4. A search through Amazon.com calls up 106 titles under the category of

"mixed race." These books tend to fall under one of three categories: children's books such as *What Are You?: Voices of Mixed-Race Young People*, *Why Am I Different?*, and *The Colors of Us*; psychological studies such as *In the Best Interests of the Child: Culture, Identity, and Transracial Adoption*, *The Interracial Experience: Growing Up Black/White Racially Mixed in the United States*, and *Edgewalkers: Defining Cultural Boundaries on the New Global Frontier* (a book which one reviewer claims offers "'suggestions' for reconciling a multicultural person's identities and patterns of thought/behavior"); or memoirs like *The Color of Water: A Black Man's Tribute to His White Mother*, *Divided to the Vein: A Journey into Race and Family*, and *Black, White, and Jewish: Autobiography of a Shifting Self*. Over half of the titles in these categories deal specifically with the Black-White mix.

Works Cited

Bureau of the Census, U.S. Department of Commerce. *United States Census Form D-1 (UL)*. Washington, D.C.: U.S. Department of Commerce, 2000.

Campo-Flores, Arian, et al. "The New Face of Race." *Newsweek*, September 18, 2000, pp. 38–41.

Hall, Stuart. "What Is This 'Black' in Black Popular Culture?" In *Black Popular Culture*, ed. Gina Dent, pp. 21–33. Seattle: Bay Press, 1992.

Omi, Michael. "Foreword." In *The Sum of Our Parts: Mixed Heritage Asian Americans*, ed. Teresa Williams-León and Cynthia L. Nakashima, pp. ix–xiii. Philadelphia: Temple University Press, 2001.

Williams-León, Teresa, and Cynthia L. Nakashima. "Introduction: Reconfiguring Race, Rearticulating Ethnicity." In *The Sum of Our Parts: Mixed Heritage Asian Americans*, ed. Teresa Williams-León and Cynthia L. Nakashima, pp. 3–10. Philadelphia: Temple University Press, 2001.

———, eds. *The Sum of Our Parts: Mixed Heritage Asian Americans*. Philadelphia: Temple University Press, 2001.

I

Issues and Trends

1. AMERICAN MIXED RACE
The United States 2000 Census and Related Issues

Naomi Zack

INTRODUCTION

The average American, and many scholars as well, still believe that there is some coherent biological basis for the racial categories of Black, White, Indian, and Asian, and that relevant scientists have specialized information about the nature of that basis. Race, however, is a social construction on all levels. Not only are the links between so-called biological race and culture the result of history, tradition, and current norms, but the existence of biological racial taxonomies is itself the result of such social factors. If human races existed, then more people would be properly described as mixed race than are commonly thought to be. But, since human biological race is a fiction, so is mixed race.

Nonetheless, no matter how it is parsed, "race" remains a powerful social mechanism for distributing status and privilege in the United States, and the growing numbers of so-called mixed, biracial, or multiracial individuals are likely to remain an interesting and complex problem of taxonomy and identity for some time to come. Readers of this journal (book) are likely to approach the subject of race from legal backgrounds, with expectations of concrete arguments and specific advocacy.[1] As a philosopher, however, I offer a discussion that is more conceptually driven.

In Part I, I consider the treatment of race, and in particular, mixed race, in the U.S. Census. The logical and empirical weaknesses of commonsense beliefs about race and mixed race become evident through an examination of the Census 2000 questions pertaining to race. If common sense and the Census are vague and erroneous about the biological basis of race, this raises the question of what is precisely true. Therefore, in Part II, I offer a summary of current scientific findings about biological race. These findings indicate that the main problem with "race" in common sense is a failure to recognize that there is no biological basis for racial categories. But, since such commonsense illusions about race exist, it is important to note that they have been accompanied by a general denial of official recognition of mixed-race identity. This denial has supported ungrounded notions of racial purity. If race is (falsely) believed to be real, then mixed race ought to enjoy the same social status. Therefore, so long as beliefs in pure races persist in society, there would seem to be a need for a theoretical foundation that could be used for political and policy arguments that allow for the recognition of mixed-race identities. In Part III, I consider how neither the traditional individual-based model of pluralism, nor its group-based multicultural contender, supports mixed-race identity claims. Returning to the gap between common sense and science, in Part IV, I consider education and activism as ways of achieving mixed-race identity recognition, on the heuristic grounds that such recognition will ultimately disabuse Americans of their false beliefs in the biological reality of race.

I. THE U.S. CENSUS

As David Goldberg argues, although the U.S. Census is now broadly regarded as a valuable resource for corporate planning and a basis for many different kinds of government allocations and representation, it has not provided a stable system of racial categorization from decade to decade. There is, thus, no precise numerical basis for historical comparison of racial demographics. The shifting racial taxonomies have not reflected changes in scientific consensus about race, but have expressed political power, social attitudes, and economic interests. Racial categorization first appeared in the 1850 Census, when under the general group of free persons, Whites were not counted by race under "Color" and mulattoes were counted separately from Blacks. By the 1890 count, distinctions were made within the mulatto group down to "one-eighth or any trace of black blood." The "one-drop rule," whereby Black designation resulted from any Black ancestry, no matter how remote, became the social rule of the land by 1900, and it was adopted by the Census in 1930 (Goldberg 1995, 240; Williamson, 98–129). Anthropologists use the term "hypodescent" to describe practices, such as the one-drop rule, for categorizing children with mixed racial parentage by assigning them to the parental racial category with the lowest social status (Davis). Hence, the American one-drop rule also required that any degree of blackness in mixtures between Black and Chinese or Black and Indian ancestry result in Black designation. As applied beyond the Black category, the one-drop rule required that mixtures of White and Asian or White and Indian result in Asian or Indian designation, respectively. In the 1980 and 1990 Censuses, a new formulation developed—ethnicity, as Hispanic or non-Hispanic (replacing what was formerly labeled "Spanish"), came to be counted separately from race, but the one-drop rule remained in effect for racial categorization.[2]

In all of the census counts through 1990, an individual's race was supposed to be indicated by checking only one of the boxes presumed to correspond to the main social racial categories. Thus, there was no allowance for mixed-race identification, although the category "other" was recognized in the 1980 and 1990 censuses, and on many local record-keeping forms. During the early 1990s, advocates for the federal recognition of mixed-race identities succeeded to the extent that the "check only one box" rule for race was rescinded in the Census 2000.[3] This appeared to be the beginning of official recognition of mixed race in the United States. Consider the text of the Census 2000 short form questions 8 and 9, which pertain to ethnicity and race.

NOTE: Please answer BOTH questions 8 and 9.
8. Is Person 1 Spanish/Hispanic/Latino? Mark X the "No" box if not Spanish/Hispanic/Latino.
__ No, not Spanish/Hispanic/Latino　　　　__ Yes, Puerto Rican
__ Yes, Mexican, Mexican Am., Chicano　　__ Yes, Cuban
__ Yes, other Spanish/Hispanic/Latino—*Print group*

_____

9. What is Person 1's race? Mark X *one or more races to indicate what this person considers himself/herself to be.*
__ White
__ African Am., or Negro
__ American Indian or Alaska Native—Print name of enrolled or principal tribe _____
__ Asian Indian　　__ Japanese　　　__ Native Hawaiian
__ Chinese　　　　__ Korean　　　　__ Guamanian or Chomorro
__ Filipino　　　　__ Vietnamese　　__ Samoan
__ Other Asian—Print race _____
__ Some other race—Print race _____
(Bureau of the Census)

Several aspects of questions 8 and 9 are theoretically interesting, if not fascinating. In question 8, the general category, "Spanish/Hispanic/Latino" is not identified as racial or ethnic, and it is presumed that respondents already know the criteria for self-inclusion in one or another of the subcategories. Common sense alone yields many such criteria: language, national origin, culture of origin, culture of marriage or adoption, ancestral national origin, name (both given and surname), and appearance. No allowance is made that a person might identify as more than one of the subcategories, such as Cuban and Puerto Rican, or that a person might be both Spanish/Hispanic/Latino and not-Spanish/Hispanic/Latino, for instance, German and Spanish.

In question 9, the phrase "considers himself/herself to be" clearly bases racial categorization on self-identification. It is remarkable in this regard that no guidelines are available for making this identification, for instance: race of ancestors, culture of origin, geographical origins of ancestors, or appearance. The list of racial boxes does not distinguish between presumptive biological racial groups and racial groups based on national origin. That is, "White" and "Black" are presumptive biological groups, whereas all of the other listed groups refer to national origin. The designation "other Asian" suggests that respondents already know that the group names from "Asian Indian" to "Samoan" refer to Asians, although "Asian" itself is nowhere defined.

The lack of either explicitly structured taxonomies or criteria for membership in specific categories suggests that those who composed the census form assumed that Americans have unequivocal and ready answers to questions about their identities in the Spanish/Hispanic/Latino category and in terms of race. And since these answers were deemed worthwhile to collect, it must have been further assumed that they were accurate according to some *unstated* criteria for ethnic and racial categorization. If there are no independent criteria for racial identification, apart from ordinary practices and perceptions, which, as we shall see in the next section, are not coherent, then the data collected through the census cannot be as informative as they purport to be.

While mixed race is not mentioned explicitly in question 9, those who identify as mixed usually do so on the basis of known ancestry of more than one race. Therefore, the Census 2000 almost explicitly, and for the first time in American history, allows for mixed-race identity in ways that *appear* to do more than create subcategories within nonwhite races; i.e., the one-drop rule does not *appear* to be active in this enumeration. Although, without an application of a one-drop rule, there is a dizzying array of possible racial categories. In March 2000, when the government began distributing the census forms, the *New York Times* reported that the five racial categories and their possible combinations would yield sixty-three recognized racial categories, a number that would be doubled by the options in the "Spanish/Hispanic/Latino" category. Official plans, however, for interpreting the data tell a different story. Anita Hodgkiss, deputy assistant attorney general for civil rights, commented on the Clinton administration's policy concerning interpretation of the data: "The

first allocation rule is that if you are white and anything else, you are al-
located to the minority." Sally Katzen, counsel to the director of the Bud-
get Office, reported that this allocation rule "reflected a determination
that people who have suffered discrimination in the past should be subject
to certain protections" (Holmes 2000b). Thus, the justification for this
application of the old one-drop rule is that it is a response to lobbied requests by civil rights groups that the new classifications not "dilute the
power and protection of minorities in the enforcement of antidiscrimi-
nation and voting rights laws" (Holmes 2000b). The pill of hypodescent
is thus turned into a placebo, sweetened by referring to all of the racial
categories other than "White" as "minorities," rather than "nonwhite."
One local paper went so far as to paraphrase Hodgkiss's statement in a
headline that turned "minority" into a noun: "Census Will Count Mixed-
Race People as Minorities" (Holmes 2000a).[4] While the word "minority"
may now be a euphemism for "nonwhite racial group" or even "member
of a nonwhite racial group," its traditional literal meaning is "the smaller
number in a political body" or "the group having less than the number of
votes necessary to control" (Webster's, 536). But few who work toward
and hope for racial egalitarianism in the United States believe that when
nonwhites, both presumptively pure and mixed, are no longer numerical
minorities, racial equality will thereby automatically be achieved. Indeed,
in South Africa, as well as many locales in the American South, Blacks
have been racial majorities under conditions of extreme antiblack racism
and oppression (Omond).

It should be noted that despite the rich array of possibilities for racial
identification, the Census 2000 does not allow respondents to reject racial
identification completely or even to identify as "mixed" without specify-
ing how they are mixed. The use of the one-drop rule in interpreting biracial and multiracial categorization will be received as supportive of the
rights of those who belong to groups that have suffered race-based discrimination in the past. But the new one-drop rule, like the old, which was
instigated to make sure that everyone who might possibly qualify for race-
based discrimination would be forced to do so, does not seriously allow
for the recognition of mixed-race identity. Paradoxically, an examination
of the flimsiness of all presumptively biological racial identity illuminates
why the recognition of mixed-race identities is important.

II. CONTEMPORARY SCIENCE AND RACE

The contemporary biological human sciences do not support commonsense notions of racial taxonomy. While such notions vary and cannot

often be stated with precision, until very recently, American school-children have been taught that there are three main human racial groups—Black, White, and Asian—a taxonomy that was upheld in anthropology textbooks and general-reader encyclopedia entries under the word "race" throughout the twentieth century. Obvious biological facts that are now broadly accepted undermine such notions, as do more sophisticated accounts of the history of *Homo sapiens* in population genetics. Let us begin with the broad facts. In the eighteenth and nineteenth centuries, biologists posited racial essences inherited through the blood as a physical as well as psychological and cultural determinant of racial identity.[5] This notion has never found empirical support. No specific essences of race have ever been identified for the main social racial groups, either in the blood or any other component of human physiology or genetics. The lack of proof for the existence of racial essences makes it highly improbable, if not impossible, that there is any general racial factor for each of the racial groups that determines more specific traits associated with racial membership (Zack 1994, 114 n. 1). The lack of general racial factors means that there is no known biological method by which racial identities could cause either specific physical racial traits or nonphysical psychological or cultural traits associated with race. There is also independent evidence that the nonphysical differences associated with race are the result of historical events, tradition, and culture, evidence that anthropologists have accepted since the 1930s.[6] For instance, human talents are distributed irrespective of racial groups. Many traditions develop as the result of historical events, and there are cultural commonalities between racial groups and diversity within them.

The recognized environmental and historical causes of those cultural and psychological traits associated with distinct racial groups means that the human capital represented by culture is in principle attainable by all human beings, regardless of their designated racial groups. This "equal opportunity" view of human culture is widespread among scholars, scientists, and others concerned with social justice and remedies for racism. A recent expression of this view is the 1998 American Anthropological Association "Statement on 'Race.'" Prior to this pronouncement, the United Nations sponsored statements on racism that were published in the 1950s and '60s.[7] During the last third of the twentieth century, however, the egalitarian view of the acquisition of cultural assets was often opposed by members of nonwhite racial groups who sought to support the identities of their groups on the basis of cultural traditions and practices valued by them. The right to distinctive race-based group cultural identities has come to be generally accepted as a necessary component of democratic pluralism, and it is usually referred to as "multiculturalism."[8] In ordinary usage, except when the term "ethnicity" is used as a synonym for "race," the cultural aspect of group identity is called "ethnic" if the group in question is racially white (e.g., Italian, German, and Jewish *ethnic* identities as developed in the United States) and "racial" if the group is African American, Asian American, or American Indian (e.g., Black, Asian, and Indian *racial* identities). Some contemporary scholars view ethnicity as a matter of culture and race as a matter of (presumptive) biology. Insofar as race is biologically false, but ethnicity is pervasive in daily life and universal as a narrative and social science subject, the restriction of biology to "race" and culture and psychology to "ethnicity" is useful for analytic purposes.[9] This line having been drawn, it can safely be said that distinctive ethnic practices, which are often assumed to be linked to distinctive racial identities, are in themselves worth preserving. The right to participate in, maintain, and pass on the distinctive ethnic practices of what are, mistakenly or not, thought to be different racial lineages is often part of what is claimed by those who advocate for the recognition of mixed-race identities.

Just as there is independent evidence of the causal separation between race and culture that precludes biological determinism, there is also evidence of great (relative) biological diversity within the main socially determined racial groups. Contemporary biologists agree that there is greater diversity within so-called racial groups than between them. Within *Homo sapiens*, there is an average genetic difference of .2 percent, or 1/500. The racial part of this difference is 6 percent, which is .012 percent, or less than 1/8000 of any human's genetic material (Appiah, 68–69; Templeton, 632–650; Angier). Furthermore, the physical traits in which human beings differ in ways identified as racial do not all get inherited together but disperse and recombine at conception, when individuals are formed, with half of their genetic material coming from each parent. The lack of racial essences, the high degree of variation of presumptive racial traits within racial groups, the great genetic similarity of all humans, and the facts of genetic recombination preclude the possibility of an empirical foundation for biological racial identity (Montagu).[10]

Thus far, I have discussed the possibility of a biological foundation for race based on similarity or difference among human groups and individuals existing at the same time. Population genetics tracks human migrations since the origin of modern *Homo sapiens* in Africa. From the perspective of this migration, or diaspora, the traits of skin, hair, and skeletal structure associated with race are viewed as *clines*, because they vary continuously over large geographical areas and on that basis exist in continua rather than discrete categories. L. Luca Cavalli-Sforza and his colleagues, who worked on mapping human evolutionary history, have found it possible to identify human geographical groups in ways that roughly correspond to races (1994). But since the classifications are based on probable ancestry, rather than similarity or difference, they do not provide an objective foundation for race, unless location in a certain place at a certain time is arbitrarily used to indicate racial identity. For instance, the current evolutionary account posits original ancestors of modern humans as occupying Africa approximately 140,000 years ago. About 70,000 years ago, some members of that group are believed to have migrated to Asia and, after that, to Europe and the Americas (Cavalli-Sforza 2000, 57–66). On this model, there is no independent way to divide humans into Blacks, Whites, and Asians. The question of how to classify human beings based on the continental origins of their ancestors can be answered only by making arbitrary classifications based on time spans of habitation. Neither can it be claimed, without begging the question, that we are all Africans because our ancestors originated in Africa, if by "African" is meant "Black" or "Negro" in a racial sense.[11]

Given the great degree of human migration and intermixture between groups with different ancestral origins, some writers have claimed that we are all mixed race. (But note that there cannot be mixed race or mixed races unless there are races beforehand.) Had human history been different, with less migration and more isolation between groups, human races might have evolved. But this did not happen, and not even stringent regimes of White purity and segregation have succeeded in accomplishing it. Most writers on the subject of American Black-White miscegenation, for instance, estimate that 70 to 90 percent of African Americans have White ancestry—whatever that could mean in *racial* terms, given the lack of any biological foundation for race itself (Blackburn, 3).

Despite the lack of biological foundation, what is thought of as racial distinction continues to have a powerful social effect on reality in American life. This is because the social categories of race are the result of history. The modern concept of biological race was invented during the period of European colonialism in order to establish and perpetuate European domination over the inhabitants of Africa, Asia, and the Americas.[12] It is in this social, economic, and political context that demands for a different system or order of racial recognition, by individuals who view themselves or their children as mixed race, must be addressed.

III. MODELS OF PLURALISM

Keeping in mind that racial categories are social constructions, two models for pluralism in American contexts emerged in an attempt to provide justice for those whose group identities were disadvantageous. The first model was developed in response to ethnic diversity during the great waves of European immigration in the early twentieth century. Ethnic pluralism, at that time, was based on a melting-pot ideal of equality and nondiscrimination in public life. Individuals of different national origins, languages, and customs were expected and encouraged to adopt the identity of generic, nonethnic Americans in public and civic life.[13] The second model of pluralism was driven by race-based egalitarian projects beginning in the 1960s. Members of nonwhite racial groups, particularly African Americans and Native Americans, have argued for the right to retain and have their nonwhite identities as fully functional in civic and public life.[14] It is not accidental that the subject of the first model is an individual who can be conceptualized as ethnically neutral, whereas the subject of the second model is a group defined by its ethnicity or race. Thus, the first pluralistic model emphasizes public neutrality of *ethnic* identity, and the second pluralistic model emphasizes public distinctiveness of *racial* identity. Inasmuch as the first model has individuals as its subject, it has been closer to the legal model for rights in the United States. The second, group-based model has functioned more as a moral critique of the individual legal model than as a legal model itself.

The discourse of rights in American history has always focused on the rights of individuals and not even individuals as members of particular groups. Thus, both the civil rights legislation and revision of immigration laws in the 1960s addressed the rights of individuals to be free of discrimination. For example, the Civil Rights Act of 1964 prohibits discrimination against *individuals* on the grounds of race in all major American institutions, the Voting Rights Act of 1965 protects the voting rights of all Americans as *individuals*, and the 1965 Immigration Act forbids the exclusion of *individuals* based on race or national origin (Glazer, 136).

In recent decades, this individual subject of rights in situations of racial discrimination has been criticized as a symbol of an impossible ideal because positing such a subject assumes a nonexistent neutrality. The critique is that individuals do not appear in public and civic contexts with undetermined racial identity, so that it can be stipulated that their race is not to be a reason for discrimination.[15] Rather, racial identity is believed to be immediately attached to individuals at all times, in all places, and in ways that shape how laws are created and applied. This belief has led to arguments that the subjects of egalitarian legal discourse ought to be affirmatively identified by race from the outset rather than negatively protected on the basis of race after the fact.[16]

The Census 2000 becomes even more interesting in terms of the individual model as compared to the group model. The census form is meant to be filled out by individuals about themselves. The protest against the interpretation of multiple boxes without the application of one-drop rules was brought not by individuals but by an organization, the National Association for the Advancement of Colored People (NAACP) (Holmes 2000b). The NAACP has vested privileges to protect and represents the rights of African Americans as a *group*. African Americans are a recognized racial group with a social history, traditions of liberation, and at this time, hard-won recognition of their civil rights. In recent years, the arguments against official mixed-race identities have often been implicit within racial scholarship, varied discussion fora, and the media. These arguments include: a multiplicity of recognized mixed-race categories will create social confusion; in the case of Black and White mixed race, individuals allowed to be "not-Black" will defect from membership in the Black community, to the detriment of neighborhood and family ties; the recognition of people who are mixed with Black ancestry may deprive Blacks of political representation and moral power as a special interest and advocacy group because they will be fewer in number; and mixed-race people have a long history of wanting the best of both worlds, both White privilege and special consideration for being members of minority groups—and it is not fair that they should have these unique advantages.[17] A critique of these objections to mixed-race identity would include: social confusion about race is not a bad thing if racial categories are confused and unfounded to begin with; special interest coalitions are possible among nonwhite groups; the historical advantages of mixed-race people occurred before Black Americans had a recognized voice, but this is no longer the case; and mixed-race people tell a different story about their alleged advantages.[18]

Most important is the question of whether mixed-race individuals have a right to be recognized as members of groups different from the nonwhite groups in which they have partial ancestry. On an individualist model of pluralism, they would seem to have the same right to claim racial identities as do individuals who identify as members of groups falsely believed to be racially pure. The 126 possible categories of mixed race enabled by the current census, however, do not yet exist as recognized groups. Therefore, on a group-based model of pluralism, mixed-race people have not yet been constructed as rights-bearing subjects. This is partly why mixed-race identities are at this time perceived as deviant and antisocial by the "mainstream." Another reason is that the U.S. Supreme Court struck down all remaining state laws against racial intermarriage in its 1967 opinion in *Loving v. Virginia*, and the national phenomenon of mixed-race individuals born in legal marriages is relatively new. But despite the novelty, this group of mixed-race children has been both publicly visible and fast growing—estimated to have increased from 500,000 in the mid-1960s to over 2 million in the late 1990s.[19]

A comparison of the majority opinion in *Loving v. Virginia* with a decision in *Jane Doe v. State of Louisiana* (hereinafter the Phipps case), brought in opposition to the one-drop rule, is instructive in regard to the workings of the individualistic model of pluralism. In *Loving v. Virginia*, the appellee argued for retention of antimiscegenation law in the state of Virginia on the grounds of the desirability of "racial integrity" (11). The Court's decision was based on the premise that marriage is a basic social liberty, which could not be regulated on what Justice Warren called the "invidious" basis of racial difference alone (12). Inasmuch as a liberty is what individuals are not constrained from doing by law, this decision would seem to be an application of a more general doctrine of individual rights.

Now consider the Phipps case, decided by the Fourth Circuit Court of Appeals in Louisiana and refused review by the Louisiana Supreme Court and the United States Supreme Court. Susie Guillory Phipps was denied White identity because, at the time of her birth, her parents had considered themselves and her to be "colored" (371). This ruling was made despite the fact that Phipps looked White, thought of herself as White, and "had twice married as white" (371). The Louisiana appellate court noted that racial classification of individuals was "scientifically insupportable" and claimed that racial perceptions were purely social (372). The relevant question was taken to be whether Phipps's parents had correctly recorded her race based on social perceptions, and it was concluded that they had (372).[20] The higher courts apparently did not disagree. In this case, an individual's choice of racial identity is not accorded the same protection from regulation as is the choice of a marriage partner. Neither is a racial identity claim or denial taken to be justified or not justified on the basis of group rights. If Phipps is Black as an adult because, according to social perceptions at her birth, it was correct to consider her Black at that time, then the courts seem to be implicitly deferring to tradition as a basis for the assignment of racial identities.

A judicial deference to tradition in matters of racial identity puts mixed-race identity claims in a kind of legal limbo between the individual and group-based models of pluralism. Individual rights are not recognized and protected from the invidious bias of race, as they were in *Loving*. But, in addition, group rights do not exist. There cannot be claims on behalf of members of the group(s) of mixed-race Americans unless the existence of the group(s) is recognized. Phipps, to be sure, was going beyond a claim for mixed-race identity, because she believed that her racial identity was White. But the recognition as White of someone who appears to be White but has Black ancestry is in fact less transgressive of the social racial order than the recognition of that person as mixed, because the category of White is already recognized. It is amazing and often overlooked that the courts are willing to acknowledge the social and nonbiological nature of racial categories. There is no indication that beyond this, however, they are willing to oppose custom. There is no basis on which to expect that remedies for either false notions of race or lack of recognition of mixed-race identities will be developed through common law.

IV. MIXED-RACE RECOGNITION AS A HEURISTIC DEVICE FOR SOCIAL CHANGE

The First Amendment allows people to think and say what they choose. One result of this right is that there is no legal basis on which false beliefs can be excluded from the domains of public or private discourse. This is a good thing insofar as it limits government propaganda, censorship, mind control, and so forth. But the First Amendment creates challenges for those who have reason to believe that the public is in error about a major aspect of life in the society. Such error can be corrected by education, which is easily accomplished when students are consenting adults. But the education of children depends on the consent of their parents, and false ideas about race, taught early in life, are often defended by parents on emotional and moral grounds. The public has never been taught, either informally in public fora or systematically at different levels of the educational system, that contemporary biology offers no support for its persistent anachronistic belief in the existence of human racial divisions. And at this time, any widespread primary and secondary school instruction about the scientific flimsiness of race is likely to be strongly opposed by the same established interests who have opposed relinquishing one-drop rules in interpreting the Census 2000 data. Anything that disturbs the ontological premises underlying the racial status quo, no matter how liberating it may be in principle, will at this time be perceived as a threat to the gains justly secured by nonwhites on the group-based pluralistic model. That a widespread revision of received opinion about the existence of race may undermine racist thought and behavior is almost beside the point, insofar as it appears to be either a merely theoretical enterprise or a threat to the liberating aspects of the status quo.

Nevertheless, widespread realization of the scientific emptiness of human racial taxonomy would be a great social good, because it could undermine human interactions based on the belief that some groups are different from others in the manner of a subspecies. Despite the celebration of diversity and its positive private and political uses, when diversity has been *racial* in the United States, it has never been viewed as mere variety, but as a natural-kind type difference lending itself to comparison in terms of human worth.

The reality of human biological diversity is both subtle, in that we are all overwhelmingly similar, and vast, in that no two of us are exactly alike genetically (except, perhaps, for identical twins). The rules for established racial groupings differ according to the race at issue: Whites have no nonwhite ancestry;[21] Blacks have at least some Black ancestry;[22] Asians encompass a multiplicity of national origins;[23] and Indians have recorded Indian ancestry to an approved "blood quantum."[24] Despite the different bases for the received racial identities, appearance is the rough guide, which is considered to be the normal indicator of racial identity. In this sense, the major racial groups are socially intelligible. Recognition of even a fraction of possible mixed racial identities, however, will render racial identities unintelligible, at a glance, at least to those who take the new complexity of categories seriously. If racial identity is widely accepted to be something that cannot be accurately determined at a glance, racial divisions will begin to crumble on epistemological grounds alone.

Even if mixed-race identities are not officially recognized, mixed-race identity advocacy is not likely to go away. There are two national organizations devoted to mixed-race recognition, AMEA (Association of Multi-Ethnic Americans)[25] and Project RACE (Reclassify All Children Equally),[26] as well as numerous local organizations and groups on college campuses. Also, magazines and Internet sites increasingly serve as a virtual community for mixed-race individuals and their families. Although self-identified mixed-race Americans are likely to remain a small (numerical) minority for some time to come, their existence is subversive to the imaginary taxonomy. What exists only in the imagination may be vulnerable only to what disturbs the illusion on the same imaginary level.

However, mixed-race identity tends to support the family-history aspects of racial identity, which are real. Many of the narrative accounts of mixed-race heritage attest to this, particularly famous cases, such as: James McBride's novel, *The Color of Water: A Black Man's Tribute to His White Mother;*[27] the story of Thomas Jefferson's paternity of Sally Hemings's children (Gordon-Reed); and Tiger Woods's self-designation as "Cablinasian."[28]

In conclusion, it should be noted that there is no constitutional provision, body of law, or established case precedent according to which Americans must identify themselves racially. Also, the racial categories which are offered as choices on official forms are not established by law, but by the vague dictates of administrative policy. In the past, such policy has followed what administrators have understood to be custom and public opinion, and the courts have upheld these understandings. But custom and public opinion are never as stable as traditionalists would like them to be, and the twenty-first century may very well sustain exactly those historical processes which will unravel the false taxonomy of race established during the eighteenth and nineteenth centuries and attenuated during the twentieth. And if the past is a guide, as custom and public opinion change in these matters, so will the courts.

Notes

1. This article first appeared in the *Harvard BlackLetter Law Journal* 17 (Spring 2001): 33–46, and is © 2001 by the President and Fellows of Harvard College and the *Harvard BlackLetter Law Journal*.

2. See Goldberg for further citations on the history of the census. On the legal history of the application of the one-drop rule to mixed-race categories, see Naomi Zack, *Race and Mixed Race*, 77–85. For discussion of the empirical and logical problems with the one-drop rule, see Zack, *Race and Mixed Race*, 9–18, and Zack, *Thinking about Race*, 5–6.

3. For discussions of the grounds for mixed-race recognition see Fernández; Graham.

4. This was substantially the same as Holmes's article in the *New York Times*, but condensed slightly and given a slightly different title, which reads as though "minority" is not only a name for a group but for an individual member of a group.

5. Discussion and sources for the blood-based essentialist notion of race can be found in Hannaford and in Zack, *Race and Mixed Race*. For direct sources, see excerpts from Bernier; Voltaire; and Kant. See also Howells's 1940 historical survey of attempts to construct scientific racial classifications.

6. See Levi-Strauss; UNESCO.

7. See UNESCO; American Anthropology Association. See also Zack, "Philosophical Aspects of the 1998 AAA Statement on 'Race.'"

8. For an analysis of multiculturalism in this sense, see the following: Goldberg 1996; Webster.

9. On the contemporary distinction between the terms "race" and "ethnicity," see Michaels 1995b, 32–62; Corlett, 83; Zack, *Race and Mixed Race*, 67–75.

10. The facts about genetic recombination can be found in contemporary high school biology textbooks, although Ashley Montagu first applied them to presumptions about racial heredity in the early 1940s.

11. See Gordon, 82–83.

12. See Smedley.

13. See Walzer.

14. See Glazer.

15. See Williams.

16. See Gutman, 110.

17. See Brown.

18. See Zack, "Mixed Black and White Race and Public Policy"; Zack, *Race and Mixed Race*, 20–28.

19. See Root. It will be interesting to compare the figure of 2 million, based on children with married parents of different races, with the data gathered from the Census 2000 questions, which include adults (Bureau of the Census).

20. To view Walter Benn Michaels's interpretation, with which I agree, see Michaels, "The No-Drop Rule."

21. See Ridgeway.

22. See Davis.

23. See Arisaka, 209.

24. See Wilson.

25. See Fernández, 192. Fernández founded AMEA.

26. See Graham, 185. Graham founded Project RACE.

27. See also Johnson.

28. See, e.g., Strege; Gutman.

Works Cited

American Anthropology Association. "AAA Statement on 'Race.'" *Anthropology Newsletter* 9, no. 3 (1998).

Angier, Natalie. "Do Races Differ? Not Really, Genes Show." *New York Times*, August 22, 2000.

Appiah, K. Anthony. "Race, Culture, Identity: Misunderstood Connections." In *Color Conscious*, eds. K. Anthony Appiah and Amy Gutmann, pp. 68–69. Princeton, N.J.: Princeton University Press, 1996.

Arisaka, Yoko. "Asian Women: Invisibility, Locations, and Claims to Philosophy." In *Women of Color and Philosophy*, ed. Naomi Zack. Malden, Mass.: Blackwell Publishers, 2000.

Bernier, Francois. "A New Division of the Earth" (1684). Reprinted in *The Idea of Race*, ed. Robert Bernasconi and Tommy L. Lott. Indianapolis: Hackett, 2000.

Blackburn, Daniel G. "Why Race Is Not a Biological Concept." In *Race and Racism in Theory and Practice*, ed. Berel Lang. Lanham, Md.: Rowman & Littlefield, 2000.

Brown, Ursula M. "Between Two Worlds: Psychosocial Issues of Black/White Interracial Young Adults in the U.S.A." In *Leading Issues in African-American Studies*, ed. Nikongo BaNikongo, pp. 89–104. Durham, N.C.: Carolina University Press, 1997.

Bureau of the Census, U.S. Department of Commerce. *United States Census Form D-1 (UL)*. Washington, D.C.: U.S. Department of Commerce, 2000.

Cavalli-Sforza, L. Luca. *Genes, Peoples, and Languages*. New York: Northpoint Press, 2000.

———, et al. *The History and Geography of Human Genes*. Princeton, N.J.: Princeton University Press, 1994.

Corlett, J. Angelo. "Parallels of Ethnicity and Gender." In *Race/Sex: Their Sameness, Difference, and Interplay*, ed. Naomi Zack. New York: Routledge, 1997.

Davis, James F. "The Hawaiian Alternative to the One-Drop Rule." In *American Mixed Race: The Culture of Microdiversity*, ed. Naomi Zack, pp. 115–132. Lanham, Md.: Rowman and Littlefield, 1995.

———. *Who Is Black?* University Park: Penn State University Press, 1991.

Fernández, Carlos A. "Testimony of the Association of Multiethnic Americans." In *American Mixed Race: The Culture of Microdiversity*, ed. Naomi Zack, pp. 191–200. Lanham, Md.: Rowman and Littlefield, 1995.

Glazer, Nathan. "Individual Rights against Group Rights." In *The Rights of Minority Cultures*, ed. Will Kymlicka, pp. 123–138. New York: Oxford University Press, 1995.

Goldberg, David Theo. "Introduction." In *Multiculturalism: A Critical Reader*, ed. David Theo Goldberg, pp. 1–41. Malden, Mass.: Blackwell Publishers, 1996.

———. "Made in the USA." In *American Mixed Race: The Culture of Microdiversity*, ed. Naomi Zack, pp. 237–257. Lanham, Md.: Rowman and Littlefield, 1995.

Gordon, Lewis. *Existentia Africana: Understanding African Existential Thought*. New York: Routledge, 2000.

Gordon-Reed, Annette. *Thomas Jefferson and Sally Hemings: An American Controversy*. Charlottesville: University of Virginia Press, 1997.

Graham, Susan R. "Grassroots Advocacy." In *American Mixed Race: The Culture of Microdiversity*, ed. Naomi Zack, pp. 185–190. Lanham, Md.: Rowman and Littlefield, 1995.

Gutman, Bill. *Tiger Woods: A Biography*. New York: Simon Pulse, 1997.

Gutmann, Amy. "Responding to Racial Injustice." In *Color Conscious*, ed. K. Anthony Appiah and Amy Gutmann. Princeton, N.J.: Princeton University Press, 1996.

Hannaford, Ivan. *Race: The History of an Idea in the West*. Baltimore: Johns Hopkins University Press, 1996.

Holmes, Steven A. "Census Will Count Mixed-Race People as Minorities." *Alabama Times Union*, March 11, 2000.

———. "New Policy on Census Says Those Listed as White and Minority Will Be Counted as Minority." *New York Times*, March 11, 2000.

Howells, W. W. "Physical Determinants of Race" (1940). Reprinted in *This Is Race: An Anthology Selected from the International Literature on the Races of Man*, ed. Earl W. Count. New York: Henry Shuman, 1950.

Jane Doe v. State of Louisiana. 479 So. 2d 369. Louisiana Court Appellate. 1985.

Johnson, Kevin R. *How Did You Get to Be Mixican: A White/Brown Man's Search for Identity.* Philadelphia: Temple University Press, 1999.

Kant, Immanuel. "Of the Different Human Races" (1777). Reprinted in *The Idea of Race*, ed. Robert Bernasconi and Tommy L. Lott. Indianapolis: Hackett, 2000.

Levi-Strauss, Claude. "Race and History." In *Race, Science and Society*, ed. Leo Kuper, pp. 95–134. New York: Columbia University Press, 1965.

Loving v. Virginia. 388 U.S. 1. 1968.

McBride, James. *The Color of Water: A Black Man's Tribute to His White Mother.* New York: Riverhead Books, 1997.

Michaels, Walter Benn. "The No-Drop Rule." In *Identities*, ed. Kwame Anthony Appiah and Henry Louis Gates, Jr., pp. 401–412. Chicago: University of Chicago Press, 1995.

———. "Race into Culture: A Critical Genealogy of Cultural Identity." In *Identities*, ed. Kwame Anthony Appiah and Henry Louis Gates, Jr. Chicago: University of Chicago Press, 1995.

Montagu, Ashley. "The Concept of Race in the Human Species in the Light of Genetics." *Heredity* 23 (1941): 243–247. Reprinted in *The Idea of Race*, ed. Robert Bernasconi and Tommy L. Lott. Indianapolis: Hackett, 2000.

Omond, Roger. *The Apartheid Handbook: A Guide to South Africa's Everyday Racial Policies.* Harmondsworth, Middlesex, England; New York: Penguin Books, 1985.

Ridgeway, James. *Blood in the Face.* New York: Thundermouth, 1990.

Root, Maria P. P. "The Multiracial Experience: Racial Borders as a Significant Frontier in Race Relations." In *The Multiracial Experience*, ed. Maria P. P. Root, pp. xiii–xxviii. Thousand Oaks, Calif.: Sage Press, 1996.

Smedley, Audrey. *Race in North America: Origin and Evolution of a World View.* Boulder, Colo.: Westview Press, 1993.

Strege, John. *Tiger: A Biography of Tiger Woods.* New York: Broadway Books, 1997.

Templeton, Alan R. "Human Races: A Genetic and Revolutionary Perspective." *American Anthropologist* 1998: 632–650.

UNESCO. "Four Statements on the Race Question." In *Race, Science and Society*, ed. Leo Kuper, pp. 341–364. New York: Columbia University Press, 1965.

Voltaire, Francois-Marie. "Of the Different Races of Men" (1765). Reprinted in *The Idea of Race*, ed. Robert Bernasconi and Tommy L. Lott. Indianapolis: Hackett, 2000.

Walzer, Michael. "Pluralism: A Political Perspective." In *The Rights of Minority Cultures*, ed. Will Kymlicka, pp. 139–154. New York: Oxford University Press, 1995.

Webster, Yehudi O. "Introduction." In *Against the Multicultural Agenda: A Critical Thinking Alternative*, pp. 1–11. Westport, Conn.: Praeger, 1997.

Webster's New Collegiate Dictionary. 1960.

Williams, Patricia. *The Alchemy of Race and Rights.* Cambridge, Mass.: Harvard University Press, 1991.

Williamson, Joel. *New People: Miscegenation and Mulattoes in the United States.* Baton Rouge: Louisiana State University Press, 1980.

Wilson, Terry P. "Blood Quantum: Native American Mixed Bloods." In *Racially Mixed People in America*, ed. Maria P. P. Root, pp. 108–125. Newbury Park, Calif.: Sage, 1992.

Zack, Naomi. *American Mixed Race: The Culture of Microdiversity*. Lanham, Md.: Rowman and Littlefield, 1995.

———. "Mixed Black and White Race in Public Policy." *Hypatia* 10, no. 1 (1995): 120–132. Reprinted in *Leading Issues in African-American Studies*, ed. Nikongo BaNikongo, pp. 121–134. Durham, N.C.: Carolina University Press, 1997.

———. "Philosophical Aspects of the 1998 AAA Statement on 'Race.'" *Anthropological Theory* (December 2001): 445–465.

———. *Race and Mixed Race*. Philadelphia: Temple University Press, 1993.

———. "Race and Philosophic Meaning." *American Philosophical Association Newsletter on Philosophy and the Black Enterprise* 1 (1994): 114–120.

———. *Thinking about Race*. Belmont, Calif.: Wadsworth, 1998.

2. MISCEG-NARRATIONS

Raquel Scherr Salgado

I. DELIBERATIVE DISCOURSES

September 13, 2001, two days after 9/11, I pull into a gas station in El Cerrito on I-80 West, only two exits before I reach my home in Berkeley. I am more attentive than usual in getting from here to there. It does not matter where here or there is really. It is more a matter of making it from A to B. You can pay dearly these days for travel.

I pump my gas, and as I am about to get into my car, two thirty-something baseball-capped men strut by me. "We should kill all brown people," says one to the other. He looks at me. "That will solve the problem for sure."

At first I think, "The guy must be joking." After all, we are next door to Berkeley, the most liberated town in the world. But then I try to re-capture the baseball cap's train of thought. Brown people killed us; there-fore we must kill brown people. If nothing else, bin Laden has reminded us that there is power in simple logic, as has Bush's decree: "Wanted: Dead or Alive." We must get rid of ambiguity, says one guy to the other, muscles hard, rippling. Black or white, dead or alive, yes or no, new and old are easy constructs to understand. Anything that rests in between, in-terstitial, undefined, intercultural, or simply unconstructed, like brown, neither black nor white, is unreasonable because it clouds and complicates matters. We must draw the line somewhere, says the baseball cap, or we will be confused and forced to deliberate.

Like the two men, and the rest of the population, I too watched the at-tacks. The spectacle of planes crashing in machinelike sweeps into global centers had the look of video games. The analogy points less to the lack of verisimilitude than to a lack of logic. The event was rather more a case of the real mimicking the virtual, a regress of *simulacra*, to use Baudrillard's term. It was also devastation and destruction—spatial and temporal, symbolic, historical, and political—a deliberate act of oppressed against oppressor, of David against Goliath, of box cutters against advanced technology. *De terrore. Locura completa.* Sheer terror, the insanity of it. An incomprehensible narrative—there simply are no words for it. Spectator of the spectacular, I watched, over and over again, planes strike buildings.

Then came the reactions to the tragedy. Though the guy in the cap and I saw the same images, the inferences we reached were different. He concludes, "Kill all brown people," those no-good evildoers. I see white people, black people, brown people searching for loved ones. I feel oddly patriotic. Black, white, colored, poor, and rich. We are all in this together. At the same time I can imagine the counternarrative: New York is the world center, a multinational marketplace. The world encroaches on us, economically, culturally, politically. If we don't act now, they say, we will miss our fifteen minutes of media protest and our chance to show that, however small, we can be as savage and powerful as any other nation.

The more I weigh, counterweigh, question, construct, deconstruct, the less anything makes sense. I concentrate on the instant in which planes crash, fires flash, and smoke hangs heavy in the air. I begin with a question. I assay, suppose, propose, weigh, and still end with a question, a *no se que*—all thoughts contingent on the "I-don't-know-what" of the moment. The events want a narrative but there is no narrative—no plausible beginning, middle, and end. There is no answer. There is only deliberation, a spin of emotion and thought that keeps me stupid for a moment. But much later similar deliberations free me from thinking that we should kill all men who wear baseball caps. The same deliberations persuade me to write about deliberation and how deliberation is brown.

Indeed I believe my deliberations emerge from the fact that I am brown and grew up at a time when crossing the color line was opprobrious if not illegal. As a mixed-race individual I have lived in nuance and negotiation. I embody contradictions. My deliberations, then, arise from habit. I have also come to inhabit them. They are highly individualized, self-centered, and self-conscious. They should not be confused, however, with the appraisals of therapeutic discourse, which mistake self-esteem for awareness of self. For those who are mixed race, contingency is identifiable with self. Deliberative discourses, though driven by the urgency of emotions, by the kinetics of emotion, so to speak, turn away from the spectacle of self qua self.

Emotions guide and direct thought. The aim of deliberation is to mediate impulse by making emotion concrete in the moment it is able to communicate itself and become self-conscious. A "deliberative" act of writing, for example, might reveal the very moment or impetus that transmutes emotion to thought. But a deliberation is less answer-oriented than it is question-centered, and even when it moves toward an answer, which for intelligibility it must, it sees the answer as provisional, contingent always on the next question, which an answer necessarily opens up. Deliberation moves into the world of the observable and understandable and back again to self.

While deliberations, then, arise from self, they are not, in our usual sense of the word, self-centered, because they seek, through the self, the other, and try to make concrete the nuances, contingencies, and complexities that drive thought and that inspire social or worldly deliberations.

I think of a well-known passage in an Orwell essay that engages and evokes such deliberations. In "Looking Back on Civil War," Orwell writes of seeing his enemy, a fascist officer, jumping from a trench and "running half-dressed . . . holding up his trousers with both hands" (199). Orwell reveals that the detail saved the man. "It was true that I am a poor shot," he writes. "Still, I did not shoot partly because of the detail about the trousers. I had come here to shoot at 'Fascists'; but a man who is holding up his trousers isn't a 'Fascist,' he is visibly a fellow-creature, similar to yourself, and you don't like shooting at him" (199). By focusing on detail, Orwell both justifies ("because of the detail") and describes a humanizing feature that makes him look beyond the general and through the other, to self. Orwell captures perfectly the moment of emotional judgment, the act of deliberation that allows him to see the interplay between originality and cliché (catching someone unguarded, with his pants down in the double meaning of the phrase), between the humorous and the serious, self and other, life and death. Deliberation of this sort requires imagination, for it seeks to understand the "other," and in some way absorb its experience.

Orwell, however, does not speak from the perspective of a writer, eager to disclose self, but rather from that of a writer who wants to show how an act of reflection which understands the other through self can change one's view of the world. It is in this sense, then, that I speak of deliberations. Deliberations seek coherence and continuity, but contingencies lie at their center. It is, after all, Orwell's recognition of contingency that allows him to humanize his enemy. But these contingencies are not the same as the procedures of Postmodernity and decentering theories, which in their scrutiny of modernity rely on verbal contingencies and rhetorical display and wit. Rather, deliberations are vigilant for details that illuminate contradiction, contingency, and paradox as a perpetual condition of existence and of the expression that lets existence be communicated to others. By recognizing paradox not simply as an intellectual paradigm but as integral to human thought and existence, deliberative discourses can begin to topple both judgments (such as "we should kill all brown people") and theoretical play that lead only to intellectual and moral dead ends.

I would like to suggest, apropos the many fracturing critical ideologies that have emerged in the past couple of decades, that mixed-race (brown) writers, because of the contingencies they inhabit, have been in the unique position to understand the specific nature of those contingencies, though they have yet to describe and chart it. Moreover, the task of charting mixed-race experience becomes increasingly difficult because (as the baseball cap makes clear) mass migrations to and from the United States have made those of us who are brown less geographically localized and also more racially and ethnically muddled. Indeed, Mexican, Middle-Eastern, Indian, White-Asian, Puerto Rican, Black-White, for example, who live and work side by side often find it difficult to identify, by phenotype alone, even members of their own ethnic group. (I am reminded of an event years ago, when a Japanese woman, thinking my Mexican mother was Japanese, spoke to my mother in Japanese.) As a result, because of the way mixed race exists in the world, any mixed-race theory must remain deliberative at every moment. I want to suggest further that the very uncertainty inherent in experiencing mixed race makes theorizing difficult, inasmuch as theories necessarily stand outside experience, working instead to define, categorize, and classify. Mixed race sees itself in constant shift, fluid in every instant, incorporating in its movement conflict and contradiction, and the tension these produce. Mixed race, therefore, needs a negotiating theory that emerges in fact from mixed-race experience and that predisposes mixed-race individuals, who have grown up in a racialized society, to live in nuance and negotiation. Often mixed-race theory is best expressed through more pliant genres such as the reflective essay or memoir that move between and beyond theoretical categories. Finally, modern mixed-race theory, by necessity, incorporates the anthropological "other," which always looms large in any concept of race.

Having said this, in what way are we to write about mixed-race experiences? Can we theorize about them at all? I think we can and we have. For the mixed-race person, however, a mere theoretical position is incomplete, since it cannot capture the affect and deliberation in which she inevitably engages when she moves in the world. Even Postmodern theories that find articulation in verbal play, and thus appear to demonstrate the inevitability of contingency and paradox, do not grasp fully the tension that holds the paradox together or describe the moment of the paradox and examine in it a tension *sui generis*.

I want to argue, then, that mixed-race experience begins with the consciousness of that tension, the moment of deliberation. For that reason, mixed-race theorists are well positioned to examine the very point of tension and intersection as the legitimate location and origin of contemporary theory—a theory that may serve to explain what we might call transmodern experience.

II. THEORIZING CONTINGENCIES AND SUBJECTIVITIES

Although they lie beyond the scope of my discussion here, both Postmodern and identity theories (however contradictory in the manner and the mapping of their discourses) contribute to an understanding of mixed-race experience and discourse. Postmodern theories, advanced first by Jacques-Marie-Émile Lacan, then by Jacques Derrida and others, posited that language structures consciousness of the "other." In their critique of language, "post" theories set in motion the idea that identity may be fluid and categories unreliable. However, though these theories may have established a theoretical framework for discussing the contingencies of mixed race, they have shown little concern with the nuances and intersections of human thought and emotion—the deliberations of which I speak above—and with the historical and cultural forces of racial politics.

Postcolonial theories do well by offering a pointed cultural, historical, and political critique. However, these theories have an interest in maintaining a perception of racialized identity, and since recognition of mixed race threatens notions of alterity, the theories largely limit conversations that may take place across color lines and ignore the political and social implications of these conversations. Moreover, mixed-race individuals' embodiment of self-other, their undermining *en cuerpo* of binary categories, renders notions of the "other," which are so crucial to "post" theories, no longer a radical concept. Indeed recognition of mixed race inevitably will unsettle all cultural theories of estrangement and dichotomy.

Even early on, when cultural theorists partial to the rhetoric of Postmodernities explained the important split between colonized and colonizer (and thus self and other), these theorists were challenged by writers who had a stake in expressing the experience of peoples disempowered because of race. In 1987, for example, the same year that Gayatri Spivak published *Other Worlds: Essays in Cultural Politics*, in which "peripherality," "marginality," and "positionality" gained a permanent place in the vocabulary of postcolonial theory, Barbara Christian, critic of Afro-American literature, pinpointed the critical (and cultural) split occurring between theory and literature by asking whether theories of the day in fact might not be undermining the emergence of Black and other ethnic literatures. "I have seized this occasion," she wrote in her essay "Race for Theory," "to break the silence among those of us critics, as we are now called, who have been intimidated, devalued by what I call the race for theory" (124). She observed further that these "New Philosophers," heirs to Postmodern theorists, had hijacked literature by creating theories that were hegemonic and in the tradition of Western thought (125). "My concern," she wrote, "is a passionate one, for the literature of people who are not in power has always been in danger of extinction or of cooptation" (130). Her critique was not too far off the mark, especially given the hegemony of antifoundationalist theories, themselves often remarkably rigid and essentialist, that were rampant in the academy precisely at the moment, as Christian claimed, when Western literature had "become pallid, laden with despair, self-indulgent, and disconnected" and when Black and other ethnic-centered literatures were "bursting with vitality" (124). Christian saw non-Western literatures in all their vitality as a direct challenge to the nonintelligibility of the theoretical discourse. "[L]iterature," she wrote, "is an affirmation that sensuality is intelligence, that sensual language is language that makes sense," and that theory lacks intelligence, because it lacks "pleasurableness" (125).

The concerns Christian articulated were very different from the concerns of a critic like Gayatri Spivak, for example, who claimed that "we operate with no other consciousness but one structured by language," that we cannot own because "we are operated by those languages." Theorists like Spivak discounted both the emotive impulses that may drive language and thought and the sensuality that may derive from these (1994, 520).

Although as language qua language, then, "post" theories had been liberating in their play, they raised their revenue by taxing those who have been most marginal and peripheral. Critics like Christian found little accommodation with texts whose language was abstruse, whose theories were intelligible only to the initiated, and whose concerns about the politically disenfranchised were minimal. It is not difficult to understand how those who had been marginalized because of the color of their skin and had struggled for recognition of personhood would see a travesty in the new philosophies that declared with so much authority that "A self does not amount to much" (Lyotard, 15). Christian argued for the need of "writer-critics" such as Ralph Ellison, Richard Wright, Mary Chesnutt, Alice Walker, and Zora Neale Hurston, because they voiced collective concerns and thus provided "necessary nourishment for their people" (125). "Now I am being told," Christian wrote, "that authors are dead, irrelevant . . . that . . . they produce texts as disembodied as angels" (125).

Pace Foucault's technologies of the author, Postmodern theories did not reduce the author (for he declared himself with no uncertain authority), but rather they reduced the reader, colonized her, so to speak. The "post" theories that Christian opposed, then, were counter texts to a literature that seeks to remain performative, deliberate, empathic, sensual, and thus viscerally, emotionally, and intellectually graspable by others. Her critique becomes instructive for what it can tell us about the objectives of a deliberative discourse that makes emotional engagement a condition of political engagement. Those of us who have not been legitimated need to believe we can "possess" language and the authority to use it.

Unlike Postmodern discourses that saw subjectivity as governed by language and thus "decentered," the identity theories that were emerging at the time understood the political power of language either to delegitimize or legitimize identity and thus sought a language of "engagement" that mobilized emotions. However, while identity literature, like Postmodernities, has been important to mixed-race discourse, more recently it, too, has suffered from excesses by coming dangerously close to indulging the writer's racialized emotions in a self-congratulatory fashion, and thus losing the literature's potential for successful transmutation of emotion into thought. A deliberative model is determined by four guiding elements: context, contingency, emotion, and transmutation of emotion to thought, which implies recognition of otherness in self or self in otherness. Identity, deliberation shows us, can never be absolute or simple.

Killing Rage, by bell hooks, an otherwise interesting collection of essays on Black identity, provides an example of a literature unable to transmute emotion to thought in the fashion of deliberative discourse, because it indulges the writer's emotions and offers as remedy a narrow strategy, thus taking the sting out of the complex interaction between self and other. Angered at several "racialized incidents" that she experiences on a plane flight, hooks describes how she finally directs her racialized anger toward a White man who refuses to move, although he is perfectly aware that he is sitting in the wrong seat. "I felt a 'killing rage,'" she admits. "I wanted to stab him softly, to shoot him with the gun I wished I had in my purse. And as I watched his pain, I would say to him tenderly 'racism hurts'" (11). The experience leads hooks to review the literature and history of Black rage and its effects, including the repression of rage among economically successful Blacks, who, hooks claims, become complicit in their own colonization by Whites.

The irony in hooks's desire to softly stab and tenderly talk to the White man who has aroused her "killing rage" (the words themselves reminiscent of Roberta Flack's "Killing Me Softly") is not lost on readers, who soon realize that the wordplay in the title instructs us how to read her text. "Confronting my rage, witnessing the way it moved me to grow and change," bell hooks confesses, "I understood intimately that it had the potential not only to destroy but also to construct." Later on she concludes, "Racial hatred is real. And it is humanizing to be able to resist with militant rage" (16–17). But the resistance hooks advocates is oddly borrowed from the White middle-class self-help discourse, which speaks, as does hooks, of self-actualization. "Sharing rage," she writes, playing once more with the title of her essay, "connects those of us who are older and more experienced with younger black and non-black folks who are *seeking ways to be self-actualized and self-determined*" (20, emphasis added). In short, she transforms her killing rage into a therapeutic resolve to kill racial hatreds, indeed a laudable goal, and imagines arising from this a "beloved community . . . formed not by the eradication of difference but by its affirmation, by each of us claiming the identities and cultural legacies that shape who we are and how we live in the world" (265). The link hooks establishes between her "radical politicization and self-recovery" is especially interesting, given her warning about the complicit and self-colonizing behavior of successful Blacks (11). But most important, by validating emotion qua emotion, hooks's text demonstrates how to make the personal political, and the political therapeutic, thus falling short of letting her readers discover the psychological and political complexities of racialized emotions. Rather, she turns expression of rage into step one of a therapeutic process.

While rage, as hooks and others have shown, has a singular place in Black literature, her observations in this particular case tend to aestheticize emotions rather than encourage social or political change. Therapeutic discourses, I would argue, promote an aesthetic of self that decontextualizes and depoliticizes social problems and, instead, locates sources of problems within the "client" who undergoes these therapies, thus quieting any potential social dissent, since blame lies not with the system but with the client who hasn't adapted to the system. Discrimination, oppression, and cruelty *should* arouse passions and outrage among dispossessed groups, just as they should arouse outrage in those who witness these acts.

Literature of rage succeeds in its protest only when it engages both pro-
testors and nonprotesters to think of its source and imagine the human
damage rage creates. James Baldwin's *The Fire Next Time*, for instance,
historicized and politicized the "prolonged religious crisis" that brought
him to the emotional, sexual, and intellectual moment of recognition that
"Yes, it does indeed mean something—something unspeakable—to be
born, in a white country, an Anglo-Teutonic, anti-sexual country, black"
(30). At the moment he recognizes his separation from the White world
and the unspeakable pain it engages, his narrative explodes by dramatiz-
ing his suffering, legitimating his rage, and locating his body as the site of
these experiences in a way that has implications beyond self. He describes
his anguish, which he claims "cannot be described," by moving precisely
into a description and, then, in the peak of emotional crisis, expanding
that very moment into an eternity that moves like the toss and turn of
oceans against shores:

> One moment I was on my feet, singing and clapping and, at the same
> time, working out in my head the plot of a play I was working on then;
> the next moment, with no transition, no sensation of falling, I was on
> my back, with the lights beating down into my face and all the vertical
> saints above me. I did not know what I was doing down so low, or how
> I had got there. And the anguish that filled me cannot be described. It
> moved in me like one of those floods that devastate counties, tearing
> everything down, tearing children from their parents, and lovers from
> each other, and making everything an unrecognizable waste. All I re-
> ally remember is the pain, the unspeakable pain; it was as though I
> were yelling up to Heaven and Heaven would not hear me. (29–30)

One cannot help but read Baldwin's expression of self-loss and recognition as a political indictment of personal devastations that racism has
caused. At the same time, between the anguish he "cannot describe" and
the "unrecognizable waste" that agitates him, Baldwin describes in detail
an apocalyptic vision of humanity-wide rather than personal devastation,
and speaks for "unspeakable pain" by embodying its rhythms and making
his anguish recognizable to all. He thus collapses the boundaries between
self and other, between moment and eternity, and lays the groundwork
for his social and political critique, which ends, fittingly, with an allusion
to a slave's rhythmical re-creation of a biblical song: "God gave Noah the
rainbow sign / No more water, the fire next time!" The power of these final words and the fear they invoke lie not in the fact that they represent a
warning (though they do that, too), but rather in the fact that Baldwin has

made his own fear and vulnerability palpable to Whites (*intelligent*, as Barbara Christian would say, in its sensuality). Knowledge is finally about experiencing the other in the self. It is sensual and embodied—a knowing in the gut, so to speak. Baldwin's readers cannot help but experience the very moment of his pain and devastation, and understand their complicity in it. Unlike hooks, then, who confesses her rage (in a personal and self-congratulatory style common to confessions), Baldwin testifies about his experience and gives reasons for it (the audience witnesses and hears him, like it or not).

Here, as in Orwell, language works against its very abstraction. Racism, as a word or concept, Baldwin suggests, is too devastating to its victims to remain abstract, and too abstract to its perpetrators to leave unembodied and unfelt. Using detail, description, metaphor, rhythms, and sound, Baldwin animates language and offers the illusion, at least, that anguish is graspable. Indeed, when he raises his voice to declare his own voicelessness and unintelligibility—"as if I were yelling up to Heaven and Heaven would not hear me"—Baldwin not only makes his audience witness his own social, political, and racial alienation, but also helps them to recognize their own fear and vulnerability, sources of all human anguish and alienation. "Can Heaven hear *any* of us?" Baldwin finally forces us to ask.

In the end, Baldwin's testimony about the impossibility of testimony, which teases us with its legal and religious implications, displaces his detailed description of anguish and leaves us instead witnessing a desperate and solitary voice yelling wildly in the wilderness. Baldwin teaches us that the first experience of alienation originates not in vision and specularity, as Lacan might claim, but in voice—in the phonation that instructs us that we are forever alone. Indeed, when we hear ourselves born to the world, we perceive how distant and separated even from ourselves we are. When we write, our voice remains elusive, and we seek, if nothing else, its embodiment—as if this embodiment, this phonation of voice, were the purest, loneliest form of our existence.

For mixed-race writers who experience the "what?" and "who?" of worldly alienations, Baldwin offers some good lessons. Because the impulse of language is toward abstraction, it should be our interest as writers to pull language together, to force it where it does not want to go, to dictate to it and, at the same time, to acknowledge the very tension that inheres in the opposing inclination of language to describe and to conceptualize. This lesson is especially important for us, because as mixed-race individuals we have lived in the push and pull of categories; we have been constructed as one race then reconstructed as another, neither this nor that, not quite, not other, always under the tyranny of categorizing discourse, always gazed upon and theorized about. We have been interpreted, read, reviewed, critiqued, co-opted, denied, imagined as not authored and not authorized.

Baldwin shows us, then, that critique can be embodied and that theory, which, as its etymology suggests, relies on specularity and speculation, and the categories that emerge from these, might be better represented by polyphony: the multiple "voicings" of thoughts, ideas, and actions (not to be confused with montage, polyphony's pictorial counterpart, since montage relies on superimposition of images). Unlike theory, which works to prove an idea that it has observed at a distance, polyphony inhabits the moment—no periphery, no distance, only movement, tension, center, and brown. Polyphonic and deliberative writing recognizes sound, rhythm, imagery, imagination, memory, perception, sensation, and reason, as they move in and out of thought. Pulsations of thought like pulsations of the body, these are sensual intelligence.

III. MISCELLANY: MISCEGENATION, *MESTIZAJE,* AND TRANSMODERN DERACINATIONS

When I was a child there were two words about which I was intensely curious. One was "miscellaneous," the other "miscegenation." It might have been the sound of the words, much more melodious and sophisticated, for example, than "mistake," though I suspected they meant something similar. I discovered the word "miscellaneous" in the title of a journal, *The Miscellaneous Man*, that my father kept in the literature rack of the Steppenwolf, a Beat bar for "subsistentialists" he opened in Berkeley in the late 1950s. I still have the first issue of the journal, edited and published by William J. Margolis, with an inscription on the title page that reads:

> The miscellaneous man is the individual man, the human being who, as a dynamic entity, never quite fits under any label and is constantly bulging out of categories. He stands alone, but not aloof; self-sufficient, and yet cooperative. He is searching constantly for a closer approach to truth; criticizing those things, which to his mind and to his animal nature are false. He is seeking and testing creative approaches to the problems that face individual men and women that limit their humanity and chain them in a cage of mere existence.

The inscription, naïve and idealistic, serves as a companion to the cover art, which displays a shadow of a miscellaneous man who bulges with minidrawings in black of men and women dancing, reading, painting, playing trumpets, and bending under the weight of bundles—workers with cargoes. The journal, in its dynamism and mishmash of essays, poetry, short stories, and drawings, captures well 1950s West Coast bohemia, but I think I was attracted to the journal because its miscellaneous look spoke to me. Its cover, shadow set on brown, was noisy with contradictory activity.

My interest in miscegenation arises from another, yet related, story that has to do with my mother, my father, and my mixedness, or *mestizaje*. I use the term miscegenation to suggest its political and social history (and my own), and the Spanish term *mestizaje* to claim what (not who) I am.

I was born in 1947, the year before the California Supreme Court case of *Perez v. Sharp* declared state antimiscegenation laws unconstitutional. I came of age in 1968, a year after the Supreme Court, in *Loving v. Virginia*, struck down antimiscegenation statutes, and the year that ethnic power movements, along with the Vietnam War, gained a center stage in my campus life at Berkeley. But antimiscegenation and Jim Crow laws played a part in my life long before I was born. Let me explain.

Before joining the Sixty-fifth Infantry Battalion in Camp Wolters, Texas, in 1943 to fight the Nazis, my father brought my Mexican mother to this country by bus. As a couple they were verbally threatened, forced to use separate facilities, and prohibited from renting a room together. A couple of years earlier, my father, a young lawyer from Baltimore, had barely escaped with his life for attempting to unionize cab drivers in that city. To make a quick exit, he had hopped the rails to the West Coast, and hitchhiked to Mexico. Two years later, when he came back with a non-white-looking woman, his wife, and insisted that my mother be allowed to use the same facilities as he, he was threatened again. The White Southern bus driver, with whom he began his trip into the South, took my father by the collar of his shirt and told him that there had just been a lynching in the Alabama town through which the bus would be crossing, and that nigger-loving Jew boys should beware and not push their luck. Unable to find rooms in hotels that would accept them as a couple, my parents spent their honeymoon sleeping on park benches.[1]

My mother, born on the coast near Acapulco to a fourteen-year-old girl who rolled cigars for a living, was of mixed Indian, Dutch, and Spanish ancestry, though she looked Asian (when my father's family met her they likened her to Mme. Chiang Kai Shek). My grandmother's other children had a darker look. My aunt looked Gauguin-Tahitian, her dark skin flashing against her white teeth and black-black hair, and my uncle looked like a mix of Indian and coastal Black, his hair crimped, his eyes

Indian, and his skin a husked coconut brown. Of my mother's father, I know that he was the son of an Indian, head of a *capulli*, a tribe in the mountains of Guerrero, and of a widowed Spanish woman from Galicia, who owned a hacienda in Quetzala where the Indian traded his wares. I have a picture of my grandfather that shows him with black hair slicked back, sharp black eyes, beaked nose, high cheekbones, full lips, and dressed in a French suit. He took his pleasures with my grandmother, and my mother was born of these. My mother called herself mestiza. I saw Asian in her look.

My father was Jewish, born of a Jewish mother from Vilna and a Jewish father from Odessa, neither of whom spoke English or each other's language, but who both had the Russian pogroms in common. My father was blue of eyes and wide of smile. He was light-haired as an adolescent (though this did not protect him from posted signs that said: No Dogs or Jews Allowed), bald when I knew him, and bearded in his later years.

I had two brothers, who had my father's features and my mother's eyes. I thought my older brother looked like a mix of Marlon Brando and James Dean, and my younger, like a darker, wavy-haired, slighter version of my older brother—"more Indian," people said, "his eyes, yes Indian eyes." It is hard to describe any of us except by media images that were popular at the time, precisely because we were not a type. Though my hair is wavy like my father's, I have my mother's features, and Asian-yellow or dark brown skin, depending on the sun. I have been asked in different stages of my life whether I was Italian, Moroccan, Brazilian, Filipina, Eurasian, or "some Black mix," depending on when and where I was. A talent scout asked me, as a thirteen-year-old in Miami Beach, if I was Puerto Rican. Hollywood, he said, giving me his calling card, was interested in exotics. That same year, White classmates at Garfield Junior High School in Berkeley, later named Martin Luther King, called me Aunt Jemima. In the mid-1970s I was once mistaken for Bianca Jagger, though I think that is only because brown icons were rare and because I was Bianca-dark from lying in the summer sun. Never has the first guess been Mexican or Jew. I have always been a "what are you?", a guessed-at person, a question mark. Early on I learned that I resided at the end of a question, hooked onto empty space that I had to fill with some answer. Self was created at the moment of answer, and the answer depended on where I was and with whom. I thought of myself as an interrogated subject (Louis Althusser would have said "interpellated"), a "look" always waiting to be policed, questioned, qualified, and defined. To legitimate myself, I practiced how to answer not in the affirmative or negative, but in the narrative.

My mother, on the other hand, saw herself both as mestiza and Mexican. She did not separate the two. The Mexican concept of *mestizaje*, rooted in the mix of Spanish, Indian, and African, acknowledges the reality of racial mixing. This does not mean a hierarchy of color does not exist (in some Mexican circles marrying dark is still considered marrying down, but Mexicans also say money bleaches the skin). Nevertheless, to be too white in Mexico brings reminders of cruel foreign usurpations. To be Mexican is to be a mestizo. Mexicans can be adamant about this. "*Soy Mexicana*," my mother would say. She never became a U.S. citizen.

But since I was a child I have been sure of nothing except that I would be subject to scrutiny, by anyone, anywhere. In the summer of 1960 my father sent my mother, younger brother, and me by Greyhound bus to visit his family in Miami Beach. As we boarded the bus, he told my brother and me to "Write down what you see, and let me know how Negroes are treated." Our political education was important to him. During the 1940s he had fought against antidark laws in Miami, and the day after we left he was subsidizing Freedom Riders to ride a Greyhound south.

The trip was without drama until we reached our transfer point in the South, where the bus on which we would spend two days and a night was divided between front and back, White and Black. My brother, mother, and I gravitated toward seats at the back of the bus. I do not remember whether we were directed to sit there or took the seats to avoid being questioned and looked at disapprovingly (you internalize such fears). This was during the years of the Aunt Jemima taunts, and I know I felt out of place in the White zone. A short time after we sat down the person in back of me began to kick my seat. I tried to ignore it, but what began as occasional taps escalated into violent kicks. Finally, I turned to confront an angry middle-aged Black woman. "Excuse me," I said, "can you please stop kicking my seat!" "You all belong at the front of the bus," she said, before she stopped kicking. I looked around to see where we might belong. A Black man sat right in front of us, and in front of him, whiteness. We were sitting behind the color line. Though I looked like "Aunt Jemima" to my classmates, I must have looked White to the woman. I wondered whether she would have expressed such contempt for us had we been White. I was confused. But the reaction of other passengers to the small commotion we had caused told me we were not welcome in the front of the bus either.

"Mexicans not welcome." I read this somewhere right around those days. The "welcome" dangling at the end of that injunctive might have made me think it was better than prohibitions like "No dogs or Jews allowed" or "Colored Only," the latter visible every place we went in the South. But the untidy negative "not welcome" suggested that we were contaminated and to be feared. Even then I understood "not welcome" to mean please leave, please do not come back, please disappear, please you are an embarrassment, please do not touch me—please you are the face of shame, a sham. Such has been antibrown sentiment.

I was not altogether wrong. Mestizos have had no place in the legal strategies of this country. In 1930, only thirty years before my freedom ride through the South, Texas sociologist Max Handman wrote that "American society has no social technique for handling partly colored races. We have a place for the Negro and a place for the white man: the Mexican is not a Negro, and the white man refuses him an equal status" (Moran, 57). These observations were the cutting edge of political, scientific, cultural, and sociological theories of the day. About the same time Handman was writing this, Hitler was developing techniques and technologies to rid his nation of degenerate elements. The new sciences had facilitated such reasoning. But legal scholar Rachel Moran has observed that such reasoning existed in learned circles well before Handman identified it. After the Treaty of Guadalupe, she writes, "Leading scholars . . . warned that American democracy would be in jeopardy if the color line were compromised" (57). They were afraid of a mixed-race country like Mexico. And on the continent, around the same time the Treaty of Guadalupe was signed, and European nations were burgeoning and establishing dominions around the world, French theorist Arthur de Gobineau laid the theoretical groundwork for atrocities of the twentieth century when he theorized that "Nations die when they are composed of elements that have degenerated" (Taguieff, 113). But let us not stop here. Mixing had been associated with moral corruption well before it took hold in modern nation-states. According to an old Arab adage: "God created the White man and God created the Black man; the Devil created the *métis*" (Taguieff, 223).[2]

Degenerate, immoral, impure, the *métis* is proof of deracination, transgression, of border crossings, of translocal yearnings, and of sexual urges. She has contravened the laws of the tribe. For empire builders of the nineteenth century, *métissage* served both as a warning against such transgression and as a way to ensure national allegiance. *Métissage* was a construct that anticipated the decentering effects of imperialism. Indeed, anthropology emerged in Europe during the explosion of empire and colonization not simply because colony and empire facilitated the study of the "other," but also because early anthropology provided an ideological framework to separate the self from the other, the "they" from the "us" of Western societies (the representation of the noble savage had served the same purpose). Moreover, new technologies aided in under-scoring the separation. One of the initial uses of photography, for example, whose emergence in 1839 was contemporaneous with the expansion of imperialism, was to record for scientific study the phenotypic distinctions between self and other. This was the beginning, one might say, of a different way of seeing, where the observer rather than the observed deciphers, constructs, manipulates, and then passes judgment on his subject of study, and where for the observing culture, other cultures are reduced to a distinct and concrete image robbed of human complexity. The fear of *métissage* is precisely the fear of weakening the distinction between self and other, a fear of transmodernity, one might say, of loss of self to other, a fear, in short, of human sexuality and the complexity it can tap. As an ideology, then, racism exists to police sexuality. Abel Bonnard concluded as much when he said, "Racism is the refusal to be further bastardized" (Taguieff, 213).

Brownness demonstrates, then, the effect of border-trespassing economies and imperialist movements that inadvertently license, to use Baudelaire's words, the *déregulation de tous les sens*. Depending on one's perspective, this deregulation of sensual experience may be one of the few positive effects of a deregulated economy, since it will become increasingly impossible, despite what Pierre-André Taguieff calls the "mixophobia" in Western societies, to regulate brownness (213–229). Nevertheless, even today intellectual and theoretical discourses tend to skirt the matter. A while back, discussing the subject of brownness with a philosophe Argentine friend of mine, I made an off-the-cuff observation, "*Solo la sensualidad dice la verdad, porque la sensualidad no tiene ego.*" Disturbed, she turned my statement into a question. "Only sensuality conveys the truth because sensuality is devoid of ego?" she asked, mocking me. "What kind of nonsense is that?" she snapped. "You know there are no universal truths. You know everything depends on where you're coming from." Then she got up from the table at which we were sitting and abandoned me to her café au lait.

Another Argentine raised quite frankly the issue of Mexico's mixed-raced phenotype. "Mexicans are not a good-looking people. Don't you think?" she asked, perhaps forgetting that I was mestiza (or was it I who was forgetting that people in Argentina, symbol of a European non-mestiza nation, might not be accustomed to such looks). I suddenly remembered the rallying cry "Black is beautiful," a call of a people in their battle for recognition. Behind the battle scenes, of course, sensuality was playing its leveling game. But twenty-five years later I was still fighting the same battle in a discreet conversation with a colleague at an academic cocktail party.

If I have been indulging in the *lookism* I denounced earlier, it is because the mixed-race person lives within the assumptions her appearance opens up, and these can depend on weather, age, or social, cultural, or political perceptions. *Lookism*, or the capacity to be called into existence by others' perception about how we look, is central to "mixed-racism" and any theory that examines it, since how we look ("you don't look American"), we are told again and again, is largely what we are. In this country our identity is in the eyes of the beholder. My mother must have felt great confusion when she crossed the border and in the passing of one moment to the next became "colored."

While my brief résumé parallels the story of racism in this country during the last half century, I use it to suggest the individuality, contingency, and deliberation in which mixed-race individuals engage the moment they awaken to self. In this sense, mixed-race children's impression of self is very much the opposite of children who learn to identify themselves in the world by naming, categorizing, differentiating, and ordering. The mixed-race individual traces her awareness of the world not by asking causal questions ("Why?"), but by having to explain a self ("*What* are you?") that knows "self" only as a contradiction, a friction, a tension, an inconclusiveness, and a disorder that comes to an end only at the moment the tension is conceptualized. We are self-imagined. This is very much a view counter to the imaginary one we have of innocent childhood. In fact, the inter-race—and "inter-raised"—child must engage in deliberations, posing and answering questions that adults are reluctant to pose: Why do we exist *between* this and that? The narratives of mixed-race writers reveal this deliberation not because the narratives are fragmented, as texts of Modernist and Postmodernist writers might be, but rather because as mixed-race individuals we have always resided at the nexus of paradox, crisis, conflict, and tension. Indeed, our refusal to engage in the self-other dialectic and to find location (or be situated) in any geographical space makes us a center that moves—in a word, makes us what I have been calling transmodern.

IV. MISCEG-NARRATION AND COUNTERNARRATIVES

Narratives of mixed-race individuals, by mixed-race individuals, have existed for a long time. I think, for example, of Nella Larsen's *Passing*, or James Weldon Johnson's *The Autobiography of an Ex-Colored Man*, or of more recent writers like Charles Mingus, Frank Chin, Julia Alvarez, Lisa See, James McBride, and Gregory Howard Williams. Yet in this media era of the sound bite, Tiger Woods perhaps most forcefully captured the contemporary mixed-race narrative when in 1996 he declared in an answer to the question "What are you?" that he is "Cablinasian," a combination of Caucasian, Black, Indian, and Asian. His narrative had particular resonance not simply because of his immense popularity, but also because photo ops showed him in the company of his father and mother, both of whom he clearly resembles and who, as a Black and Asian couple, move beyond Western/non-Western paradigms of Black and White or self and other. If anything, this is a coupling of "other-other." The combination of visual message and textual identification—the word Cablinasian itself difficult to pronounce, incongruous in its spelling, and, at first sight, nonsense—made all the sense in the world to someone like me. I saw the narrative as rich, full, and poetic. Tiger Woods's words rendered a Lewis Carroll–type performance where sound is sense, where declaration is act, where a picture is worth many words (the multimedia help multirace narratives, especially where they can be commodified), and where deliberation lies at the center. It was a transmodern narrative, an imaginative political statement, eschewing location and designation, and transmitted worldwide. Tiger Woods's "translation" of self as a Cablinasian transcended the very word he had invented by demonstrating the limitation of words and the absurdity of categories that try to locate identity.

Of equal interest was the immediate attempt by the media and politicians to deconstruct the text, particularly because the text dovetailed with the controversy over whether or not to convert the category of "other" to "mixed race" in the 2000 Census. In July of 1996 mixed-race activists led by Georgia-based Project RACE (Reclassify All Children Equally) had marched on Washington to lend support to the effort to reclassify the Census. Yet even this event did nothing to mollify Tiger Woods's critics, who saw his assertion as not fitting the Black/White binary of identity politics. Blacks attacked Woods's placement of Caucasian first and Black second because he seemed to be giving a preference to his White ancestry, even though his father, designated by colorists as Black, accompanied him everywhere and news commentators had often referred to him as Black.

Still, many of those who opposed including a multirace category in the Census were upset. Darryl Strickland reported in his article "Interracial Generation: 'We Are Who We Are'" that civil rights groups, including the Lawyers' Committee for Civil Rights under Law, the National Association for the Advancement of Colored People, the Urban League, and the Joint Center for Political and Economic Studies, urged that "the OMB [Office of Management and Budget] should not rush to institute the multiracial category when there [was] clear potential for increasing the racial segregation, discrimination and stigmatization of black Americans" (Strickland). In the same article Eric Rodriguez, a policy analyst at the National Council of La Raza, which counts 2 million Hispanics in its membership, was quoted as opposing the addition of a multiracial box: "We're not sure what it does, how it's counted, and what it means." Joseph Lowery, head of the Leadership Conference, echoed these arguments, saying, "We would be hard pressed to fight for racial justice if we were not able to identify people defined in certain categories" (Strickland). Inadvertently, no doubt, Lowery in his support of categories validated the Census and its function as a powerful counternarrative to Woods's own.

The census has been, since it began, a major narrative of racial categorizing. A 1988 Census Bureau study, for instance, summarizes nicely the changing story of race (Martin et al., 3–4). In 1850, "White," "Black," and "Mulatto" were used. In 1870, "Chinese" and "Indian" appear with the caveat "Be particularly careful in reporting the class *Mulatto*. The word here is generic, and includes quadroons, octoroons, and all persons having any *perceptible* trait of African blood" (Martin et al., 3, emphasis added). In 1890 these become separate categories, and the category "Japanese" also appears. In 1930 the Census designates as "Negro," "any person of mixed White and Negro blood . . . no matter how small the percentage," and classifies as "Mexican," "All persons born in Mexico, or having parents born in Mexico, who were not definitely White, Negro, Indian, Chinese, or Japanese." In 1940 the narrative shifts, and reclassifies Mexicans as White, unless they show "observable characteristics of another race." Clearly in 1942 my mother did, thus the prohibitions against her. In 1960 the Census adds Filipino, Hawaiian, Aleut, and Eskimo to its growing list, and in 1970 the ethnic option of "Hispanic" is included. By 1980 the Census is populated by a large portion of the world, as "nine separate Asian and Pacific Islander categories such as Asian Indian, Guamanian, Samoan, and Vietnamese" appear (Martin et al., 4). But in the 1980s the plot thickens, becomes Postmodern, and, as if taking its cue from postcolonial narratives, opens up the category "other race," to designate as "others" those of us who simply do not fit. Asserting their *mestizaje*, Latino self-classification in the "other" category rose from "700,000 in 1970 to 5.8 million in 1980" (Martin et al., 5). In 2000, the Census offered the following categories: American Indian or Alaskan Native, Asian, Pacific Islander, Black or African American, White, and Other. This categorizing fiction rejects the "multiracial" category, or the "cablinasianizing" of the United States. In a strange twist, some civil rights groups resisted the new changes in the Census, and declared that mixed race is not an acceptable category. Try as we might, our national narrative simply cannot get rid of the rhetoric of "other."

The anti-multirace protests, however, are not unjustified. There is a lot at stake in census categories, not least of which, as the civil rights advocates maintain, are laws that protect politically disadvantaged groups. But equally important, the clash between category and self-perception has come into the open because minority groups are achieving results in this categorizing narrative. The existence itself of the controversy—the idea that the mulatto, the mutt, the half-breed sons and daughters of the devil should want to declare their identity—is proof of the grassroots success of identity politics. While the census narrative by necessity, then, shows a shifting to self-identification, civil rights advocates, having become victims of their own success, need to collude with the government to maintain their gains. *Clearly, it is also in the government's interest to keep the dualism active and engaged, precisely because it keeps nonwhites in their place. Identity politics is double-edged.*

It is in this context, then, that I find Woods's narrative pertinent. The uproar that Woods caused exposes the conflict at the center of identity politics. Allowing individual choice and differences threatens to undermine political consensus—the inescapable conundrum of modern politics. Certainly, at the moment that Orwell decides not to shoot his enemy, we experience how personal choice can change political intent and prejudice. But can this be sustained? Perhaps, if individuals, like Woods in this case, challenge orthodoxies, realize that self cannot be separated from other, and work collectively for change. But, too often, especially in this country, which is built on an imagined individuality, we often see individual well-being as a condition opposed to collective action—as if one negates the possibility of the other. We must invent another vocabulary, which sustains individual choice, but also galvanizes individuals to work collectively for economic, educational, political, and social justice. If we don't, we may imagine we have made individual choices, but in fact we will have doomed ourselves to the same categorical thinking that has made "White" and "other" so convenient. Woods's narrative subverts color and racial categories, and voices instead the human desires that cablinasianized him. Try as we might to construct categories, they cannot ultimately resist human urges to defy them as mechanisms of identity. If only for a moment, then, Cablinasian opens the imagination and triumphs as a narrative.

As Tiger Woods shows us, since brown does not have to battle White, it has no stake in being essentialist—in other words, it does not have to protect the dualism that continues to foster racist policy, but rather can choose to affiliate at will. Moreover, since mixed-race people are interested in protecting their own freedoms, it is common for them to support nondiscriminatory strategies. For example, as a result of who I am and the deliberations that ensued from my experience with the baseball caps, it became impossible for me to support any racist policy in the wake of the September 11 disaster that visited our country. These men's discriminatory remarks, then, determined my strategic position against stricter policy regarding immigration to the United States, even though the attackers and their associates maintain a deep hatred of groups with which I affiliate. I fear more racist sentiment in this country than I do terrorist attacks and the need to be "secure" from them.

V. ANTHOLOGIES AND MEMOIRS: "VOICED" NARRATIVES

In 1994, a couple of years before Tiger Woods's declaration, Lise Funderburg edited *Black, White, Other*, one of the first popular books on the issue of mixed race. The anthology, little more than a book of "voices" that "bear witness directly to the reader" about mixed-race experience in this society, compiles narratives which reveal the difficulties that mixed-race children confront, if they are born with phenotypes different from other siblings; or the confusion they may experience when their own prejudices or fears lead them to identify with one parent and not the other; or the ostracism a mixed-race child experiences because she does not look Black enough or White enough to quiet group prejudices (15). "I really started to become Anti-white," a young mixed-race woman reveals (39). Another who fails to look Black enough describes a very different experience: "I couldn't participate in that [the Black] world . . . because I'm mixed" (136). "I identify as I do mainly because the outside world says I have no choice," says yet another young woman (134). In the mingling of voices, Funderburg's anthology reveals the tension her subjects experience when they realize how much of their self-perception is at variance with the public identities forced on them. Most important, the testimonials demonstrate that the discourses of difference, ethnicity, and culture—the main discourses of the day—are products of an ideology of othering.[3]

Funderberg's decision to preface what she calls "self-portraits" both with biographical data, such as the subject's age and employment, and with photographs of the subject seems out of place in this book, especially since the anthology otherwise claims that "racial identity is defined not . . . by appearance, but by how people choose to define themselves" (170). In fact, the photos end up anchoring the subjects' narratives to their appearance and thus inadvertently functioning as racial designators. Not surprisingly, black-looking subjects, who felt more prone to institutional discrimination, tended to identify with Blacks, despite their desire for other affiliations, whereas light-skinned biracials were largely not accepted by Blacks, even though they may have identified themselves as Black. The editorial subtext thus reveals that racial politics still depend on being "other"-identified (which is exactly the narrative that Woods resists) and that a mixed-race individual's racial affiliation is, in many cases, not voluntary, because the mixed-race individual has not yet been permitted to escape the Black-White consciousness of appearance. The unintended consequence of Funderberg's use of photos shows how difficult it is not to succumb to the demands of "lookism" when dealing with mixed race within a culture that still operates according to a Black-White binary. While this editorial decision undermines the subversive goal of voice-based testimony, it is hard to imagine how else the editor might have handled the problem, since the reader, too, expects the subjects to fit racial categories. It is interesting that the closer to White that a subject looked, the greater flexibility she had to determine her affiliation. Anthologies, as genres, lend themselves well to the polyphonic interplay of editorial and authorial voices. In Funderberg's text this interplay deepens our understanding of the difficulties that inhere when speaking and writing about mixed race.

Indeed, the polyphony inherent in anthologies makes the anthology an excellent conduit of choice for the melange of voices and genres that mixed-race discourse should encourage. Like thought, polyphony moves not from beginning to end, but continuously everywhere—voices, bodies, and thoughts meet and mingle. For early mixed-race theorists the need for polyphony was both pragmatic and theoretical. "Theorists-of-color," wrote Gloria Anzaldúa in her preface to her groundbreaking anthology *Haciendo Caras (Making Face, Making Soul)*, "are in the process of trying to formulate 'marginal' theories that are partially outside and partially inside the Western frame of reference [. . .] theories that overlap many 'worlds.' . . . In our literature, social issues such as race, class and sexual difference are intertwined with the narrative and poetic elements of a text, elements in which theory is embedded" (xxvi). Anzaldúa's own anthologies "embedded" theory in poetry, political manifesto, and personal essays so that even here new "layered" and polyphonic discourses emerge. She thus transformed the anthology into a mestizo genre par excellence, the misceg-narrations of which I speak.

In both of her early anthologies the mixed-race subject emerged as a "theorizing" and interstitial subject who oftentimes found herself pinned between the voice of one culture and the voicing of another. By "embedding" emerging theories into different genres, brown writers (as the title *Making Face* suggests) mimicked and mocked univocal Western theory, which knows where it is going before it gets there. In their multiple "voicings," Anzaldúa's anthologies replicated mixed-race experience—now one thing, now another, clearly authored but rarely by the same writer. It showed again and again how mixed-race theorists prefer the anthology as a genre particularly because they know that their experiences, far from being unicentered, assume no singular place of origin, only a vague sense of destination, and, because crossings of boundaries necessitate contingencies, no contract with the past. Mixed-race writers live the reality of an anthological moment.

As I have suggested earlier, if mixed-race theory has a narrative, it is embodied in the tension, conflicts, and deliberations that inhere in discursive genres like the personal essay or memoir, which remain the voiced alternatives to official histories or systematic philosophies. This preference is consistent with the task before us, since the objective of the personal essay or memoir, to paraphrase Montaigne, is to show thought in its physical labor, making the self and others a condition of work.[4] As I have shown elsewhere, the memoir is a narrative of an ahistoric and fragmented self trying to find a form and a moral center; in its very labor the memoir, like the essay, is a narrative of the present, not the past, the "now" rather than the "then."[5] Thus, unlike cultural theorists, who become the center of their discourses as a way to "locate" themselves vis-à-vis their subjects, mixed-race writers return to self at the point the self engages the other. As I suggested earlier, I believe this intersection, this polyphonic instant, to be the original point of departure for all theory, itself a recognition of the solitude and separation that accompany being let into the world.

For these reasons, mixed-race writers tend to reject fashionable metaphors of "positionality" that express separation between self and other in favor of metaphors that emphasize the movement within which and from which these connections arise.[6] The mixed-race writer understands herself existing not simply in one single moment but also in the flux and multiplicity that these contingent moments may generate in her transit. It is in the recollection of these moments that she reconstitutes herself as a subject.

VI. MEMOIRS: NEGOTIATING AND THEORIZING SUBJECTS

Three memoirs, James McBride's *The Color of Water: A Black Man's Tribute to His White Mother*, Gregory Howard Williams's *Life on the Color Line: The Story of a White Boy Who Discovered He Was Black*, and Sara Suleri's *Meatless Days*, illustrate the history and development of a negotiating and theorizing subject that becomes increasingly transmodern. In 1996, the same year Tiger Woods declared himself Cablinasian, James McBride's and Gregory Howard Williams's memoirs made the bestsellers list—mixed race was coming of age and being "outed." Both memoirs expose the conflict and moral turmoil of living on the color line. Williams's narrative covers the period before pre-identity politics and Jim Crow, and McBride's speaks of the identity politics that emerged during the Black Power movements of the late 1960s. The memoirs reveal how interdictions against mixed race obliged both writers to create a counterimaginary to the binary of race. Despite the humiliations and tensions created by race and the constant "repositioning" that laboring within these tensions requires, the writers demonstrate the self as it begins to reconstitute itself in thought—mobile and transforming, neither White nor Black.

Life on the Color Line demonstrates the devastating powers of language and law to shape perception, indeed to destroy lives. Williams, who spends his first ten years as a White boy living in segregated Virginia with his White mother and his "Italian" father, involuntarily crosses the color line from White to Black when his mother leaves his father and he and his brother accompany their father to live with his Black family in Muncie, Indiana. Right after the confused children meet their grandmother and great aunt, his father reveals that he is not White, but Black. "I saw my father as I never had seen him," writes Williams. "Before my eyes he was transformed from a swarthy Italian to his true self—a high-yellow mulatto. My father was a Negro! We were colored! After ten years in Virginia on the white side of the color line, I knew what that meant" (32–33). Categorizing has had the power to achieve radical transformation. In fact, Williams's alienation from the White world becomes complete only when it is named. Frustrated by his lack of prospects for work, Williams's father denounces his mother. Williams recalls that "The harshness of Dad's words shocked me. Though we hadn't heard from her in almost a year, labeling her a 'white bitch' pushed her over the line and banished her totally" (67). He is now prepared to reject his mother and complete his crossing from White to Black. Williams shows us that unlike race, which is equivocal, the word is law.

But self cannot be isolated from the contingencies that create it. Williams begins to inhabit his blackness not only because the law recasts him as Black but also because he begins to understand his community, which in turn allows him to see that the cruelty of Whites is out of kilter with his moral sense. Despite the laws against it, he will eventually see himself as mixed race, but not before he reconstructs the history of its representation.

He learns soon enough that he is the outcome of multiple crossings of the color line, of multiple layerings of race and of multiple dissimulations, all persistent themes in mixed-race narratives. He learns that his grandfather was the White "young master of the household," for whom his grandmother worked. Of her own father, his grandmother tells him, "My daddy was Shan Higginbottom. He was an Indian from Bristol. He was just a little bit colored" (61). And of his own father Williams tells us that, though mixed, he "masqueraded as white" (63). This narrative of pedigree sums up the history of mixed race in the United States.

While tales of passing are common to mixed-race narrative, Williams uses these to critique the way mixed race has been forced to constitute itself. He recognizes the historical and economic circumstances that led to the phenomenon of passing, but rejects passing because of the duplicity it entails and the alienation and self-devastation that it creates. His father's tale becomes a counternarrative to his own. At one point Williams's father, justifying his reasoning for passing, contends that "Coloreds don't like half-breeds either" and that as a half-breed Williams would do well to "learn to bob and weave" (38, 67). Indeed, Williams's life as a half-breed becomes absorbed in bobbing and weaving, in ducking enemies on both sides of the color line, so his father's argument seems to have some merit. But when his father later tells him that to escape this hell of blackness he must learn to pass for White, Williams protests, "But I don't want to be white." Even though he "hadn't wanted to be colored . . . too much had happened to [him] in Muncie to be a part of the white world that had rejected [him] so completely" (157). This deliberation, perhaps a reflection itself of a historical moment that separates him from his father's generation of mixed-race individuals, is not based on logic but on emotion and identification. Williams chooses to endure the economic, geopolitical, social, and personal consequences of his "descent" into blackness and makes us see that while the mixed-race individual, like the "passer," has no real community, creating his life as he goes, mixed race operates with consciousness of its alienation and solitude in a way Williams's father cannot.

In his rethinking of mixed race, Williams discovers two things. First, "passing" prohibits any radical change in thinking about the subject of race because it is directed by fear of being found out. Second, the privileges afforded to Whites cannot be obtained by dissimulation, because privilege in its most basic sense is the privilege not to have to dissemble but to do as one pleases, to be none other than self. This is finally Williams's objective. Ten years later, when he finally sees his mother, who asks him and his younger brother to "forget we were 'colored' boys . . . [and] to move back into her life without a past, without roots, without feelings for the people who had sheltered and cared for us," he concludes that passing is not an option. "I knew that was something we could never do," he says of himself and his brother (281). Williams *consubstantiates* his narrative (in the way that Montaigne intends when he says he consubstantiates his book). He exists in narration, in the finding and knowing that he is not the "bestial mongrel mulatto, the dreg of human society," that he was called in the early days.

McBride's story begins where Williams leaves off. Williams's work unsettles us because it suggests that we are all vulnerable to misidentification and categorizing fictions of the self and, perhaps even worse, to both the tyranny and deceptions of others. Unlike Williams, who in the 1950s has no choice but to declare himself on one or the other side of the color line, McBride makes explicit how the mixed-race individual must be none other than a theorizing subject. McBride, who looks Black and identifies as Black, discovers in the middle of the Black identity movement of the 1960s that his mother is a White Jewish immigrant who during the 1940s crossed the color line into blackness, a counterstory to the better-known tale of passing, or "ascending," from Black to White. In much the same way as Williams's memoir is a descent into blackness, so McBride's memoir is, at first, a descent into whiteness, an unwilling recognition that he is White, too.

McBride's memoir, a tribute to his Jewish mother, alternates between his mother's voice and his own. The double-voiced narrative, which begins with his mother's oral history, moves slowly like a call and response between two cultures, between spoken and written narrative, between argument and counterargument, between a racist past and a racist present, between White and Black, between mother and son. "[C]onflict was part of our lives," McBride observes, "written into our very faces, hands, and arms" (79). Where Williams lays claim to a genealogy of mixed race, McBride is less concerned with racial history than he is with how he embodies mixed-race individuality, or what he comes to see as a "contradiction that survived in its essence" (79). He writes his memoir to explore precisely that contradiction, or point of tension.

McBride's mother narrates her past reluctantly ("You want to talk about my family and here I been dead to them for fifty years") and only at her son's urging. She tells McBride, among other things, that she is the Polish Jewish immigrant daughter of a rabbi and that she abandoned her home, family, and culture deliberately, so she could cross the color line and marry McBride's father, a Black Baptist reverend, and, after his death, McBride's Black stepfather, both of whom she loved. We find out that she, her spouses, and her twelve children lived in great physical deprivation, but survived. We find out as well that she is defied by her son simply because she is White. Until the moment of her narrative she has existed as an ahistorical subject alienated from her past.

Unlike Williams, McBride, who grows up in a Black neighborhood, believes from the start that he is Black, only to discover, in a moment of spiritual crisis, that his mother is White, something she had kept from him ("When I would ask her if she was white, she'd say, 'No, I'm light-skinned'") because of her own rejection of her family and her desire to be part of her Black community (15). Whereas Williams is alienated from his mother, McBride's memoir is an enactment of his reconciliation. But the polyphonic crisscrossing of voices, like the crisscrossing of race, gives the narrative a tension, a fighting voice one might say, which is finally what remains with us. Nevertheless, early in his childhood, McBride anticipates his transcendence of the racial divide. His mother, he tells us, "would occasionally do something in church that I never saw her do at home or anywhere else . . . bow down her head and weep" (39). McBride asks his mother why she cries, and when she tells him that she cries because she is happy, he puts his own spin on it:

> I thought it was because she wanted to be black like everyone else in church, because maybe God liked black people better, and one afternoon on the way home from church I asked her whether God was black or white.
>
> A deep sigh. "Oh boy . . . God's not black. He's not white. He's a spirit."

"What's a spirit? "

"A spirit's a spirit."

"What color is God's spirit? "

"It doesn't have a color," she said. "God is the color of water. Water doesn't have a color." (39)

This episode, which gives the memoir its title, begins the drama of McBride's painful and sometimes cruel rejection of his Jewish mother and the White world she represents, and triggers his deliberations about race. The memoir in this sense is a polemic about the nature of race, which significantly begins not with a question about who God is but rather what color God is, a question that will take the whole narrative to answer. Despite McBride's initial rejection of whiteness (a posture consistent with the radical, and much needed, identity politics of the late 1960s), his mother's observation that God is the color of water lingers with him. He asks the questions his working mother does not have the time or leisure to ask and, as her listener and interlocutor, finally understands that she has been right all along. For a child the logic might seem irrefutable: God is the color of water; I am made in the image of God; therefore I am the color of water. But race is not subject to logic. Only in his back and forth with his mother, one life pitched against another, does he come to understand that he is neither Black nor White.

McBride's narrative suggests that to understand race, mixed race in particular, one must remain engaged and become an interrogating and theorizing subject. It suggests further that to remain radical, one must refuse the categorizing tendencies of any orthodoxy, especially in this case the binary categories of race. It is by this questioning that McBride discovers that like God, like his mother, he is the color of water and that there is meaning beyond the racist and restless world in which he lives. This meaning, as the parable of God's color suggests, is liquid as water and absorbs all colors in its transparency.

Unlike Williams, who sees his role as a mediator between races, McBride realizes that to live at the interstices of race is to move, like the color of water, in the space between categories, in the space where contingency and paradox stir. In other words, one must be, like thinking itself, unbounded, displaced, and vigilant. Deliberative discourse is a radical venture because it requires that one be radical at every moment.

Literary critic Sara Suleri, in her memoir-theory *Meatless Days*, demonstrates the radical possibilities of this discourse. Born brown in Pakistan to a well-connected Welsh mother and a diplomat Pakistani father, and now teaching in the United States, Suleri expresses precisely the dislocated and increasingly transmodern nature of mixed-race experience. She jostles the rules of her narrative in a certain imitation of the dislocation she feels and in the act uses voice, as if it were music, to remind us that we are already too separate from ourselves and that racial, gender, linguistic, and political categories work to exacerbate this tragic human condition. Here she both lives in language and performs it:

> Living in daylight, after all, is not so different from living between two languages: it is a lie to say that some people only live in one, for to know a couple of different languages is merely a matter of demonstrating the pangs of intimacy that beset our mouths each time we speak. Coming second to me, Urdu opens in my mind a passage way between the sea of possibility and what I cannot say in English: when those waters part, they seem to promise some solidity of surface, but then like speech they glide away to reconfirm the brigandry of utterance. So snatches of discourse overheard in the streets seem fraught with robbery, a low-income level making each voice belligerently protest, "I need, I need, a different speech!" Speaking two languages may seem a relative affluence, but more often it entails the problems of maintaining a second establishment even though your body can be in only one place at a time. . . . Urdu like a reprimand disturbs my sense of habitation: "Do you think you ever lived on the inside of space," it tells me with some scorn. . . . Living in language is tantamount to living with other people. Both are postures in equilibrium that attend upon gravity's capacity for flotation, which is a somber way of looking out for the moment when significance can empty into habit. For significance is that which must be bailed out all the time; it must be peeled away with onion tears in order that habit can come bobbing up like mushrooms on the surface of a soup. (177)

Suleri's prose reveals, all the more, linguistic dislocations and the racial, political, social, and theoretical dislocations that these linguistic dislocations may express. At the same time, her reminiscences, thoughts, and prose move in a current that absorbs and transforms literary, cultural, race, and gender theory, so that it is unclear where one discourse begins and another ends. Theoretical terminology, for example, appears unexpectedly now and then and because of its displacement often resonates with the emptiness of buzzwords, while remaining subservient to her voice and whatever significance she decides to bail out. Her prose then moves in pitch from the high notes of intellectual discourse to the low notes of mundane observations, from prose to poetry, making us conscious of language from moment to moment, as though each word, though running with the current, had an individual life of its own.

Suleri's relation to language, a central subject in her memoir, is complex. The language she uses itself supports her theory that there is always a gap between intimacy and utterance, a certain staging of self when we talk, an experience of alienation as we hear ourselves go public. In the passage I quote above, for example, the economic and social metaphors seem incongruous in what on the surface seems to be a lyrical meditation on the nature of language and memory. The sudden presence of these metaphors within the passage interrupts her meditation, suggesting that language participates in the world of economic exchange and that her command of English and Urdu is a mark of her class privilege, a possession, to use Pierre Bourdieu's expression, of linguistic capital. At the same time, as her memoir-critique makes clear, money has yet to eradicate race, and in most of the world, still, to be brown or black of skin is to assume a poverty that all the affluence in the world cannot remedy.

Nevertheless, Suleri tells us, she first experienced the power of language because of race. At one point in her narrative, she remembers herself as a seven-year-old in London being asked by her Pakistani father why, unlike her sister Ifat, she has no friends:

> [A] happy formulation crossed my mind: "It's because Ifat's white, and I am brown," I suggested brightly. I knew that I had given him, essentialized, a scrupulous rendition of school-ground politics, but Papa the politician was outraged. Ifat, who could pass as English, had one hurdle less to cross than I did in our Chiswick school—she and I had talked about it many times. But Papa could not stomach such a bald fact, launching instead into a long and passionate speech about the ancient civilization that inhered in my genes, about how steadily I should walk in such proud pigmentation. "[Y]ou are my wheaten daughter," he declared, "wheaten, and most beautiful!" (160).

The anecdote takes place in the middle of a meditation on race. Her Pakistani father sees the treachery of race within an historical context (he is Pakistani and brown, and has lived as the colonial "other"), whereas, taking the liberty perhaps of one who is White, her English "mother loved to look at us in race . . . [and] seemed subdued with awe at the commingling of color that with our bodies we flung onto her, comminglings in which she had colluded to produce" (161). Suleri observes, though, that her mother seemed at the same time to retreat from the joy, as though in the "aftermath" her mother would be asked to consider: "What will happen to these pieces of yourself—you, and yet not you—when you dispatch them into the world?" (161).

While her mother meditates then on the very sexual, embodied "commingling" of race that she has helped to produce, her father reminds Suleri that color is a marker of difference and inferiority: "Oh dear, I thought, looking down. How could I tell him that I was only trying to locate a difference, a fact that shaped my day much as weather did the wet chill of an English spring. I had not the language to face up to his strong talk, and so looked down instead, almost as though he were right to assume that I had felt ashamed, inferior. 'Never call color by its proper name,' I told myself, at seven" (160).

If her parents play out the division and fears emboldened by racialized thinking, Suleri's resolution to see language as the perpetrator of division is also to see language's ability to liberate. "To be engulfed by grammar after all," Suleri writes, "is a tricky prospect, and a voice deserves to declare its own control in any way it can, asserting that it is an inventive thing" (155). In the very moment of connection and dissolution of logical sequence, in the dislocation, Suleri suggests, we can find our voice.

While in many respects Suleri's description of dislocation and difference is reminiscent of Orwell's account of deliberation where habitual perceptions are displaced, her memoir-critique testifies more specifically to the dislocation that comes from mixed-race experience. What makes Suleri's work so theoretically interesting is the way she taps into current transworldly experiences of mixed-race individuals. Speaking of memory, Walter Benjamin observed that the transience of the moment had the power to reduce time. Suleri's work reproduces that transience. Her prose floats in and out of the reader's consciousness, capturing for the reader the fluctuation of dislocated experience—she is in New Haven when she remembers London or in Pakistan when she imagines the United States. Her memory is one of continuous displacements and transmigrations, of quick movements back and forth from one "habitation" to another. Time, space, and geography shrink under the pressure. These transmigrations capture the perspective of all misceg-narration, since mixed race talks about itself, when it talks about itself in any way, as transmigratory and deterritorialized. As mixed-race individuals, we have always been transmigrants, and it is only in this shifting and moving—with all its dangers and its disaffiliations or "happy" shapings—that we best express who we are.

Memory moves outside of space and time. Suleri's work shows us that memory has the infinite capacity to deterritorialize both the mind and body. But as the memoirs we have examined show, these are not mere aesthetic experiences; they are lived as well. Perhaps this is why in moments of her own deliberations Suleri remembers her mother telling her: "Daughter, unplot yourself; let be" (156).

VII. TRANS-ACTIONS, TRANSMODERNITIES, AND TRANSIT LOUNGES
i. Montaigne

The brilliance of the essay as conceived by Montaigne lies in its modernity: in its perception that the writer has the capacity to capture the contingent, fluid, undetermined, chaotic, insecure, and otherwise unknown nature of daily human action and to communicate in a theory no grander than explaining it to himself. The nub of Montaigne's philosophy rests in his belief that everything in life is unplotted and contingent or, as he puts it, that "all things are in constant motion . . . both with the common motion and with their own." Thus his aim as a writer is not to "portray being," but to "portray passing. Not the passing from one age to another . . . but from day to day, from minute to minute" (610–611). Contingency and motion are the only certainties. And they cannot be served by abstraction and formal systems of philosophy or any grand theories, which disguise the daily details of life. The theorizing subject alone, as Montaigne so clearly states, must consubstantiate the theory ("I am myself the matter of my book").

Montaigne perceives, then, that individuals best understand themselves when confronted with the nuanced, spontaneous, and unpredictable daily behavior of another—much like Orwell, who in a moment sees himself in his enemy and decides not to shoot him, or like those of us who might see ourselves in the detailed description Suleri gives of living "on the inside of space," unplotted and contingent, hoisting herself on bits and pieces of memory as they float in and out of her consciousness.

To be consistent with its philosophy, then, the essay is theory in performance, or the performance of theory. It moves always with the consciousness of how the actor engages the "other." It is deliberative discourse, par excellence. It weighs, assays, and considers the individual at the very moment of her transactions in the world. It is a theory of exchange.

ii. Montaña

Even here, within the scope of this exchange, Montaigne's perceptions are entirely modern. Both transmigrations and transmodernity exist in exchange (indeed exist as a result of economic transaction). There is a tacit agreement that there will be an exchange between local and foreign, city and country, goods and services, self and other, real and imagined. The mixed-race subject feels better in cosmopolitan places, where people are more worried about exchanges than the color of skin. Mixed-race people prefer New York City to Modesto, California. Exchanges are not always good, if executed under coercion. Tiger Woods is a product of the desire for freer fleshly exchanges.

Paradoxically, however, with the quickening of transactions, the individual, subject of Montaigne's scrutiny, begins to shrink into anonymity in a proportion inverse to the growth of his identity. The mixed-race subject, on the other hand, who has eschewed type casting, has now a chance to take center stage.

Mixed-race theorists have been well positioned to describe transmodernity, especially because the contingencies of mixed-race experience are coincident with the contingencies of this global moment. Moreover, those theorists who have chosen to deal specifically with the transmodern as a subject of inquiry commonly examine issues that emerge from practical experiences. For example, they typically question the validity of identity constructs in the global modern, they encourage negotiation, and they support the nomadism of migration as a way to dismantle the parochialism of traditional cultures. For the mixed-race theorist, the only center that holds is the thinking subject as it transacts in the world.

As to this transaction, philosopher and cultural critic Anthony Appiah well remarks, in his collection of critical essays *In My Father's House: Africa in the Philosophy of Culture*, that in order for a transaction to work, it must consist of a "negotiable middle way," a position consistent with his upbringing as the son of a Ghanaian father and an English mother. For instance, when speaking of exchange, he argues that oral and written cultures must seek exchange. He reveals the inconsistency of romanticizing oral cultures with the very tools of literacy and argument. Western cultures are known because they are written and they are argued. "It is literacy that makes possible the precise formulation of questions," he maintains, "and it is precise formulation that points up inconsistencies" (130).

Appiah reflects further that his education is a result of exchanges because his moral, aesthetic, and philosophic education have been guided by "a Lebanese uncle, American and French and Kenyan and Thai cousins," and, more recently, by his Norwegian, Nigerian, and Ghanaian brothers-in-law, and he has come to see the world as "a network of points of affinity" (viii).[7] The transmodern space Appiah describes reflects a nonterritorial cosmopolitan consciousness, which inspires him to explore further the radical possibilities of an "intercultural project" that combines African with Western ideas. To this end, he argues against myopic theories that think in the binary of Western and non-Western. "If there is a lesson in the broad shape of this circulation of cultures," he observes, "it is surely that we are all already contaminated by each other. . . . The postulation of a unitary Africa over against a monolithic West—the binarism of Self and Other—is the last of the shibboleths of modernizers that we must learn to live without" (155).

Appiah's use of the metaphors of "circulation" and "contamination" here is curious for what those words suggest about the paradigm of "liquidity" (the color of water) that mixed-race theory invites.[8] Indeed, the former, fluid and generous, and the latter, evoking contagion and death, suggest that traditional "cultures" are under strain. Social scientist Arjun Appadurai, another theorist interested in the convergence of racial identity and global modernities, supports this view when he argues that we should distinguish between the noun "culture" and the adjective "cultural," because the noun brings "culture back into the discursive space of race" (11).

In his collection of essays *Modernity at Large*, Appadurai suggests further that a national culture based on territorial boundaries is fast becoming obsolete because it no longer adequately describes either local or global anxieties, which he claims have been produced by the convergence of transmigrations and by the rise of the electronic media—both conditions that have helped to disseminate lifestyle, culture, identity, and even nationalisms of a new sort. As a result, he suggests, new nonterritorial ethnic boundaries are resurging, facilitated by cosmopolitan networks of affinity.[9] We are thus at the center of a transmodern paradox where racial boundaries reemerge in a transmuted form, like the monstrous inventions of crazy scientists that I used to see on the screen as a child, where chemicals and blobs threatened to engulf all of humanity. So race reemerges, again to threaten. But Appadurai takes heart imagining that, despite the drawbacks, transnational models like Amnesty International can serve good ends.

Unfortunately, as a brown man married to a White American and father of a mixed-race child, his transnational experience looks different from the theoretical model he draws. Although he was at first "content to live in that special space allotted to 'foreigners' (especially Anglophone, educated ones like [himself], with faint traces of a British accent)," he comes to recognize that in the past few years, "it has become steadily less easy to see [himself], armed with [his] Indian passport and [his] Anglophone ways, as somehow immune from the politics of racial identity in the United States," because "[t]he net of racial politics is now cast wider than ever before on the streets of the urban United States," and his "own complexion and its role in minority politics, as well as in street encounters with racial hatred, prompt [him] to reopen the links between . . . diasporic identities and the (in)stabilities provided by passports and green cards" (169, 170). In the "ugly realities of being racialized, minoritized, and tribalized in everyday encounters," Appadurai writes, "theory encounters practice" (170). Despite the value of his theories, Appadurai discovers that being brown in this country subjects you to being theorized by others.

While Appadurai suggests that brownness as a negative condition has recently reasserted itself, the truth is that brownness, forced underground by the polarity of Black-White, was always a perceived threat to stable identities and only recently has been allowed to resurface. The United States has never liked "Black," though it has had to tolerate it in order to maintain "White" power. But the United States dislikes brown even more because it undermines our "self-other" national race-based imaginary.

I am reminded again of Montaigne. In his famous essay "Of Cannibals," he tells of a story told to him by a traveler who had made his way across sea and mountain to the jungles of Brazil, where he encountered prisoners of war roasted and eaten by their captors (150). Despite their death sentence the prisoners urged their captors to eat them. One captive even convinces his captor that "[these, his own] muscles, this flesh and these veins are your own . . . the substance of your ancestors' limbs is still contained in them. Savor them well; you will find that you taste of your own flesh" (158). Registering no shock, Montaigne proposes that in eating their enemies the captors eat the flesh of their flesh, itself having been eaten on a previous occasion by the very same enemy. Montaigne suggests in his use of this anecdote that, to get rid once and for all of otherness, the most wise and radical act of all would be to ingest the "other."[10] This is deliberative discourse. This is misceg-narration. This is radical politics.

iii. Climb Every Mountain

The events of September 11th have shown, if nothing else, how fragile identity is and how, despite mass migration and mass media throughout the world, which introduce us to world populations and make us imagine multicultural needs, there is still, as Appadurai suggests, a parasitic though increasingly fragile relation between the claims to identity of modern nationalism and modern globalism. While mixed-race theorists may envision the obsolescence of race and traditional cultures that encourage race-based thinking, identities reassert themselves precisely because they are imagined. This being the case, as mixed-race writers we must continue to propose counterimaginaries and deliberative procedures, which see in details larger human movement without ridding themselves of the tension and paradox that inspire them. This call-and-response discourse can help us to deal with moral and political problems whose complexity is often masked by the media, and postnational ideologies that have the capacity to propagate facile and false public imaginaries.

But we must be cautious, for mixed race itself is not immune to these facile imaginaries and co-optation by the media. In 1993 *Time* featured on its cover a computer-generated image of "the" mixed-race individual. As I looked at all the unidentifiable mixed-race faces, I imagined for a moment that my time had finally arrived. At last, *por fin*, I might identify my unidentifiable self. But the computer image on the cover gave a cyber quality to the mixed-race "look," and the cover spoke as if mixed blood were not a reality, but rather an American invention that would be "appearing soon" in local public theaters. Exactly seven years later *Newsweek* made *Time*'s prediction a reality by celebrating the hyphenated "Age of Color." The cover and feature article exhibited photos of "New Americans," including a picture of a "Nigerian, Irish, African-American, Polish Jewish toddler," "A Lebanese, Dominican, Haitian, Spanish woman," and a "Trinidadian Sicilian man" *(Newsweek*, September 18, 2000). The commodification of mixed race, of the United States as the transnational imperium, of these "new" Americans, who in fact have been hundreds of years in the making, may seem on the surface a cause for celebration. But it is mostly evidence of the United States' capacity to reinvent itself, to stretch its cultural capital worldwide, to seek dominion everywhere. In fact, just as easily as we might have congratulated ourselves in September 2000, exactly one year later, brownness, manipulated by media images, became opprobrious again. On September 11, 2001, we of mixed race suddenly became unenviable and, contingent creatures that we are, an undesirable brown mishmash of miscellaneous, suspicious, war-mongering bastards created by the devil.

A month and a half after the attack I was sitting in the transit lounge at the San Francisco airport waiting to board a flight for Mexico, when four armed guards approached an older dark-skinned man and demanded to see his passport. Frightened, he turned to walk away, "*no entiendo*, I don't understand" he muttered, "*Dejenme*. Leave me alone." Two guards grabbed him, while the other gently explained, in politically correct jargon, which the older man did not understand, that they were not going to harm him, they simply wanted to ask him a few questions. I overheard one guard say to another guard that someone had reported seeing an older Middle Eastern–looking man acting suspicious. Policing identities in transit lounges—one certain location in this uncertain world of a transnational project—has become legal again. And those of us who are brown once more will be forced to think of our brownness as a marker of ambiguous identities, even though it is not. "What are you?" I heard one of the guards ask the man. "What are you here for?" I thought the question rather stupid. Clearly this was a transit lounge and the man was going back home. He was in transition, so to speak, in that vast space of nowhere where we spend more and more time.

Returning from the same trip, and passing through customs, I noticed that of all the United States Customs officials who were in charge of overseeing identities that day, only one of them was White—a frizzy and dark-haired, brown-eyed woman in her early thirties. I thought for a moment that maybe *Time* and *Newsweek* had gotten it right. The United States has changed its color, and in the pandemonium this causes no one knows who is who anymore. Were it not for the badges it was difficult to tell the difference between the non–United States citizens who were entering the country and those who were guarding its entrance. Brown people were policing brown to protect the men in the baseball caps.

Notes

1. It was still a time when, as Gordon Allport wrote in his famous 1934 study on racism, "Legal intermarriage, where possible at all, is rare and is bedeviled by social complications that create grave problems even for the most devoted couples" (374).

2. In contradistinction to *mestizaje*, which expresses the social reality of mixing, and a self-identification of a nation such as Mexico as being of mixed race, I

identify *métis* with racist ideology that is based on fear of mixing. Werner Sollors observes that, unlike *mestizaje*, racial dualism does not allow for such "fluidity and tended to make invisible the fact of interracial mingling" (122–123). The invisibility of interracial mingling is crucial to the self-perception of *mestizos*.

3. Philosopher Pierre-André Taguieff maintains that "Discourses of racizing intention and militant antiracist discourses meet in using the same language games, in taking recourse to the same foundational evidence, and in aiming for the realization of the same values" (7).

4. The distinction I make between the memoir and the essay is one primarily of perspective. In the memoir we know about the subject by how the subject perceives his existence in the world, in other words, how the subject makes self as it interacts with others the condition of his work; in the essay we know about the subject by how the subject perceives the existence of the world, in other words, how the subject makes others the condition of his work.

5. See "Memoir at St. Brieuc," on Camus's memoir novel, *The Last Man* (557).

6. While in the text I quote above Anzaldúa uses geographical metaphors ("We are articulating new positions in these 'in-between,' Borderland worlds"), she emphasizes, as do other mixed-race writers, the "in-between" space, the activity itself of border crossings.

7. It may be a coincidence that Appiah, Suleri, and Appadurai all have fathers who were active in the independence movements in their respective countries, but I think it is worthy of notice. Suleri's Pakistani father was an important political journalist who supported the independence of Pakistan; Appadurai's father was a war correspondent in Bangkok, who allied himself with Subhas Chandra Bose, in Pakistan's nationalist struggle for independence; and Appiah's father was a defender of Pan-Africanism and solicitor of the Supreme Court of Ghana. All of these authors, privileged to be sure, were transnationals growing up in the wake of independence movements and postcolonial authorities, and all of them teach in the United States without having surrendered their cultural affiliations with their independent homelands, whose struggles for independence they witnessed from both within and without. It is not surprising that they understand the legacy of fabricated boundaries and educational exchange. They are children of upper and educated classes. The exchanges that the First World asks of people in Third World countries are unequal and often coercive.

8. In his study *Liquid Modernities*, Zymaunt Bauman uses the metaphor of liquidity "to grasp the nature of the present, in many ways *novel* phase in the history of modernity" (2). McBride's own metaphor to describe the obsolescence of identity (which is the color of water) echoes Bauman's use of the metaphor to represent instantaneous, nonbounded, continuous changing modernities. Even though Bauman uses the metaphor to describe how the global powers profit from the ability to move freely across territorial boundaries, I use the metaphor to show how mixed race profits from the same opening of boundaries through which power moves—the analogy stops here.

9. These politics and reinvented boundaries, for example, promote the logic that we are seeing now among Islamic fundamentalists: the cause of Arabs must be the cause of all Muslims.

10. "I think there is more barbarity in eating a man alive than in eating him dead; and in tearing by tortures and the rack a body still full of feeling, in roasting a man bit by bit, in having him bitten and mangled by dogs and swine (as we have not only read but seen within fresh memory, not among ancient neighbors, but among neighbors and fellow citizens, and what is worse, on the pretext of piety and religion), than in roasting and eating him after he is dead" (155).

Works Cited

Albrow, Martin. *The Global Age*. Stanford, Calif.: Stanford University Press, 1996.
Allport, Gordon. *The Nature of Prejudice*. Massachusetts: Perseus, 1979.
Anzaldúa, Gloria. *Making Face, Making Soul: Haciendo Caras*. San Francisco: Aunt Lute Foundation Book, 1990.
Appadurai, Arjun. *Modernity at Large*. Minneapolis: University of Minnesota Press, 1996.
Appiah, Anthony. *In My Father's House*. Oxford: Oxford University Press, 1992.
Baldwin, James. *The Fire Next Time*. New York: Random House, 1991.
Bauman, Zymaunt. *Liquid Modernity*. Cambridge, UK: Polity Press, 2000.
Benjamin, Walter. *Illuminations*. New York: Shocken-Harcourt, 1969.
———. *Reflections*. New York: Shocken-Harcourt, 1986.
Christian, Barbara. "Race for Theory." In *Contemporary Literary Criticism*, ed. Robert Con Davis and Ronald Schleifer. New York: Longman, 1994.
Danqua, Meri Nana-Ama. "Life as an Alien." In *Half and Half*, ed. Claudine Chiawei O'Hearn. New York: Pantheon, 1998.
Derrida, Jacques. *Disseminations*. Trans. Barbara Johnson. Chicago: University of Chicago Press, 1981.
Funderburg, Lise. *Black, White, Other*. New York: William Morrow, 1994.
hooks, bell. *Killing Rage*. New York: Henry Holt, 1995.
Johnston, Jill. *New York Times Book Review*, April 25, 1993.
Lyotard, Jean-Francois. "The Postmodern Condition: A Report on Knowledge." In *Theory and History of Literature*, vol. 10, trans. Geoff Bennington and Brian Massumi. Minneapolis: University of Minnesota Press, 1984.
McBride, James. *The Color of Water: A Black Man's Tribute to His White Mother*. New York: Riverhead Books, 1996.
Martin, Elizabeth, Theresa DeMaio, and Pamela Campenelli, eds. *Context Effects for Census Measures of Race and Hispanic Origin*. Washington, D.C.: Center for Survey Methods Research, U.S. Bureau of the Census, 1988.
Montaigne, Michel de. *The Complete Essays of Montaigne*. Trans. Donald Frame. Stanford: Stanford University Press, 1965.
Moran, Rachel. *Interracial Intimacy*. Chicago: University of Chicago Press, 2001.
Nuestros Cuerpos, Nuestras Vidas. Translated by Raquel Scherr Salgado and Leonor Taboada. Boston: Boston Women's Health Book Collective, 1974.
Orwell, George. "Looking Back on the Spanish Civil War." In *Essays*. New York: Knopf, 2002.
Scherr Salgado, Raquel. "Memoir at Saint Brieuc." *Modern Language Notes* 112, no. 4. Baltimore: Johns Hopkins University Press, 1997.

Sollors, Werner. *Neither Black nor White Yet Both*. New York: Oxford University Press, 1997.

Spivak, Gayatri. "Feminism and Critical Theory." In *Contemporary Literary Criticism*, ed. Robert Con Davis and Ronald Schleifer. New York: Longman, 1994.

———. "Teaching for the Times." In *Dangerous Liaisons*, ed. Anne McClintock, Aamir Mufti, Ella Shohat. Minneapolis: University of Minnesota Press, 1997.

Strickland, Daryl. "Interracial Generation: 'We Are Who We Are.'" *Seattle Times*, May 5, 1996.

Suleri, Sara. *Meatless Days*. Chicago: University of Chicago Press, 1989.

Taguieff, Pierre. *The Force of Prejudice*. Translated by Hassan Melehy. Minneapolis: University of Minnesota Press, 2001.

Williams, Gregory. *Life on the Color Line: The True Story of a White Boy Who Discovered He Was Black*. New York: Penguin, 1996.

II
Multiracial Subjects

3. A PASSIONATE OCCUPANT OF THE TRANSNATIONAL TRANSIT LOUNGE

Adrian Carton

> We find ourselves in the moment of transit where space and time cross to produce complex figures of difference and identity, past and present, inside and outside, inclusion and exclusion.
>
> —Homi Bhabha, *The Location of Culture*

The fraying red, white, and blue bunting fluttered robustly against the humble gray backdrop of the concrete wasteland that we called home. Like a lost cuckoo viewing the world from another's nest, I felt awkward and disturbed that this comical carnival with all its delusions of grandeur was considered a part of our everyday lives. Strings of Union Jacks were hung up next to old socks on washing lines and over garden fences. I remember it was a brilliantly sunny day, unusual for an English summer, and the cool breeze carried the smells of sherry trifle and watercress sandwiches around our housing estate through the meandering tables that had been set for the great occasion of our monarch's twenty-five years on the throne. The year was 1977. We all received a free commemorative mug, and the fact that we had the whole day off from school seemed to add to the occasion. Some of the boys played marbles in the gutter, quite unimpressed by the pretension of it all, while the elderly stayed inside behind the armory of their net curtains—silhouetted shadows observing the proceedings in solitude.

Some of my friends in grade six won tickets in a lucky dip for a bus trip to central London to feel the vibrancy and revel in the pomp and splendor. The ones left behind rehearsed the old pantomime of imperial glamour and were encouraged by our teachers to take our places in a play where we would never be real actors, to sing the joys of an anthem that somehow did not include us in its words. Mrs. Naib, my Indian math teacher, whispered in my ear as she surreptitiously dropped a hot cauliflower *pakora* into my lap, "Where did you learn those words, it's not

'Land of *Pope* and *Tory*!'" We never knew the real words to anything we were made to sing and made up the verses to all the common hymns and anthems so that in the end they all sounded like football chants. Comedy and satirical banter provided the antidote for the symbolic violence that imposed upon us a national imaginary that was premised on the notion of a continuous, homogeneous, pure racial heritage.

My friends Ryan and Seema sat on either side of me and my sister in a noticeable corner of the table that ran for what seemed like miles into an infinitesimal point in the distance. The ridiculous Jubilee party hats were far too large for a child's crown and we looked ridiculous with them as they dropped below our brows. In front of us lay the fruits of a hundred Christmas and birthday parties rolled into one. Ryan's parents were from Barbados and he ate only yam curry so his mother prepared one especially for him and we were all jealous. Seema brought wonderful hot *puris* wrapped meticulously in aluminum foil and *channa dhal* served in a shiny stainless steel dish that glistened in the sun. I dipped my egg and watercress sandwiches into the *dhal*, causing squeals of laughter from the surrounding audience. We were, to quote Harry Goulbourne, the "opposite side of the postcolonial coin" (27–28), and children of the Empire's evacuees.

The frolic of the street party continued into the late afternoon as the men swilled beer and complained of the state of the country. Streamers were thrown in an exaggerated fashion and the general hum was interrupted only by a couple of skinheads who threw a can of Coke in what seemed to be our direction. We all went to Seema's house to watch television and to eat piping-hot *chappatis* with apricot jam followed by *mango kulfi* encrusted with little pistachio flakes and piping-hot, sugary tea. This was followed by a game we called "airport," in which we played out our fantasies of international travel, or, rather, international escape, by mimicking air stewards or passengers on a 747. The gangway was located as a path between two rows of three kitchen chairs. One would be the passenger while the others pretended to serve drinks. During this enactment of desire, we were assigned essentialist nationalities as part of the play of cosmopolitanism. Seema insisted on being Air India and got her own way because she had the unusual privilege of actually having experienced the real thing in her frequent trips to Varanasi with her father, while Ryan was West Indian Airlines and they chose me to manage the transit lounge. Neither here nor there, neither English nor foreign, neither departing nor arriving.[1] Forever on the boundary, I would manage this cultural space of traveling identities where people were not fixed in national paradigms or categories of racial difference. A placeless place, the transit lounge reflected my own liminality and hybridization as much as the protocols of the game that required me to enact it. For here was a game where space and time mingled into a haze as complex as the memory of hybrid recollection itself. This metaphor of the transit lounge would haunt me in my searches for my Eurasian origins for many years to come. Whereas my sister fulfilled her fantasies and eventually became an airline flight attendant in the Gulf, I became a passionate occupant of transnational transit lounges.

The house still smelled of fish and chips, and the thin polystyrene tubs of bright yellow curry sauce were still scattered on the side of the sink when I arrived. Dad once told me that in Bombay, which in our imaginations was an exotic and subliminal version of any English seaside resort, people ate fish curry on the beach followed by vanilla ice cream, but we never believed him. This place seemed far, far away in a landscape of generational memory that slipped by us. Our Indian referents and associations did not come from India. Our constructions and enactments of "Indianness" were developed in exile, removed from the gaze of the mother culture, renegotiated in the diaspora where India was an imagined dream brought to life by frequent visits to the Bengali supermarkets in Brick Lane or further ventures to Southall, Leicester, and Birmingham. Those visits were among a very few things that constituted "Indianness" in our condition of exile. In these markets, it seemed, Dad would come alive and talk with an accompanying swaying of the head that appeared to come from another temporality as he bargained vigorously for the best deals. To be "British Asian," as it was termed, was to be Indian. To be Indian was to have the appearance of *being Indian*, whether you were a child of a Gujurati Indian bus driver, a Pakistani teacher, a Sikh from Uganda, a Hindu from Trinidad, a Christian from Fiji, a Bangladeshi waiter, or a mixed-race person from Mauritius, Burma, or Guyana (Hall). As with British Jews before us, who had to assimilate or develop a pan-Jewishness that incorporated German, Russian, Latvian, and Polish alike, diasporic identity was imagined from a common homeland that was not a country but an idea (Khilnani, 150–195; Kaviraj, 14). Moreover, it was an idea that encompassed and accepted difference and heterogeneity against the intransigent host culture in order to construct our sense of place.

But in the quest for a stable sense of self in a world which marked racial difference in terms of binaries, causing multiculturalism "to atrophy in its own apprehension of difference" (Suleri, 4), and where interracial subjectivity was hidden in the interstices of cultural boundary marking, where was I situated?

In the Hindu epic the *Mahabharata*, Bhisma asks his grandfather how to recognize a "half-caste." His grandfather's response articulates the moral transgression that racial hybridity represents in orthodox Hindu culture:

> The baseness of a man born of miscegenation is easily detected by his un-Aryan conduct; indiscriminate habits, cruelty, the non-observance of rituals proclaim the low origins of these men—they can never hide their baseness. (Abel, 28–29)

I had always been uncomfortable living in England, although I had known no other country. My friends were Indian and I tended to embrace all things Indian. After all, we lived in an area with a very high immigrant population, settled mostly by West Indians, Punjabis, Gujurtis, and Sikhs who had escaped Idi Amin. Women could buy *bindhis* at the local corner shop along with *ghee* and henna dye. *Diwali* was usually celebrated alongside Guy Fawkes Night. My sister and I often made coconut *barfi* in the house, which we took to school and shared with the others.

Yet, even this identification seemed comic to an extent. In the eyes of first-generation Indians themselves, I was an embodiment of the ethnicity that dare not speak its name. I was someone who had defied ancient caste laws, terrorized the purity of the moral order, and vilified the sanctity of the kinship networks that have kept the private memory of Indian history so dynamic for thousands of years. I was someone whom Parama Roy describes as a "hyphenated Indian" (87), a visible reminder of transnational, cross-cultural sexual relations long before the terms themselves came to be used in a postmodern context. For the second generation, I was just another member of the gang except that some of the more middle-class Asian boys referred to me euphemistically as a "coconut," or "brown on the outside, white on the inside," as Jtinder used to say. In the essentialist quest for origins to legitimate cultural difference, where was the hybrid home? In "Confessions of a Eurasian," an anonymous Eurasian, writing in the 1830s, shares his feelings concerning the notion of "home":

> To me there was no home. It was a lifeless term that awakened no sentiment and presented no picture. What heart beat for my return? (382)

My father told me stories of India in glowing terms without being romantic or sentimental, although unlike other Indian or Pakistani immigrants he held onto no myth of return (Anwar, 21). He loved to watch the horse racing at the local pub with the other men as life revolved around pints of bitter and the weekly fate of Arsenal. My mother, born in rural Norfolk, used to play darts on the ladies' team and then drag him home when she was finished. He said there were lots of boys like him at school and the other children called them "Crannys." At that time, I never understood what that meant and certainly had no racial consciousness of being "Anglo-Indian" or "Eurasian." A separate ontological and epistemological category to confer legitimacy to the multiracial self had not entered my syntax of self-description or framed the hue of my internal gaze.

To other eyes, we were "Tash." That is, regarded as cheap, untrust-worthy, and promiscuous:

> Young lower-caste girls used to sleep with British soldiers, you know, just like that, for nothing more than a pair of stockings or a bar of chocolate. Shameful, you know. That's how you people came to be here. You are only eight annas. Not sixteen.

This was how Mrs. Naib eloquently explained my background to me one morning as I was struggling through an exercise on adding fractions. I never understood the concept that the sum of the parts had to equal the whole and I questioned philosophically why the total could not be greater and stronger than the sum of its parts. I would never be a mathematician, it appeared.

The Portuguese used the term *mestico* from about 1546. The British in-troduced the derisive term *half-caste* from about 1789 (Yule and Burnell, 401, 604–605). The fight for self-identification commenced in Bengal when it was decided at a meeting in 1823 that the term *East Indian* would be used to describe people of mixed origins (Goodrich, 123). However, at the same time, some preferred the term *Indo-Briton*. The British in India were always called *Anglo-Indian*. John Malcolm first used the term to de-scribe Eurasians in 1826, as a protest against the use of the derogatory "half-caste":

> There has been much discussion regarding the name by which this race ought to be distinguished, and latterly some amongst them have thought that of Half Caste, by which they have long been known, is opprobrious. It certainly is not so, any more than Creole, or men of colour, when applied to persons of mixed race in the West Indies; amongst names chosen by themselves, that of Anglo-Indians appears to be the most descriptive and unexceptionable. (441)

It was not until 1898, however, with the formation of the Imperial Anglo-Indian Association that the term Anglo-Indian was used by people of mixed origins to affiliate themselves with British interests in India, as illustrated in the deputation leader's triumphant comments:

> Britishers we are and Britishers we ever must and shall be. Once we relinquish this name [Anglo-Indians] and permit ourselves to be styled "Eurasians" or "Statutory natives of India" we become estranged from our proud heritage as Britishers.[2]

As it was officially used from 1911 for government purposes and in the Government of India Acts of 1919 and 1935, the colonial term Anglo-Indian is defined as applying to those having European descent on the male side only:

> [e]very person, being a British subject and resident in British India, of (a) European descent in the male line who is not comprised in the above definition, or (b) of mixed Asiatic descent, whose father, grandfather or more remote ancestor in the male line was European. (*British Parliamentary Papers*, 107)

From the above definition, according to Vijay Gaikwad, "it can be easily seen that the term *Anglo-Indian* cannot be used for anyone whose father is an Indian and mother a European" (43). *Eurasian* as a term was used from 1878, though it generally has not been favored by people of mixed race in India, being seen as a derogatory or clinical term. In places such as Burma or New Zealand, however, where European descent was not specified along lines of gender, the term has not carried with it the same baggage. For example, in a memorandum to the Simon Commission in 1920, the Eurasians of Burma, who were called Anglo-Indian by the colonial government, reemphasized the use of the term Eurasian with this definition:

> Any person of mixed European and Indian or Burmese descent, whether of legitimate parentage or not, or whether the European strain be derived from the paternal or the maternal side. (Dover, 137)

The debate over the uses of terms to reflect the diverse nature of the community has been a feature of intellectual life to this day, whether it be between East Indian and Indo-Briton or between Anglo-Indian and Eurasian. The nomenclature itself has been a changing amoeba, reflecting specific historical circumstances and specific loyalties, but it has always referred to the identity of Anglo-Indians born in India and it has been largely their debate. Just before Independence in 1947 there was an attempt to give the community in India the name *Britasian,* but the idea failed to gain either acceptance or momentum (Dutt, 16).

The transformation of an invented racial binary into a pleasing hyphenated duality reflected the British colonial context in which hybridity was articulated.[3] As the famous Eurasian poet Henry D'Rozario commented in the early nineteenth century, the names used to describe people of mixed European and Indian origin have been largely British political terms utilized by an ethnic elite striving for civic acceptance and not cultural terms encompassing the multiplicity of European and Asian heritages from which the community draws its origins.[4] The act of interpellating individuals as hybrid subjects was an integral part of the subject-constituting program of the colonial state and its naming practices.

However, many feel that the term Anglo-Indian does not reflect the racial diversity of both our European and Asian backgrounds, regardless of where we were born and through which gender our ethnicity is carried. French and Portuguese Eurasians from India, in particular, are categorically anglicized to fit the protocols of communal affiliation. Under the banner of British colonial category formation, the specific modalities and localized expressions of multiple hybridities were repressed (Shohat, 110; Carton, 1–3). Furthermore, the question of what to call people of Anglo-Indian origin who were not born in India or what they themselves would like to be called, is sadly missing from the debates. Missing, also, are the growing communities of postcolonial children who have European mothers and Indian fathers and who either identify as "Indian" in India or else, in the diaspora, are generally lost to the British, Canadian, and Australian host cultures. As with the construction of other second-generation immigrant subjectivities, it is in the contact with a largely hostile host culture that ethnic self-consciousness is produced and consolidated.[5] In this sense, the postcolonial hybrid generation has no name.

O ENGLAND! WHO ARE THESE IF NOT THY SONS?[6]

On another summer's day in June 1950, my father arrived in Southampton from Bombay as a young boy with his mother. He was born in a town called Jhajha, northwest of Asansol in what is now the state of Bihar. His mother was a Scottish-Burmese Eurasian from Mandalay and his father identified as a Bengali of French extraction, from the settlement of Chandernagore, which France handed back to India in 1950, three years after independence from Britain. My two Eurasian grandparents, both called "Anglo-Indian" by the British and domiciled Europeans in India, despite the fact that neither had any English origin at all, straddled the rigid dichotomous categories borne of colonial occupations, and their existence spoke much of an historical narrative that revealed a more diverse and heterogeneous multiracial population than that pictured in the discourses of imperial history. Rather than a monolithic metaphor of British colonialism, my own history reflected how varied, contested, and fractured were the subjects created by different colonialisms (Stoler, 199). The family moved to Auntie Hannah's place in Bombay in 1944 amidst the chaos in Bengal due to the great evacuations from Burma after the Japanese invasion. My grandfather was killed, like many other Indians, in a war defending the glory of the British Empire from the threat of Japanese fascism.

My grandmother said that when they arrived in England, no one seemed to know that Eurasians existed and they were consequently greeted as quaint curiosities, as comic Asians in European drag who transgressed the conventions and categories of the colonial order of things. My grandmother remembered the British immigration officials referring to them as "those dark people from Bordeaux," not really knowing where Bombay or Burma was. Yet, she herself was always reticent to declare who she was and preferred to remain a mysterious bundle of contradictions and curiosities. Forever the mimic and the chameleon, burning frankincense in front of icons of Mary the Virgin, Buddha, and Shiva and serving hot fresh chilies with a gin and tonic to guests as a precaution against mosquitoes, she celebrated New Year's Eve in the traditional Scottish fashion and continued to prepare wonderful Bengali curries in honor of her husband, not knowing that a French side salad was totally incongruous to the entire cultural performance.

The street party and the fluttering of bunting are etched into my memory for many reasons. Although the imagery of brown faces against Union Jacks might have spoken much of a changed, multicultural, postimperial Britain, it somehow did not. Although these performances charted a symbolic realm of celebratory hybridity, those who were hybrid at the level of concrete social reality did not feel included in this exchange of cultural commodities. The entire performance of this piece of nationalist theater absorbed hybridity and cultural diversity into its own domesticated version of cosmopolitanism.

While my friends Ryan and Seema could escape the public sphere by returning home where family space was refashioned as "Barbadian" or "Punjabi," our household carried the external illusion inward as we battled between roast beef and Yorkshire pudding on Sundays and beef vindaloo with rotis on Mondays. The Anglo-Indian predicament was the desire to want to belong to both cultures amidst a barrage of racial stereotypes coming from the very cultures we imitated. Seema's father, a devout Hindu, complained of the smell of "dead cow" when he visited us, and thus she was subsequently never allowed to eat with us again. The English neighbors once complained that the smell of curry coming from our kitchen would impregnate their washing on the clothesline and demanded that we restrict "ethnic cooking" as far as possible. It seemed we could never win. We walked the fine tightrope between inclusion and exclusion, our bodies becoming the signifying boundaries of what was English and what was not, of what was Indian and what was not.

Whereas Indian migrants reinvented "tradition" as a barrier against the great British illusion, Eurasians were viewed as the impure anomalies against which purity could be imagined and glorified. Although epitomized as the tragic relics of the British Raj by some (Mukherjee, 73–74), Eurasian people actually had their own long and rich history pre-dating, and quite independent of, the British connection. Embodying a separate, dynamic, multiracial view of the world, shattering any pretension of an "East"/"West" dichotomy, making a mockery of any claim to cultural authenticity and homogeneity, Anglo-Indians demonstrate that the performances of the national imaginary are a complete farce. We transgressed ways of cultural understanding that rested on binary thinking and ways of framing identity in the language of dualism.

Margaret Thatcher came to power in 1979 and the cans of Coke turned into bricks as Indian shopkeepers boarded up their windows to prevent the damage. There was an ambiguous air of celebration and dread in the air. There were no more street parties as individualism and nationalism swept the country in a frenzy of corporate Darwinism mixed in a volatile cocktail with racial arrogance. My mother woke me up one night to tell me that the decision had been made to emigrate "far away" because she feared that things were changing. I never really thought about what that meant, apart from the exciting anticipation of being able to fly in a real plane, and my mind wandered into an adolescent denial of reality as I played records by David Bowie and, of course, our hero from Lucknow, Cliff Richard, on my plastic record player and thought of what kind of food they would serve on the plane. Mrs. Naib said they served salt and pepper in containers the size of your fingernail and this miniaturism was all I could think about for days on end. The childhood fantasy would become a reality; only I could not take Ryan and Seema with me. But were we really emigrating? To emigrate means one must move from one place to another place; from one's own country to another. But, where was my country, my place?

> They are a group balanced in unstable equilibrium between the foreign and indigenous civilizations . . . a people without a country. (Cressey, 264)

My first real transit lounge was in Los Angeles, en route to Auckland and Melbourne. It was a bright, fluorescent-lighted room filled with orange plastic chairs and smelling of bleach and cigarette ash. Little American flags were positioned on the check-in counter. The passengers in this room were of nationalities I had never encountered before: Koreans, Maoris, Australians, Samoans, Japanese, and New Zealanders. Yet they were people I felt strangely comfortable to be with. People smiled at each other across language barriers. Courtesy and helpfulness pervaded the atmosphere. An elderly nun from Auckland, who was knitting, leaned over and asked sincerely, "Where are you from, dear, India or Pakistan?" Unable to reply honestly and unwilling to reply correctly, I wanted to answer indignantly that I was born in a transit lounge, that I did not come from a real country and that countries were not real things anyway. The question "Where are you from?" seemed so intrusive, so interrogative, so violent. No one, it seemed to me, ever asked where you were going to. My mother glanced at me with a horrified look on her face and replied sternly, "We're emigrating from Britain, for a new life." The nun looked genuinely puzzled. Her question was a desire for racial origins.

This reluctance to answer the question and to deliver the requested narrative of origin hid a deeper reluctance to talk about multiracial subjectivity. Although private trauma tends to lose its emotional currency as it enters the realm of everyday public rhetoric, the question felt wrong. Furthermore, I had always found the well-intentioned liberal demand to declare one's ethnicity unfair. Invoking ethnicity is often a political move used to add currency to a certain ethnic group, usually a group that never fully invests in, or embraces, the hybridity of the multiracial. It always appeared to me, in a somewhat cynical manner, that such strategies of ethnic declaration carried with them both a demand for an explanation of origins and a fear of the ambiguities of interracial identity that needed to be controlled. However, more importantly, my reluctance to answer displayed my own intense discomfort with the notion of "home" itself. Where was "home"? Was it in the lush paddy fields just outside of Mandalay, in the brisk cold of an Aberdeen autumn morning, or near the devout Catholic church of St. Louis in that speck of French Bengal? Or was it in the dusty Anglo-Indian railways settlement outside of Asansol or in the sprawling housing estate forty minutes north of London? "Home" was all of this but none of this at once. "Home" was a potpourri of senses that came together as an imaginary homeland in Salman Rushdie's sense of the term (9–21). "Home" was the smell of cardamom and coriander. "Home" was the intense color of turmeric. "Home" was in the juice of a mango and in the calm of sandalwood. "Home" for me was a placeless place signified more by these qualities than by references to race.

The fantasy of air travel came to an abrupt end as the taxi drove through Melbourne's western suburbs—suburbs that were to be part of the reconstitution of home. I squinted through the back of the car window as both the angles and the dimensions played tricks with my eyes. Everything appeared very bright, very open, very wide, and very flat. The sun was potent. Space was vast. I could not see any kangaroos or koalas or echidnas and I remember feeling disappointed at seeing dogs and cats in the streets. I saw my first drive-in restaurant and thought we were in Nevada rather than Victoria. The sight of old green trams and of Anglo-Indian verandahs around what we called "bungalows" conjured up an historic charm that was magnetic. As we passed the factories, the houses, and the buildings and merged with suburbia, I felt like an escaped convict whom no one would find. The first few weeks at school were spent trying to dodge the tiger snakes in the paddocks that separated our house from Werribee High. I was immediately befriended by the Greek and Italian kids, who thought I was one of them and who teased the "wog with the English accent." For the first time in my life there were no Indian or Black friends to exchange glances with, but it seemed that Giovanni, Minh, and Litsa had replaced Ryan and Seema. My friend Christos told me stories of Alexander the Great, of Greek communities in India long before any other Europeans were to arrive there. These stories instilled in me a new pride for my Eurasian origins and for the history of multiracial India.

The idea that Australia was not a holiday destination but a place of permanent settlement was made easier with the aid and comfort of other immigrants in the same position, managing multiple identities and negotiating between the private world of memory and the public world of trying desperately to fit in. With all people in this position, there is an overcompensation at first as cuckoos try to be cockatoos and get hopelessly lost in the transition. I tried to use all the correct Australian sayings for things in the hope of easier acceptance, but instead this overstated mimicry provided instant entertainment for those around me. As I grappled to decipher the syntax of *Cold Chisel* and to understand Australian Rules football while gulping down mouthfuls of hot meat pies, the narratives of suburban masculinity clashed with nostalgia for campy Hindi movies, games of "airport," and the taste of fresh *masala dosas*. The symbols of interracial British hybridity and Indian reconstruction were replaced by the motifs of Australian mateship and cultural bonding.

Gradually, I grew comfortable with this idea of a third country as "freedom." Being removed from the suffocation of British culture, where the simplistic binary of "Britain"/"India" provided no real space for Anglo-Indians to be without guilt, remorse, or vanity, meant the opportunity for relief. It was almost as if a door had opened from a closed room into a field where identity was discussed, probed, elaborated, and celebrated. Indeed, as enunciated by Paul Carter, I suddenly gained an "intuition that the opposition between here and there is itself a cultural construction, a consequence of thinking in terms of fixed entities and defining them oppositionally" (101). Cypriot Greeks and Lebanese Christians told me their stories of finding in Australia a third space in which to negotiate difficult binary oppositions and manage multiple levels of identification, and I found a chord of similarity. In her book *Twice Migrants*, on East African Sikh settlers in Britain, Parminder Bhachu puts forward the proposition that the children of a previous migration wave who themselves migrate to a third space learn to negotiate their identities in a far stronger way than did their parents (38–40). I was not a second-generation Nairobi Sikh in Birmingham, but I understood the concept through Melbournians whose parents were from Beirut and Nicosia.

When the college offers started to arrive, I rang around desperately to find out who else was going to Melbourne University, but to my astonishment I discovered that I was to go alone, as no one else from my school had received an offer. So it was with a sense of fear and bewilderment that I started my first day and looked across the vast lecture hall to see a sea of bright and enthusiastic students as we listened to our first history lectures. Yet all this "history" was presented in meta-narratives of either the "European" or "Asian" experiences.

I often thought, where are those who leapt over boundaries, transgressed categories, who are denied a place in the national imagination? Where are the straddlers? Where are the Asian Europeans and the European Asians? Where was I situated?

I was fired up with so many questions. What about the poems of the Portuguese Eurasian D'Rozario? What about the socialist Eurasian Cedric Dover? What about Frank Anthony's pact with Indira Gandhi?

Was hybridity a crime? Were all Eurasians raving colonialists imbued with Raj nostalgia? What about the postcolonial generation who never had the experience of "India"? It appeared to me that both Orientalism and Occidentalism assumed similar strategies of cultural essentialism, leaving no voice for those historical straddlers that invoked ambiguity and ambivalence outside a simple split between the West and its Other (Berger, 275–276).

I believed for a while that I was the descendant of a cultural criminal and was nothing but an Indian imposter. I thought about changing my surname to "Chakraborty," our supposed Indian name on my grand-father's mother's side, in order to rubber-stamp my identity with the eth-nic authenticity so required by those around me in the academy. Like young Germans reclaiming their Jewishness, I suddenly felt the whole weight of a repressive regime running through my veins and became quite depressed. Was my grandmother no more than a servile apologist for the imperial regime? I wanted to run back to the suburbs where I was ac-cepted as a "wog with an English accent," but suddenly, in the world of polite learning and of pure categories underpinned by claims to an eter-nal authenticity, I felt like a fraud. It was time for a break. As the begin-nings of adulthood tend to beckon a search inward, I decided to become the first person in my family to go to India and see where my father came from. The bicentennial celebrations in Australia conjured up old images of the self-congratulatory Jubilee street party of my childhood in En-gland, thus telling me that it was the perfect time to go.

My second transit lounge was in Bangkok on the way to Delhi from Melbourne. It was hot and steamy. Tired backpackers lay on the floor and a baby cried incessantly. A strange faded portrait of the King of Thailand, seen everywhere in Thailand, hung above the coin-operated drink ma-chine. Small children were running up and down the length of the lounge trying to catch each other. Two Sikh businessmen with matching brief-cases appeared to be arguing over money. There was a general atmo-sphere of frustration as people grappled to make sense of the muffled Thai announcements from the loudspeakers; the three-hour break seemed like an eternity. Yet, as I often do in these transitory spaces where we are just traveling identities far from home, I felt calm and comfortable. I thought about Los Angeles and imagined that it would have been good to be born in a transit lounge. Here there were no boundaries or memories or cate-gories, just human beings in all their glorious and gorgeous diversity, im-mune from the surveillance and judgment of others, protected from the semiotics of race.

As the plane was about to land, a flight attendant asked me inquisitively "Coming from?" with acute Indian directness. I replied "Australia" confidently. "And going home for the first time?" I hesitated and replied, "Well, I guess I am." India greeted me and was no longer an idea but a concrete reality; no longer an imagined creation, a romance or a fiction, but a living modernity. I knew I had been here before.

> While respecting cultural autonomy, we should work towards the achievement of the sense in every individual that he is Indian, completely uninfluenced by considerations of religion, caste or community.[7]

The street sweepers were cleaning up the debris from the previous day's Republic Day celebrations, and, as I kicked ribbons of saffron, white, and green tissue paper, I thought how ironic it was that there was always some occasion or another in the air. And so it often happens that my memories are bound to a public event. It was January 27, 1988, nearly thirty-five years since a member of my family had stepped foot inside India. Walking aimlessly around Delhi, absorbing the kaleidoscopic sensations that permeated my vision, I felt curiously unmoved. The greatly anticipated emotional earthquake had not happened and the cuckoo seemed to have found a resting place outside the escape of transit lounges. Toward the end of that afternoon, I stopped near the railway station in the old part of Delhi to buy a newspaper. In a chance exchange, an elderly Anglo-Indian man with green eyes, dressed in an old and frayed jacket with cotton trousers and no shoes, stopped and bought some cigarettes and smiled. It was a smile of recognition that pierced right through me. I felt as if I were standing in front of a cultural and temporal shadow of myself. Gazing at an historical specter that gazed back at me, I felt as if history had turned in on itself and left me to face a past that I thought did not exist.

There were little bits of my past scattered like broken eggshell all over India as I saw the prism of colonialism from eyes that had only seen Britain and Australia. There was a slice of Marble Arch grafted onto the Bombay harbor, a lump of our council estate dropped into the Delhi suburbs, a morsel of the Werribee paddocks welded into the Rajasthan desert. The vicissitudes of time and space became interlocked as I heard the voices of a thousand Mrs. Naibs proclaim the chant of an Indian song whose melody reiterated the pulse of my childhood. Seema rode a red moped down a bumpy pink street in Udaipur and Ryan's face was grafted onto a young *Siddhi* boy in Gujarat. The gray-blue Greek eyes of Christos shone out from a handsome youth in Jullundur.

The sentimental mirrors of cultural exchange were everywhere as India became a space of familiarity and a place in which to process the past.

However, it also felt unfamiliar. At once the maternal homeland that could embrace me in a way that Britain and Australia could not, India was also irreducibly distant. Racial hybridity appeared to have no role in the essentialist caste lineages of Indian society and in the opinions of those who treasured the sacrosanct status of Indian citizenship. The politics of belonging for Eurasians was a double-sided coin: European but not quite, Indian but not quite.

The transit lounge on the way back to Australia felt altogether different as I lay on the floor and stared at the ceiling, unable to hear anything but the hum of retrospection. Mikhail Bakhtin once said that there was no internal sovereignty where the self could hide: it huddled precariously on the boundary, looking in (Emerson, 287). And on the boundary there is the transnational transit lounge, which is not represented by a name, or a category, or a passport. I close my eyes and experience the precarious boundary in the aroma of cardamom and coriander, in the color of turmeric, in the taste of mango juice, and in the calm of sandalwood. And the feeling of "home" cannot be recuperated by universalizing the experience of hybrid subjectivity or by romanticizing the colonial histories that produce hybrid subjects, but by finding that specific and localized transitory space where inside merges with outside, where the local merges with the global, where the self merges with other, and where the experience of hybridity provides a means, in the words of Paul Gilroy, "to re-examine the problems of nationality, location, identity, and historical memory" (ix).

Notes

Author's Note: A different version of this paper was originally presented at the "Selves Crossing Cultures: Autobiography and Globalisation" conference at the Centre for Cross-Cultural Research, Australian National University, Canberra, April 26–27, 2001. I acknowledge the support of Dr. Rosamund Dalziell.

1. This feeling is enunciated succinctly by Hanif Kureishi's postcolonial Anglo-Indian character, Karim, who says: "I am often considered to be a funny kind of Englishman, a new breed as it were, having emerged from two old histories. . . . [p]erhaps it is the odd mixture of continents and blood, of here and there, of belonging and not, that makes me restless and easily bored" (Kureishi, 3).

2. This is the definition given by Dr. J. R. Wallace, Anglo-Indian Deputation to the Secretary of State for India (1897). Quoted by Cedric Dover in Wallace, 130.

3. However, the reification of ethnic identities by the British in colonial India was based largely on the reconfiguration of religious, and not racial, categories. The Anglo-Indian was an exception. On the construction of ethnic categories based on religious difference, see Chakrabarty, 151.

4. Henry D'Rozario saw the terms "East Indian" and "Indo-Briton," common

nomenclature for Anglo-Indians in the early 1800s, as claims to British nationality per se and not as terms indicating cultural or racial difference. Initially, therefore, in the fight for Eurasian political and civil rights in Bengal, D'Rozario
perceived the marginalization of Eurasians who did not have British origins
(such as Portuguese and French Eurasians) to be a grave error. See *Report of Proceedings,* xiii.

5. This is not just in the case of second-generation "Anglo-Indians," but also
for second-generation "British Hindus," whose subjectivity has been reconstituted in a diasporic milieu. See Burghart, 232.

6. Spoken by the first Anglo-Indian historian of the Anglo-Indian community.
Many leaders of the preindependence Eurasian community articulated hybrid
subjectivity and culture in a wholly British paradigm, perceiving the idea of Britain to be the reference point around which interracial identity was forged. See
Stark, 74.

7. Leader of the Indian Anglo-Indian community, Frank Anthony, speaking
shortly after independence, quoted in *India's Minorities,* 51.

Works Cited

Abel, Evelyn. *The Anglo-Indian Community: Survival in India.* Delhi: Chanakya,
    1988.
Anwar, Muhammad. *The Myth of Return: Pakistanis in Britain.* London: Heine-
    mann, 1979.
Berger, Mark T. "The Triumph of the East? The East Asian Miracle and Post–
    Cold War Capitalism." In *The Rise of East Asia: Critical Visions of the Pacific
    Century,* ed. Mark T. Berger and Douglas A. Borer, pp. 260–287. New York:
    Pantheon, 1998.
Bhabha, Homi. *The Location of Culture.* London: Routledge, 1994.
Bhachu, Parminder. *Twice Migrants: East African Sikh Settlers in Britain.* London:
    Tavistock, 1985.
British Parliamentary Papers, Indian Constitutional Reforms. Appendix XI. Reports
    of the Franchise Committee and the Committee on the Division of Functions.
    Calcutta: Superintendent Government Printing, 1919.
Burghart, Richard. *Hinduism in Great Britain: The Perpetuation of Religion in an
    Alien Cultural Milieu.* London: Tavistock, 1987.
Carter, Paul. *Living in a New Country: History, Travelling and Language.* London:
    Faber, 1992.
Carton, Adrian. "Beyond Cotton Mary: Anglo-Indian Categories and Reclaiming
    the Diverse Past." *International Journal of Anglo-Indian Studies* 5, no. 1 (2000):
    1–12.
Chakrabarty, Dipesh. "Modernity and Ethnicity in India." *South Asia* 17 (1994):
    143–155.
"Confessions of a Eurasian." In *Anglo-India: Social, Moral and Political; Being a
    Collection of Papers from the Asiatic Journal in Three Volumes,* 1:363–382. Lon-
    don: W. H. Allen, 1838.
Cressey, Paul. "The Anglo-Indians: A Disorganized Marginal Group." *Social
    Forces* 14, no. 2 (1935): 263–268.

Dover, Cedric. *Half-Caste.* London: Martin, Secker and Warburg Ltd., 1937.

Dutt, Kuntala L. *In Search of a Homeland: Anglo-Indians and McCluskiegunge.* Calcutta: Minerva, 1990.

Emerson, Caryl, ed. *Problems of Dostoevsky's Poetics.* Minneapolis: University of Minnesota Press, 1984.

Gaikwad, Vijay. *The Anglo-Indians: A Study in the Problems and Processes Involved in Emotional and Cultural Integration.* London: Asia, 1967.

Gilroy, Paul. *The Black Atlantic: Modernity and Double Consciousness.* Cambridge, Mass.: Harvard University Press, 1993.

Goodrich, Dorris W. "The Making of an Ethnic Group: The Eurasian Community in India." Ph.D. diss., University of California, 1952.

Goulbourne, Harry. *Ethnicity and Nationalism in Postimperial Britain.* Cambridge: Cambridge University Press, 1991.

Great Britain. *Reports of the Franchise Committee and the Committee on Division of Functions.* Calcutta: S. Govt. Printing, 1919.

Hall, Stuart. "The New Ethnicities." In *Race, Culture and Difference,* ed. James Donald and Ali Rattansi, pp. 252–259. London: Sage, 1992.

India's Minorities. Delhi: Ministry of Information and Broadcasting, 1948.

Kaviraj, Sudipta. "The Imaginary Institution of India." In *Subaltern Studies VII: Writings on South Asian History and Society,* ed. Partha Chatterjee and Gyanendra Pandey, pp. 1–39. Delhi: Oxford University Press, 1992.

Khilnani, Sunil. *The Idea of India.* London: Penguin, 1997.

Kureishi, Hanif. *The Buddha of Suburbia.* London: Faber, 1990.

Malcolm, John. *The Political History of India (1784–1823).* Vol. 2. New Delhi: AP House, 1970.

Mukherjee, Bharati. "The Road to Ballygunge." In *Half and Half: Writers on Growing Up Biracial and Bicultural,* ed. Claudine Chiawei O'Hearn, pp. 71–79. New York: Pantheon, 1998.

Report of Proceedings Connected with the East Indians' Petition to Parliament, Read at a Public Meeting Held at the Town Hall, Calcutta on March 28th, 1831. Calcutta: Baptist Mission Press, 1831.

Roy, Parama. *Indian Traffic: Identities in Question in Colonial and Postcolonial India.* Berkeley and Los Angeles: University of California Press, 1998.

Rushdie, Salman. *Imaginary Homelands.* London: Granta, 1992.

Shohat, Ella. "Notes on the Postcolonial." *Social Text* 31–32 (1993): 99–113.

Stark, Herbert A. *Hostages to India, or the Life Story of the Anglo-Indian Race.* Calcutta: Fine Art Cottage, 1926.

Stoler, Ann L. *Race and the Education of Desire.* Durham, N.C.: Duke University Press, 1995.

Suleri, Sara. *The Rhetoric of English India.* Chicago: University of Chicago Press, 1992.

Wallace, Kenneth E., ed. *The Eurasian Problem Constructively Approached.* Calcutta: Thacker, 1930.

Yule, Henry, and Arthur C. Burnell. *Hobson-Jobson: Being a Glossary of Anglo-Indian Colloquial Words and Phrases of Kindred Terms.* London: John Murray, 1903.

4. MISCEGENATION AND ME

Richard Guzman

On August 24, 1973, my wife and I packed two-thirds of all we owned into a blue-green Dodge Dart and headed south from Hayward, California, then east at Barstow and across the Mojave Desert to travel to Virginia along the southern tier of the United States. Two years later, my brother and his Nikon camera came to visit. Charmed by the small, spidery waterfalls along the Blue Ridge Parkway, in contrast to the gargantuan pouring of the California falls at Yosemite, he crept too close to where the Tye River spilled over a forty-foot drop and fell over the main cascade of Crab Tree Falls. I heard his scream as he went down and, running back up the trail along the river, shouted his name again and again until I found him sitting upright in the pool below, water up to his armpits, his hands held high to keep the Nikon out of the water. It was too late for the camera, which would have to be disassembled and dried and re-oiled, and for the next three days he was condemned to sit on an inflated donut pillow. But when he sent us copies of the pictures he had taken before his fall we cursed our luck at having traveled so far two years earlier with nothing but a Kodak Instamatic. We went into hock to buy a Canon TLB, itself a relic today, and the Instamatic disappeared, leaving behind a handful of pictures, among which is one that has haunted me for years.

On our way to Virginia in 1973, we stopped to visit the Oak Alley estate in St. Francisville, Louisiana. The railing of the mansion porch provided just the right height and angle, so after positioning the Instamatic on the rail and walking my wife forty yards down the lawn, I walked back up to the big house. "When I get out to her and take her hand," I said to another person touring on August 30, 1973, "could you please snap the picture?" And turning around again, down I went, thinking less about the picture than the humidity.

Leaving California means discovering that the rest of the country does not dry to a golden brown during the summer. But the price of summer greens is close, smothering air. I remember a cartoon of two sinners talking in Hell. Everything is flames and perspiration, but one says to the other, "At least it's a dry heat."

The 110-degree Mojave had worn two of our tires bald and fried a sensor, so that our temperature gauge always showed us on the verge of boiling over. Slowed by false reports, we crept fifty miles, two or three miles at a time, until at some mirage of a Shell station a man named Frank discovered the error. Overjoyed by the news and Frank's apparent honesty, I bought from him, besides a new heat sensor and two new tires, a set of helper springs to buoy our back springs, which rode perfectly flat under the weight of our possessions. For years later, without a heavy load, we always bounced along.

We had planned to make the Grand Canyon the first day, but settled for Kingman, Arizona, where it was still arid. On August 28th we stepped from our motel room in Austin, Texas, into a steam bath of heavy air and drawling accents. By the time we had reached the Oak Alley estate in Louisiana, two days later, this had become my private mantra: "I shall never draw a clean breath of air again. Never ever again." This was slogging through my mind as I walked back down the lawn and grabbed my wife's hand and the picture was snapped.

* * *

Frantz Fanon, the Algerian psychiatrist whose Third World liberation theories found their home in the United States among the Black Panthers, wrote this in *Black Skin, White Masks:*

> Out of the blackest part of my soul, across the zebra striping of my mind, surges this desire to be suddenly *white.*
>
> I wish to be acknowledged not as *black* but as *white.*
>
> Now—and this is a form of recognition that Hegel had not envisaged—who but a white woman can do this for me? By loving me she proves that I am worthy of white love. I am loved like a white man.
>
> I am a white man. (63)

This begins Chapter 3, "The Man of Color and the White Woman." On days when I am feeling bad about myself and the world I grasp this idea as Truth, and the degree to which we accord this idea Truth, says Fanon, is an index of how sick, how deluded, we are.

Despite labored breathing, my brain was in full symbolic stride when I set up the Oak Alley picture. Backs to the camera, she and I walk on verdant green between twin rows of towering live oaks toward a faintly visible Mississippi levee. Our backs are to California. We are walking away from some personal problems and the hectic, motorized grind of the Bay Area. When we reach Charlottesville, Virginia, where I am to begin a doctoral program, when we see the rounded, forested mountains of the Blue Ridge, something inside seems to say, "Welcome home." But you never walk away from something without walking *in* to something else. In the Oak Alley picture: my black hair, my Filipino brown hand holding her white hand, her blonde hair draping down to the middle of her back. We are walking away from a place where those combinations do not mean that much to a place where they mean more than they should, where the foreignness of interracial marriage hangs humid, close, and thick around such couples, and the complexes Fanon describes seem smothering, especially to me.

In Charlottesville we moved mostly in university and church circles, where adjustments to us were made more easily, where we sought all kinds of shelter and found most of what we needed. I studied and taught. My wife worked on a master's and as a teacher's aide at Clark Elementary School, where one day I went to pick her up early. Because I am nervous, I dress in black sweater, taupe sport coat, and jeans, an ensemble I fancied as somewhat dashing. There is a palpable stir as I enter the lunchroom. A few hours later my wife tells me that one of her teacher friends had said, "If you don't want him, I'll take him." Like my wife, she is blonde and pretty, and my ego gets boosted like any man's would. I mention this, however, because of how rare that feeling became for men like me once they left California.

"For years, in the States," writes David Mura in his book *Turning Japanese,*

> each beautiful white woman had seemed a mark of my exclusion. The stereotype of Asian women is of a doll-like submissiveness and a mysterious exotic sensuality, qualities which make them attractive to Caucasian men who have trouble accepting women as equals. As an Asian male, I was placed in a category of neutered sexuality, where beauty, power, and admiration were out of the question, where normalcy and acceptance were forbidden. None of the women I saw on television, in the movies, or read about in books dreamed of a lover like me. (148–149)

In rare instances, like Mura's, this impotence changed. After high school, says Mura, "Without knowing how I have gained this knowledge—I can create desire, I can make them want me. Even while I fear they will shun

me, even though the small voices still echo inside me, the voices of difference, of the years without power . . ." (150). Here is the world Frantz
Fanon critiques, a world where sex rides to the supposed rescue of the
powerless. One would like to look past this entangling of sex and race, but
the influence of this tangle is undeniable, sometimes unbearably so. What
we had, and still have to a large degree, is a Manichaean vision that sees
the world arrayed in oppositions—spirit and flesh, black and white, evil
and good—and believes order depends on keeping these opposites clear
and separate. Sexuality always plays big because it blurs the lines, undermines neat categories. In a world struggling to keep Whites and people of
color strictly separated, it helps to keep a yearning for each other alive.
Those who cross the dividing lines for love—even though that love might
have contained more lust, cruelty, selfishness, or delusion than it should
have—have helped to create a new world we now glimpse at a distance, a
world more interracial, and nowhere more alive than in California.

But I had left. And David Mura grew up in the Chicago suburbs just a
few miles from where I now write. The shame of the Japanese concentra-
tion camps aside, Mura's feeling of sexual neutering would probably not
have been as great if he had spent more time in California. To put it
bluntly: I, as well as other Asian and Southeast Asian men, am sexier in
California than anywhere else. Less bluntly: our human reality—which
includes our sexuality—is a more everyday, acknowledged fact, and we
can more easily dream that we enter the dreams of women, even White
women.

In Charlottesville, however, I am sitting at a bus stop outside Martha
Jefferson Hospital, where our first child would be born three years later,
when an elderly Southern lady sits down at the opposite end of the bench
and, eyeing me gently, says, "You're at the university aren't you?" Growing
up in California, no one I knew said, "Yes, Ma'am," or "Yes, Sir" as a matter of course, but faced with this woman, the very archetype of Miss Daisy,
I say, "Yes, Ma'am," as if I had said it all my life. "What are you?" she says.
I tell her I am a graduate student and am about to tell her in which department when I realize the question is more basic than that. "What are
you?" I tell her I am from the Philippines after quickly calculating that
telling her I am from California would not have done either. "Yes," she
says abstractly, "you have that pretty brown skin, those dark eyes." This
with all the charm of that melt-in-your-mouth drawl, I hardly realize how
deftly I have been put into a certain place. I would experience such plac-
ings, some wreathed with a similar charm, over and over.

At Clark School a few minutes after my entrance has caused such a stir, for example, I sit with my wife waiting for her and others to finish eating when a little girl who has been eyeing me, and us, finally says, "He sure is more different than you!" She exhales this with a quick droop of the shoulders, overtaken by utter bafflement. This exhaled air of astonishment follows first me, then my wife and me, in the South and elsewhere. Even if innocent, it breathes these thoughts: that I, we, do not fit in any world they can imagine easily, that people do not know quite where to place me. In such an atmosphere I realize how often one is granted only the choice of *how* one will be dehumanized. If, for example, I had the choice of living with either the stereotype of animal sexuality still commonly attributed to Black males, or the neutering proffered to Asian and Southeast Asian males, I think I would choose the former. This goes beyond the dubious male fantasy of wanting to be studly. It puts me on the scale of the living. Never mind that it may be subhuman. Neutered, I feel I am nowhere at all.

* * *

Our first child, Rick, was born near the end of our Charlottesville stay under near-celebrity conditions, because my wife was one of the one-in-ten-thousand women who suffer no labor pains. Waking up on June 30, 1977, she felt merely constipated, but a push or two and the baby's head was already crowning. Weeks of Lamaze training instantly slammed into reverse, so that now the special breathing patterns became ways to help her *not* to push. Once in the hospital, the baby was fully born in about ten minutes. For the first few hours, Rick's head was somewhat misshapen because of staying in the birth canal longer than normal. Among my first pronouncements about him was: "You could use the kid for a pencil." Thus my reputation for the inability to formulate endearing phrases.

One of the nurses on the floor that morning was Sarah McPherson, an Irish redhead then married to the African American writer James Alan McPherson. Contemplating a family himself, McPherson said to me a couple of times in the weeks following, "I'd like to come look at your son." It was, is, and perhaps always will be harder for Black-White marriages. When my family moved to California from Missouri in 1956 a sign posted at the gate of Hayward's newest subdivision said, "Whites and Orientals Only." Interracially, the sentiment still stands even though it shows signs of weakening. Though not technically Orientals, Filipinos eventually came close enough to whiteness, as have other minorities, largely by virtue of not being Black.

The McPhersons had their child, and you may read a fictionalized account of the whole issue of interracial marriage in what I consider the most brilliant short story ever written, "Elbow Room," the title story of the book for which McPherson won the Pulitzer Prize in 1978. At the end, shortly after the main characters have had a son, the narrator, in response to an editorial voice that continually breaks in to ask him to clarify the meaning of the story, confesses:

> I lack the insight to narrate its complexities. But it may still be told. The mother is, after all, a country raconteur with cosmopolitan experience. The father sees clearly with both eyes . . . I will wait. The mother is a bold woman. The father has a sense of how things should be. But while waiting, I will wager my reputation on the ambition, if not the strength, of the boy's story. (241)

The editorial voice demands, *"Comment is unclear. Explain. Explain,"* but the story ends here, scant on clarity, so much hope placed on a child, the offspring of a Black mother and White father.

David Mura's book *Turning Japanese* ends similarly. A Sansei married to a White woman of English and Hungarian Jewish descent, Mura says this about their daughter Samantha:

> This split I have felt between America and Japan, this fusion of two histories, will reside in her, in a different, more visible way. I would like to think she is part of a movement taking place everywhere throughout the globe, our small planet spinning along in blue-black space. I would like to think that the questions of identity she faces will be easier than mine, less fierce, less filled with self-neglect and rage. That she will love herself more and therefore be more eager for the world, for moving beyond herself. And I know how little control I have over these wishes and their outcome. (372)

To the old story of the mixed-breed rejected as not "pure" enough by both sides of his or her heritage, McPherson and Mura offer a counterstory, and who is to say which is true? Looking at our children now, hoping the hopes parents do, I incline toward the counterstory. More accurately, perhaps we are at the meeting point of two ages, one waning, one coming to the fore, our children walking into the age of the interracial, the mulatto, the half-breed—these last two terms now losing the overwhelming negativity they once carried. At such times, it is possible to interpret things cynically and hopefully at the same time and be right both ways. You could think that Lisa Bonet, or Jada Pinkett, or Halle Berry, for example, are seen as beautiful because they are Blacks with mostly White features, or because they represent a mix, an exoticism, that is becoming more acceptable in its own right. You could think that exoticism is just another White ploy to colonize people of color, or that multiraciality really *is* not only more acceptable, but something to be desired in and of itself as a human quality.

There may be a kind of ease to this transition—a walking, as I said, not a marching—though interracial couples must still face degrees of astonishment and danger. This is not a color-blind world, but love may be as color-blind as it is just plain blind, and in this case that may not be all that bad. What I know more clearly is that there is a kind of desperateness, a foregrounded interracial anxiety, to my world now—to Mura's, to McPherson's, and to Fanon's—that I can only hope fades to the background for our children, just as it was mostly background for me growing up in California. Nor is it only that I am more acutely sensitive these days: the California I knew was a kind of interracial paradise.

Cher Mueller, a White woman, whose first child was by a Black man, used to call our church, the Free Methodist Church on Harvey Avenue in Hayward, California, a little United Nations. Besides various kinds of Whites, there were several Chinese, Japanese, Native American, and Mexican persons who passed through the doors. There were two families from Tonga. There were several African Americans as well, though when their numbers became large enough they left to form their own church, the Palma Ceila Baptist Church, in a rapidly integrating subdivision where Blacks were confined when we first moved to Hayward. The first time we went over to Palma Ceila Baptist to join their service after ours was over, the pastor, an immense man who delivered mail during the week, welcomed us with a grandiloquent speech that ended, "We now await *your* welcome." After an awkward, silent half-minute I jumped up, said we were happy to be with old friends again and I was glad Free Methodist and Palma Ceila Baptist were sister churches. And so we became.

At the church, among those who married interracially, I count Gail and Esther Wong, Kathy Martinez, Melinda Chew (who married Roy "Cookie" Matsuda), Wilma and Wanda Chui, and more. At school Larry Tong, Karen Bassett, Harry Fung—these and many more—also married interracially. Not that interracial dating and marrying were the norm, but they were not abnormal either. Nor was a racial minority whose English was "perfect"—that is to say, "unaccented." Or, for that matter, whose German was fluent, too. Wilma and Wanda's older sister Shirley Chui married Gary Fong, who taught high school German, his fastidious dress

and speech—in German, English, and Chinese—at one with the fastidious care he took of his Karman Ghia, which he always covered even during rainless California summer nights.

A few years ago in Illinois I was leading a writing seminar for Brown &
Root, one of the nation's largest engineering firms. Among the twenty en-
gineers condemned to sit under my tutelage were four Filipinos—three
men, one woman. Several times during breaks, drawn together by *pro pa-
tria* sentiments and the kinship of our bodies, we talked and laughed,
sometimes about the irony of a dark man teaching English to Whites. At
the end of our third session, one compatriot, Mike, said to me privately,
"Can you teach me to do what you do?" "What's that?" I asked. "Well,"
he said, "when you're talking with us, your countrymen, you sound like
us, but the minute you step before the whole group"—and here he
snapped his fingers with a crack that still echoes in my mind—"you're
White!" he said triumphantly.

Two days later the firm's vice president called me aside. "Can you help
Mike lose his accent? He's the brightest engineer I've got, but I can't take
him on sales calls because people won't trust him." I could not. Mike had
come to this country in his thirties, well past the age, seven or so, where
the voiceprint of an original language can be rubbed off the voiceprint of
a second. When I was six I remember my father driving our blue 1953
Plymouth rashly up our driveway on Adams Street in Neosho, Missouri.
Coming into the house and sitting down quickly at the kitchen table he
announced to my mother that she was no longer to speak the dialect (Ilocano) to the children. He was breathing hard. I have wondered at the incident, or the buildup of incidents, that caused his pronouncement. As a
result my brother and I speak an unaccented English, I lapsing into hints
of foreignness only when I am very tired. I no longer speak Ilocano,
though I still understand it, and remember hearing my parents say, in Ilocano, to relatives or friends who would resort to it to try to hide something from me: "It's no use. He knows everything you say." My brother,
being only two when the edict came down, neither speaks nor understands Ilocano.

But we are trapped both ways. Speak with an accent and for far too
many Americans the confirmation of a stereotype breeds feelings of superiority and mistrust. Speak an unaccented, or otherwise perfectly
"American," speech, and the shock, the utter novelty, breeds fear and suspicion. Or comedy. The Korean comedian Henry Chow walks on stage
dressed in sport coat, jeans, and cowboy boots. He speaks, naturally, with
a Texas drawl, saying in mock empathy, "I know y'all are thinking, 'What

is *wrong* with this picture?'" In the California I grew up in, there is a more settled familiarity, almost a profound comfort, with a much larger range of accents, so that inflections of voice have lost much of their significance one way or the other. Here in Illinois and other places where migration patterns result in a higher percentage of first-generation immigrants, I know I am often seen as an accent on legs. Walking around to random garage sales or showing up at some more formal civic event where people do not know me, I love to spy that look of surprise my articulate, unaccented speech causes. I used to speak up right away to chase off my own uneasiness, but now I often wait long minutes to make their shock that much stronger at this alien who suddenly walks into their world. Watching myself do this again and again, I hear my mind whispering more often these days, "I'm tired of this."

* * *

I do not mean to suggest that California is an interracial paradise, without its fair share of sin. Anyway, "paradise" overstates the case. It took the United States Supreme Court until 1948 to declare antimiscegenation laws unconstitutional, and it was not until 1967 that the last one was officially wiped off the books. That last law was in Virginia—it was brought down by a suit filed by a man with the marvelous name of Arthur Loving—but the effort to keep races from intermarrying operated as strongly, if not more so, in California than anywhere in the country. In 1910 California's official antimiscegenation law prohibited Whites from marrying Blacks, Mongolians, and mulattos. In the late 1920s, one Salvador Roldan sued Los Angeles County when his attempt to marry a White woman was turned down on the basis of his being a Mongolian. Filipinos are not Mongols, he replied. He won both a lower court case and a 1933 appeal made by Los Angeles County to the California Supreme Court. So in 1935, to close the loophole, the California civil code was amended by adding Malays—which I suppose Filipinos *are*—to the list of people Whites were forbidden to marry. The general sentiment was that while Filipinos might not be as bad as Blacks, they led White girls astray more easily and therefore should be watched as closely, or more so. Vigilante groups roamed, threatening to lynch Filipinos if they were caught with White women, especially blondes. In January 1930, in Watsonville, a vigilante group attacked a group of Filipinos, killing one of them, after the group had rented a hall and invited White women to the dance.

My father roamed California at the same time. Coming over in 1924 at age fourteen, supposedly to further his education, he was, to put it mildly, led astray. A compulsive gambler, in love with song and dance, he would say with false braggadocio years later that he never made it past the seventh grade. Yet all the while, when he was in the army and we lived at Fort Ord, he would take classes, which I thought were mainly hobby-related. One day he came home and handed my mother a certificate. "Your father has passed his GED test," she said to me. That was all. He said nothing. She said nothing more. It would be twenty years before I knew what a GED was. What I remember is my father's almost apologetic sheepishness, a faint air of shame enveloping the modest proceedings.

It has always been difficult to get my parents, my father in particular, to talk about the early days. "They used to mock me," he once said. "They would shout, 'Hey, monkey!' But you know what I did? I read and read. I was reading some anthropology in the Los Angeles Library one day and realized that Whites had more body hair than I did, and since monkeys are really hairy, who's closer to monkeys, them or me?" Every time we visit California, I make raids on the photo albums and come back here to impose on my friend Linda, asking her to clarify the past by wiping away the cracks and reversing the fading with all the retouching magic at her disposal. The black-and-whites of my father show him as a startlingly handsome young Filipino. Even then, marks of natural leadership show through, and to this day he is one of the most respected persons in the San Esteban Circle, the organization named after our hometown in northern Luzon. At 5'8" he is a full head taller than most of his compatriots. He has a charismatic smile, and an aura of silent-screen glamour surrounds him when he is not smiling. In one snapshot he and a White woman lie on their stomachs next to each other on a typical California backyard lawn. They are both looking up at the camera, she turned slightly toward him with a look of delight, he mugging in contorted funny face. Their bodies touch. The shadow of the photographer slants across the picture's lower right corner, and I realize with a start how many times my father must have run into, must even have been visited by, vigilantes. The rage and indignation of this, the cold blunting of Filipino-White sensuality, perhaps most of all the shame, and with that shame the heavy curtain of silence.

On my mother's side of the family there was a Filipino-White marriage that always glowed glamorously in my mind. Her youngest brother with the wondrous name Amante, meaning "beloved," married a beautiful German girl named Heidi, who, even as a youngster, I thought of as a Marlene Dietrich, only sexier and with dark hair. In 1962, when the marriage broke up and Amante had hanged himself in his kitchen with an electrical extension cord, my mother sat for three days after her return from New York in a straight-back dining room chair, hands unfolded in her lap, lips tight, eyes searching deeply into the heart of betrayal. When I showed up four years later with a White girlfriend, her mind did not have to search long before fingering a cautionary node of pain. One month later, I came home to find her sitting in the same straight-back chair, her hands, lips, and eyes set as they were in 1962. "You cannot see her again," she said. "Her father thinks I do not speak English."

Stunned, then enraged, I responded to her with a mixture of imploring and accusation. A graduate of Philippine Normal College, my mother had worked as a teacher, largely of English. In America, however, she was painfully shy, rarely attending any public events in the world outside our Filipino associations, even when her sons, in whom she took enormous pride, were key players. When my girlfriend's father, a minister, called on my parents for the first time, he could have interpreted her deep silence in any number of ways. Unfortunately, he chose to ask her if she spoke English. I think of this every time someone thinks I myself do not speak English, or speak it badly, but react mainly with irony and chagrin, perhaps because I became a professor of English and, as I said, because I sometimes relish surprising people in their misperceptions. My mother, however, took the question with an offense that struck the deepest core of her being. After days of apologies, her position softened. She grew to accept my girlfriend and, introducing her to relatives, would say as an explanatory aside: "She eats rice." Granted, rice carries a sacred aura in many cultures, but I still marvel at the calming effect these words had on my mother and perhaps many others in the Filipino community. We became a certified item, and though we each received several major honors between us when we graduated from Tennyson High School, I still deeply regret losing Cutest Couple to Janet Milan and Bob Calaway by four lousy votes.

* * *

I write about sunny California in one of the sunniest essays I have ever written, knowing full well not only the biases of my maleness and the power of my nostalgia, but also the California of Watts, and Rodney King, and O. J. Power shortages and the Gary Condit saga had steered former California governor Gray Davis away from race as a headline issue. September 11th brought it back for him and all Americans. It brought back the fact that though the measure was subsequently struck down as unconstitutional, California earlier passed Proposition 187 to block access to many essential services for its significant illegal alien population. It brought back memories of former governor Pete Wilson, whose fondness for announcing how much it took to imprison illegal aliens who commit crimes (upwards of $490,000,000) echoes louder now than when he said it a few years ago. This is also the California of the University of California, Berkeley, my alma mater, which was at the forefront of the battle to eliminate affirmative action. Bill Bagley, a regent of the university system and senior partner in the law firm for which my brother works, courageously broke with several fellow regents and his old friend Pete Wilson over this issue. His fight led to the anti-affirmative-action resolution being repealed by the University of California system. However, Proposition 209, partly a result of the battles at Berkeley, is still in force and bans affirmative action statewide. Bagley's victory may be more symbolic than real—which is still a very important thing—but the fact that such issues replaced the radical vision of the U.C. Berkeley of the 1960s reveals how deep the turmoil over race in California is.

What is the sunniest face I can put on this? For the past few years I have begun thinking that the growing backlash against race and gender politics might be the last desperate gasp of an old order. I come to this thought from many places, like James Baldwin's essay "Stranger in the Village," a work that seems to breathe behind at least half of everything I write. In it he tells of going to live in a Swiss village where people had never seen a living Black. As he walks through the village an air of astonishment follows him. The village's biggest attraction is its hot spring waters, which attract many cripples who come to "take the waters" hoping for a cure. Baldwin uses the village as a metaphor for the Western world's yearning to go back to simpler, more innocent times, to times before issues of race revealed darknesses and crippling sicknesses in the Western soul. He ends his essay this way:

The time has come to realize that the interracial drama acted out on the American continent has not only created a new black man, it has created a new white man, too. No road whatever will lead Americans back to the simplicity of this European village where white men still have the luxury of looking on me as a stranger. I am not, really, a stranger any longer for any American alive. One of the things that distinguishes Americans from other people is that no other people has ever been so deeply involved in the lives of black men, and vice versa. This fact faced, with all its implications, it can be seen that the history of the American Negro problem is not merely shameful, it is also something of an achievement. For even when the worst has been said, it must also be added that the perpetual challenge posed by this problem was always, somehow, perpetually met. It is precisely this black-white experience which may prove of indispensable value to us in the world we face today. This world is white no longer, and it will never be white again. (148–149)

This essay first appeared in October 1953. Near the end of his life, Baldwin himself began to lose hope. Now, as the gap between rich and poor in America grows, as 20 percent of America's children still go hungry each day, as the prospects for the lowest half of our lower class drop close to absolute zero, there seems more to lose hope over than to build hope on. And if, as I have implied, California is to America what America is to the world, it is entirely appropriate that California be wracked with the racial struggles it currently faces, for, to modify Baldwin slightly, nowhere have peoples of all colors been so deeply involved in each other's lives than in California. Nowhere have they settled so much, become so comfortable with each other, and thereby won the right to discover what more needs settling.

"This world is white no longer, and it will never be white again." This sentence seems to sound loudly in the imagination of the old order, causing it to lash out in denial, causing it to cling to notions of racial and ethnic purity even while most of us realize more and more each day the violence and death resulting from such ideologies. Things change in the imagination first, I tell myself. You cannot change until you imagine not only what that change could be, but also the very possibility of change itself. And yet Baldwin's sentence is not merely imaginative. It is a sentence as real as blood.

When Baldwin writes about the creation of new Blacks and Whites, he means this not only figuratively, culturally, but *literally* as well, referring to the history of White masters raping Black slaves that goes back to the dawn of slavery in the United States. In his essay "Junior and John Doe," James Alan McPherson describes "older Anglo-Saxons" who "when pressed or drunk" might tell you in private: "We're all cousins. The only difficulty is that most people don't understand just how we're related" (178–179). Recognized interracial marriage has also continued the mixing process, and the numbers have risen steadily.

In 1970 my wife and I were one of just 300,000 interracial marriages. Just over thirty years later there are over 1,300,000 interracial marriages, with about 20 percent being Black/White marriages. In late 1991 a Gallup Poll reported that for the first time in history more Americans approved of interracial marriage than disapproved. And, of course, there are the children of these marriages.

Somehow, many years ago in Virginia, our schedules never meshed, so James Alan McPherson never did get to see Rick, our firstborn, who is turning out fine. I admit the bias of thinking that Filipino/White marriages produce the most beautiful children of all; and we had four, in part because they are all boys and we kept chasing the elusive girl. I also went to four, though I still feel twinges of environmental guilt, because I felt there needed to be more of "us," not just minorities but interracial minorities, if we were to live, as we did, amid the whiteness of the Chicago suburb of Naperville. When the push for zero population growth was at its height, one Black radical labeled it a White ploy to wipe out minorities. Though not a conspiratorialist thinker by nature, I understood immediately both what he meant and what he felt.

David Duke and Pat Buchanan, those who shot Amadou Diallo and Ricky Birdsong, those who dragged a man to death down in Texas—these and countless more, to say nothing of the *institutional* racism that still grips us very firmly, make it hard to clear the haze of conspiracy from our minds. Yet as we become more "one blood" the whole concept of race is being called into question once again, and it has become increasingly evident that "race" and "ethnicity" are *social* constructs more symbolic than actual, even for people of color. The sociologist Mary Waters writes that "The ultimate goal of a pluralist society should be a situation of symbolic ethnicity for all Americans" (167). To see ethnicity, and even race, more *symbolically* is to see it as more open, fluid, and complex, thereby allowing people to construct identities which are also more open, fluid, and complex, while still fleshed out, we can hope, by ties to the best that ethnic and racial identification has to offer. Such a prospect, however, brews its own battles. For example, the racial categories that appeared on the 2000 United States Census had not changed so much that the "Other" designation had expanded into a true "Multiracial" category, but it was the first time you could identify yourself as two races, and that was enough for me to think that my boys might one day be able to list themselves as Filipino-Spanish-English Americans, which is what they are at the very least. Looking at the 2000 Census, Margo J. Anderson, professor of history at the University of Wisconsin, Milwaukee, and specialist in census issues, identifies interracial children as one of the big "sleeper" issues of this census and the future, agreeing with reporter David Mendell that "racial lines in America are blurring more with each decade" (quoted in

Mendell). Even the stigma attached to marriages between Black women and White men, what reporter Cassandra West calls "the final frontier of interracial marriage," has now been greatly diminished. In 1960 there were only 26,000 such marriages, and two decades later only 27,000, but in 2000 that number is now over 80,000 (West). Gregory Rodriguez, senior fellow at the New America Foundation, says intermarriage may be "The most important long-term social fact in America" (95).

Such multiplication of racial/ethnic choices, such blurring of racial lines, is not without huge downsides, however. The *Newsweek* cover story for February 13, 1995, highlights this growing multiracial movement in America. "Solidarity is hard to find," reports Tom Morganthau. "One third of African-Americans polled say that blacks should not be considered a single race" (64). And in a related article civil rights activist and professor Julian Bond fears that the multiplication of colors may dilute "the power and strength of numbers as they affect legal decisions about race in this country" (quoted in Cose, 72). But there are already college groups (Prism at Harvard, Spectrum at Stanford), magazines (*New People* and *Interrace*), a growing body of impressive research and writing, even support groups like the Biracial Family Network of Chicago dealing with this key phenomenon: amid the avalanche of ethnicity, it is the increase in interracial marriages and children that is shattering racial barriers in ways that we had only dimly foreseen, and in ways that no program or legislation ever could.

"This world is white no longer, and it will never be white again." Perhaps no place understands this more than California, and this explains in part why the Oak Alley picture haunts me. The ghost of another image has begun to appear to me when I look at it, and it is simply that I also see myself walking back the other way, *toward* California, accompanied this time by a throng of others so large I appear to lose myself, happily, in a national surge of walkers who are in interracial relationships or the children of such relationships. Every time I come back to California, every time I see the depth of the interracial there, something inside says, "Welcome back. You're home." More Americans seem to be hearing that same salutation, that same multiracial welcoming, whether the California they are walking toward is that actual western reach of land or a symbol that describes what more and more places in America are becoming.

Works Cited

Baldwin, James. *Notes of a Native Son.* New York: Bantam, 1964.
Cose, Ellis. "One Drop of Bloody History." *Newsweek,* February 13, 1995, pp. 70–72.

Fanon, Frantz. *Black Skin, White Masks.* New York: Grove, 1967.

McPherson, James Alan. *Elbow Room.* Boston: Little, Brown, 1977.

————. "Junior and John Doe." In *Lure and Loathing: Essays on Race, Identity, and the Ambivalence of Assimilation,* ed. Gerald Early, pp. 175–193. New York: Allen Lane/Penguin, 1993.

Mendell, David. "As Face of America Changes, Statistics Provide a Mirror." *Chicago Tribune,* July 15, 2001.

Morganthau, Tom. "What Color Is Black?" *Newsweek,* February 13, 1995, pp. 62–65.

Mura, David. *Turning Japanese: Memoirs of a Sansei.* New York: Anchor/Doubleday, 1991.

Rodriguez, Gregory. "Mongrel America." *Atlantic Monthly,* January/February 2003, pp. 95–97.

Waters, Mary. *Ethnic Options: Choosing Identities in America.* Berkeley and Los Angeles: University of California Press, 1990.

West, Cassandra. "The New Mix." *Chicago Tribune,* March 27, 2002.

5. "WHAT IS SHE ANYWAY?"

Rearranging Bodily Mythologies

Orathai Northern

"Are you comfortable with *our* people?" Aunt Grace asked me: a question that made her taller by the certainty of her *own* membership. She stretched *our* to exclude me, dressing it with Southern gravy. Aunt Grace clarified, "I mean, Frances says that Ida's son's wife, Betty [who is White], don't feel comfortable around us"—*us* referring to the same collective as the aforementioned *our*. A jury of my partner's elder aunts and uncles in rural Mississippi eyed me cautiously, but at the same time, lovingly; my blackness was on trial. Perhaps it didn't *really* matter to the elders, as they offer sweet potato pie regardless, but it mattered enough to compel the asking. Even though my partner's mother chimed in that I am adopted by a Black family, and even though I catalogued a list of immediate and distant family who are Black, the initial visual register clung quicker than the sting of the Southern heat. And later that day, the same interrogator lightly remarked, "Well, maybe you can give Betty some tips [on being comfortable around Black folks]." And I thought, *By telling her she should've been raised by a Black family? By raising a discussion about the social construction of race?* I am in constant struggle around honoring the space and place, the time and generation: the context of the asking; such a query comes from a place of familial security and a sense of cultural coalition, but a place that becomes a proving ground as well.

Traveling through the South, usually with family, brings such scenarios. But, in that instance, I didn't have the convenience of pointing to a family member for validation. I couldn't simply say, *see that's my mama* (uneasily deploying the problematic notion that my parents' racial identification necessarily determines my own). I can't bring my parents with me or always resort to a wallet-size photograph as some convenient way to authenticate my racial identification. So I am left to my own rhetorics to battle the Aunt Graces.

But the rhetorical ammunition I carry isn't always enough and it is here that I offer disjuncture, a wrestling between misrecognition and misidentification, an uneasy floating among body/culture/race/nationality. This disjuncture opens a discursive space to meditate and offer a critical framework for palimpsests of visual registers and ethnic identifications in national and international locations. Indeed, the compelling force behind Aunt Grace's query moves many of us (sometimes persistently) to ask, *Well what is she anyway?* A query homegrown in a United States context that is heavily predicated on visual registers. However, the moment of response—having to explain and attempt to push certain ingrained filters that most times prove immovable—becomes more frustrating when one is compelled to question the query.

I offer ruminations to interrogate the very query, informed by travels abroad and in domestic spaces, bearing particular guiding queries: How might we theorize this sense of (mis)recognition within United States visual registers and outside of national borders? What are the multiple levels of translation in shifting visual economies, or, translations of disparate bodily imaginations? How are the bodily mythologies in the semiotics of nativistic discourse resonant with the semiotics of United States racial discourse? In terms of international travel, what taxonomies become elided when we claim to identify with the native, inside a brown alibi, given the (power) dynamics of enabled and privileged mobility?

It is this disjuncture that shadows me and inflects the multiple contexts I inhabit. So, traveling beyond domestic borders, particularly into a Southeast Asian landscape where I was hailed as native, or at least native of a neighboring country, tweaks the identity politics I have fashioned in this U.S. context. A recent trip to Thailand and India refracted the limits and the possibilities of self-fashioning.

Last summer I spent about four days in Bangkok, a stopover on my way to India, where I traveled around for a month. During my stint in Bangkok, I was consistently hailed as Thai, by vendors or by other foreigners who needed directions. I was welcomed "home" and given quizzical looks because I couldn't speak Thai. The sense of being in a space that didn't Other me (until I opened my mouth) or mark me with some question about how I might identify proved unexpectedly liberating. I didn't refuse what this identification afforded me; in fact, I had hoped that it would allow a travel less encumbered by aggressive vendors or hawkers. Prior to arrival, I had not imagined any sense of connection on some visceral level. But the fact remained; I visually signified as Thai for native or foreign travelers, evinced by my being addressed in Thai by Bangkok inhabitants, or being greeted in Thai by other tourists. Such a signification of Thai-ness gets shelved in the United States racial matrix, where I reflexively validate blackness.

In India, I experienced a similar sense of "belonging," being hailed as South Asian. I was associated with "someplace around India." I was brown. I spent a rich month in various parts of India being consistently addressed as Nepali, Tibetan, or Ladakhi. The recurrence of this (mis)-recognition launched some ruminations about being read as native, or more to the point, reading others reading me as native, invoking discourses around nativity, tourism, and authenticity. I offer a paradigmatic moment of travel to illustrate the terms of this inquiry . . . *in India.*

I traveled as part of a tour package put together by a British tourist company. My decision to travel in this way was largely inflected by anxieties about being a woman traveling alone. So, my package included a flight from Delhi to Leh, in the northern region of India, Ladakh, which is predominantly inhabited by those who identify as Ladakhi and Tibetan. On a particular day, a trip was organized to drive up the highest driveable pass—the thrill being that given the high altitudes and steepness of the Himalayas, its "driveability" is limited and restricted. Accompanied by our tour guide—a young British man visually read as White, and a handful of other tourists who were also British and visually White—we made our way up the mountain, taking deep breaths (or gasps) over steep climbs. There were a few moments where we passed through construction sites where men were breaking rocks or tossing them onto the in-progress road. Others kept watch over burning tar, or passed tar from an oil drum in a smaller metal bucket, to eventually reach another worker who smoothed hot tar onto the road. The flame and smoke from boiling tar evoked a collective sympathy in my traveling group.

According to the guide, many of the men were from Nepal or Bihar, brought to work on the roads at such high elevations. We could see their encampments below; stretched tent circles that kept them and family sheltered. Through a window I waved and met a smile that in that moment I took as familiar, as recognition, as connection. I confess that in that moment, I felt as though there was a sense of identification. I translated their gaze as a knowing, a familiarity with my brown skin, a gaze that the Aunt Graces cannot lend or even dissemble. In that moment of presumed recognition, I translated their gaze as an epidermal identification, but without interrogating my own gaze; without problematizing the mapping of my imaginations and motivations onto their subjectivity and their gaze.

At this juncture, it is crucial to underscore the particular context of this moment; I traveled with an organized tour group under the auspices of an international touring agency whose packages are not inexpensive. Given this context, certain expectations had been preconstructed that reproduce overdetermined codes of "East" and "West." Such an industry relies on the power of spectacle: spectacularizing bodies, landscapes, consumption—food or cultural production. The space and place become a fixed site, or culture, with markers of authenticity that we are made to recognize, and that serve to validate our experience. John Urry's work illuminates the visual registers of tourism. He explains that the tourist system depends on a particular relation of signs, predicated on a constructed contrast between a tourist landscape and a nontourist landscape. Urry posits that this distinction becomes the crux of the tourist industry as well as the tourist experience. While Urry concedes that all travel experiences vary and his aim is not to homogenize the gaze, he fails to offer a sense of the possibilities of complicating that relation of signs. In short, switching the visual codes and/or spatial borders complicates the semiotics and produces a more layered as well as vexed reading of the tourist gaze. The very exercise of assigning meaning to particular signifiers, i.e., the semiotics of tourism that Urry interrogates, is grounded in an abstract tourist in a First World context.

I would argue that as the significations change and take on different nuances, the reading and relation of signs become more complex. As I witness brown bodies as a woman of color in a geographical context largely populated by bodies I read as brown, and who address me as native (or something close), the gaze—mine or the inhabitants'—is troubled and uneasy. My reading of an inhabitant's gaze and my response to that gaze are informed by my politics of location fashioned in the United States, where race and ethnicity are bound up in the visual and charged in different sociohistorical registers; where my racial identification may be subject to jury or quizzical expressions. Urry reminds us that the tourist industry relies on constructed and constructing notions of authenticity, signified by particular markers of that particular place. I would add that the industry relies on our own anxieties of authenticity—in terms of our own identity politics, notions of home-space and origin. Like the tourist industry, multitudinous "industries" in this U.S. context rely on constructed codes of race and ethnicity, e.g., advertising, federal funding, the Census Bureau, etc. Juxtaposing the tourist industry, driven by notions of native authenticity, with various United States industries predicated on visual signifiers of difference places nativistic and racial discourses in conversation: a conversation that helps to imagine the moment in Mississippi and moments in India as semiotically related.

Jonathan Culler extrapolates from Dean MacCannell's text *The Tourist*, which argues that tourists are despised, creating a problem for the industry. Culler goes on to say that in fact, "To be a tourist is in part to dislike tourists (both other tourists and the fact that one is oneself a tourist). Tourists can always find someone more touristy than themselves to sneer at" (157–158). This raises an interesting dynamic if we focus on a tourist of color from a "First World" context, for instance, traveling as I did to a "Third World" context, with other tourists read as White—i.e., American or European. The impulse of the traveler of color to identify with inhabitants read as native, and brown, cannot be divorced from a desire to disidentify with tourists based on their epidermal signification, i.e., whiteness.

Feeling enabled—indeed, privileged—to imagine a connection with the native predicated on a perceived recognition, a hail of identification, masks a traveler's own anxieties about being complicitous in a tourist industry, but more importantly, his/her own anxieties about identity politics (including notions of authenticity) and home or origin. Perhaps my impulse to read inhabitants' gaze as recognition bespeaks not only a disavowal of my own tourism and disassociation from my fellow travelers, but also a disavowal of my connection to their whiteness, and avowal of my connection with brownness, and even nativeness.

However, the play between avowal and disavowal in this context is not a far cry from Aunt Grace and rural Mississippi. Avenging my blackness to a counsel of elders tacitly implicated a repression of any Asian identification, tipping the scales to the Black side. Aunt Grace articulated a (mis)reading that I, in an Indian context, had enacted; both of us reinscribing bodily mythologies.

What is also troubling about the moment of perceived recognition is what the "native" body has been made, or even exploited, to represent. The traveler relies on the construct of the native to experience a valid or validated notion of the culture and landscape. Arjun Appadurai interrogates the construction of "native" and the currency it has come to accrue. He illuminates:

> We have tended to use the word *native* for persons and groups who belong to those parts of the world that were, and are, distant from the metropolitan West. This restriction is, in part tied to the vagaries of our authenticity over the last two centuries. Proper natives are somehow assumed to represent their selves and their history, without distortion or residue. We exempt ourselves from this sort of claim to au-

thenticity because we are too enamored of the complexities of our history, the diversities of our societies, and the ambiguities of our collective conscience. (37)

Appadurai goes on to deploy a rhetoric of *confinement and incarceration*, as the term "native" has come to signify a fixity to a place, or space, arguing that this projection of incarceration onto the notion of nativeness implicates a moral and intellectual axis. He posits, "They are confined by what they know, feel, and believe. They are prisoners of their 'mode of thought'" (37). While Appadurai's discussion is grounded in cultural anthropological discourse, his destabilization of the notion of native proves useful here, as the validated experience of the traveler—or tourist—is predicated on the confinement or incarceration of the native. This confinement, according to Appadurai, is entangled with how ethnographers, and I would add traveler/tourists, imagine the native as restricted to the landscape, a particularized space.

So, I ruminate on that particular moment in the Himalayas, waving behind a window at men I read as native to South Asia and as reading me in a resonant register; the moment reveals problematic layers of constructed notions of authenticity and serves as a site to interrogate a tourist gaze.

Following Culler and Appadurai, by reading natives' gaze as familiar, I assuage the anxieties of being complicitous in a spectacularizing activity, distance myself from the other tourists, marked as more touristy by their whiteness. Moreover, I reify my subjectivity as mobile (literally and metaphorically) and theirs as fixed, stationed—tied to the very land they labor.

And, standing before a council of elders in rural Mississippi, where the window between us is just as problematic as we (mis)read each other's bodies, they read me not-Black, and I read them as certifiable arbiters of blackness, while constructed notions of blackness and authenticity loom in collusion with the sun. The fixity of their subjectivity, then, becomes the ground on which my own sense of authenticity might take root. The fixity of my own subjectivity, which the Aunt Graces imagine, serves the same function, to affirm a secure place of identification. I will confess, though, that it is precisely in these moments of jurying my blackness that I feel most compelled to defend it; but, in my efforts to redraw lines in a defensive posture, I excise any Asian identification.

Rereading my travel journal, during the Southeast Asian excursion, I wrote that I had never felt more beautiful and appreciated on a quotidian level. Wanting to believe that I was so automatically let in. Reconfiguring how I see (my)self, my body. In an aesthetic disparate from the United

States visual economy bound to rigid codes of beauty—where I am anomalous in even subtle ways—brown skin and five feet tall were perfectly all right.

It seems that my experience in Bangkok and India provided a certain space to register and recognize how "Thai" I was, albeit simply in a visual register. I wanted to perform normativity, taken as far as my body would allow, before my language/speech or behavioral codes might reveal otherwise. I wanted a space to honor a body whose Asian significations had been disavowed and, on a more intimate level, a way perhaps to honor a biological mother and father who scratched my existence.

Having found myself in a space that received me without Other-ing, without asking for explanation, I realized that the rhetorical ammunition to defend my blackness had become so heavy. I was not obliged to prove authenticity to an interrogator who becomes taller, standing on wobbly stilts (Aunt Grace). I was not obliged precisely because I didn't feel compelled to perform a Thai-ness.

That this (public) paper has undergone many facelifts compels me to consider (personal) spaces where my critical methodologies have found little room to operate. I consider the biologism I have reinscribed in (mis)reading gazes and bodies, traveling abroad as well as in the most personal contexts and contacts in the United States.

In earlier drafts, I had drawn and presented this paper without the explicit details of identifying myself as Black, in staunch counteropposition to being the always already read (Asian) body, such as Aunt Grace's (mis)-reading. Nonetheless, the query loomed and circulated back to me via a colleague who was asked by another audience member, "Well, what is she?" I presented this paper again, naming my blackness but resolutely suppressing mention of being adopted by a Black family . . . at the (perhaps too great) risk of losing my audience because they would stop listening for rationalizing how I claimed to *really* be Black.

Can this paper effectively discuss disjuncture in various geographical contexts without explicitly naming Black identification, or naming identification without explanation? The first reading refused to name myself as such, and the second refused to explain my family tree—a breakdown I was pressed to do for Aunt Grace in Mississippi. Where is the language of cross-identification? Is there a discursive space to enunciate a multiplicity, a liminality, between Asian American and African American?

Again the *compelling place of asking*, which I had anticipated and, thus, refused to tell in my narrative. It is simply not enough to identify oneself, to claim a culture/heritage. But even among an audience mostly of color, the compelling query demands a space driven perhaps by a coalition politics, albeit based on some arbitrary racial codes. Previous versions of this paper attempted to strategically refuse obligatory naming. I had refused to give way to the pressure of singularizing, or compulsory categorization, especially to an audience mostly of color, whose racial imagination I had hoped to tweak. Weary of the place of explaining, and feeling like I shouldn't have to, peppered by a defense mechanism (Attitude), I had hoped to stand on leaving the *compelling place of asking* frustrated and pushing to critique the place of asking/needing to know. I had imagined a critique of asking, "Well, what is she anyway?" in the vein of Stuart Hall's articulation of cultural identity as a process of *becoming*, a *positioning*, rather than a fixed and immutable way of being. *Positioning* lends itself to talk about the ways in which race and ethnicity in United States contexts manipulate cross-identified individuals to privilege a singular identification.

What disallows such a transmission, or conceptualization? Cross-identification is a mouthful of roots that inquirers don't expect and aren't really asking for; roots they don't see for the contour of a fixed plant in their logic. A sales clerk asked me about my nationality (a tricky term), and I chose the most convenient answer that I figured would affirm her already read assessment, and responded that I was born in Thailand. I could've taken a more detailed path, or a path that I assumed would have disrupted her systemization (rearranging bodily mythologies), but I chose a less encumbered path. Because I can't always be responsible for dismantling visual codes of race. An African American braider advertising her service at the African Market Fair in Los Angeles recently didn't stop to give me a flyer (paranoia or misreading?). Several years ago, an Asian/Asian American student for whose high school class I subbed called me *sister*. And in that moment, in my mind, I hastily disavowed any sense of connection. Reflecting back, I didn't consider what any sense of connection might have meant for me, or for her. But in this moment, I wouldn't be so quick to disavow a connection, and would consider the ways our bodies might signify in resonant ways, or think of us as two women of color in a racial and ethnic terrain that still marginalizes bodies outside normative whiteness.

The compelling place of asking and the frustrated space of telling. An over-rehearsed space of explaining. It has never been enough to leave a blackness unqualified, narrating how a blackness came to be. A justification for being eligible, enabled to use the term, to borrow without asking. Permission is implicitly asked in the having to rehearse genealogy. There is no unproblematic space or free zone of uncalculated questions or facile responses. My response to the *compelling force of asking* is a mouthful of words and stories, a birthing and a raising, homage to one set of parents and celebration of another. I push for richer vocabularies and welcoming critical spaces where personal narrative works with, rather than against, public medium and professional theory; where I translate—unencumbered by anxieties of authenticity—fluid and complex cultural identity to the Aunt Graces.

Note

Author's Note: The author would like to thank Traise Yamamoto, Amy Ongiri, and Kenneth Williamson for insightful comments on this essay.

This essay was originally published as "'What Is She Anyway?'—Re-arranging Bodily Mythologies." *Journal of Asian American Studies* 5, no. 1 (2002): 41–50. © The Johns Hopkins University Press. Reprinted with permission of the Johns Hopkins University Press.

Works Cited

Appadurai, Arjun. "Putting Hierarchy in Its Place." *Cultural Anthropology* 3, no. 1 (1988): 36–49.
Culler, Jonathan. "The Semiotics of Tourism." In *Framing the Sign*, pp. 153–167. Oxford: Basil Blackwell Ltd., 1988.
Hall, Stuart. "Cultural Identity and Diaspora." In *Identity, Community, Culture, Difference*, ed. J. Rutherford, pp. 222–237. London: Lawrence & Wishart, 1990.
Urry, John. *The Tourist Gaze: Leisure Travel in Contemporary Societies.* London: Sage Publications Ltd., 1990.

6. RESEMBLANCE

Alice White

I don't photograph well. The likeness presented by any given photograph of me may be dismissed with this assertion.

I scrupulously avoid the camera and when faced with my photographic likeness I protest: "I photograph badly." My passport photos, the only photos I'm obliged to have taken at this point in my life, look awful—but don't everyone's? Surely, they can be disregarded.

The mirror reverses the subject horizontally, presenting maybe a semblance or an even better, but not a truly accurate, representation. The mirror in my bathroom is rippled, defective in such a way that I cannot look at my reflection without some fraction of my face, my body, being reflected back out of phase with the rest of me.

I don't know what I look like. The mirrored image does not resemble me. Or does it?

There exists one photograph of me with a blood relation. My father and I had a passerby snap our picture on M Street in Georgetown. We had just eaten lunch at our favorite Chinese restaurant. The photo was taken with my newly purchased secondhand nonreflex 120 camera using Ilford XP2, a film that supposedly has wide latitude, a film that is forgiving, especially with light. Convenient, I thought, for a camera without a built-in light meter. Nonetheless, the photo is underexposed as well as out of focus.

Social services. The blue-eyed blonde social worker is reading the report she has compiled from my file. She can only give me "nonidentifying information." Of course, I know that already. Reading the physical descriptions of my mother's siblings, green- and blue-eyed blondes and red-heads, she says, "It sounds like my family!" I resent her for saying this, though I'm not sure why. For appropriating my history? For reinforcing her whiteness? Blondeness, blue eyes, round eyes, have always been unfathomable to me; I imagine having lots of fair-haired cousins to whom I seem as alien as they do to me.

"Do I look like her?" I ask, perhaps hopefully, when I first meet my father and he speaks of my mother. He shakes his head no. Who do I look like? I look like his mother when she was my age. He remembers seeing an old photograph of her. But when I eventually meet my grandmother in her Los Angeles K-town, or Korea-town, home, she is well into her eighties, and any resemblance there might once have been has been ravaged by time. The old photos are not to be found.

Gossip. A mutual friend reports that the manager of the restaurant where my father and I dined speculates that our rendezvous may have been a date. I am incredulous. "Couldn't he tell that we were father and daughter?" I conclude that it is only his crush on me that makes him fear I would date a man thirty-seven years my senior.

My father, his mother, and I have met for lunch at my father's country club. He unexpectedly encounters an old friend. "Jane, this is my mother, and this is . . ." He hesitates and then says my name. His elision has not registered with her. I must be a family friend, or if she does note a family resemblance, perhaps a niece.

"You couldn't be more different." My sister looks like, walks like, talks like our mother, he says. My sister is dead before we meet, before my existence has even been acknowledged to her, and I am left to imagine this second incarnation of interracial desire, of Korean-German-Irishness.

"My sister could pass for White," I tell Inga. Inga thinks I might also pass for White. But that evening when we all meet up with Lina in Soho, from a short distance, with my hair like that, she doesn't recognize me, thinking me "just another Asian chick with Robby."

History. Growing up in an adoptive family of German-Russian-British origin, I do not see my likeness reflected in their faces, nor the faces of my neighbors, friends, or classmates. (I listen silently to discussions of whether so-and-so favors this side of the family or that.) In my teen years, the only point of reference for my classmates is Connie Chung—but I am sure I look nothing like Connie Chung. As a child, I had not even Connie Chung as a point of reference.

In kindergarten and first grade my best friend is a Peruvian girl named Maita. We both have long, straight dark hair and dark eyes. People think we are sisters, twins even. I do not understand how I can be mistaken for the twin sister of someone from another part of the world altogether.

Growing up, I do not know what word I should use to describe myself. The word "Amerasian" seems to be used only to refer to the children of American GIs and Vietnamese women. And nobody uses the word "Eurasian" at all.

I am nine years old. I am asked to designate my "race" on a form. I am confused about which box to check. I remember that my adoptive mother had identified me as "Caucasian" on a form I had seen, so I mark "Caucasian" until I am twenty-one. It does not occur to me that I might identify otherwise—probably because no one has ever encouraged me to consider my difference.

I am fifteen. My psychiatrist intuits that I am uncomfortable with the way I look. He tells me that in Asia, Westerners are looked down upon—they are considered ugly. I tell him I have just seen a news report on blue-eyed blonde American models who go to work in Japan, where they are considered "exotic." He tells me that this look is only popular among the lower classes. Others refer to Westerners as "round eyes." This is a derogation. He tells me that I look like a woman on the cover of a book he has. I am disappointed when he cannot find it. I want to understand how he sees me.

I first encounter the word "biracial" in a Mother's Day *Washington Post* story on mothers of "biracial" children. I am twenty-one. Why have I not heard this word before?

When I start identifying as "other" on medical forms and the like, my adoptive mother flips out. "No, you're White. I'm not even going to discuss it with you." I find her reaction bizarre and also rather shocking.

When I start identifying as "other"—specifically "biracial"—I start getting calls from Black student groups. Is it not possible to be "biracial" without being African American? I ask myself. This seems like another instance of the excruciating binarism of Western thinking.

I am offended when the media refer to "Blacks and Whites" without reference to others. Not only am I neither Black nor White—they do not even allude to the existence of one of the "races" of which I am a part. *Do I not exist?*

I encounter the word "hapa" when I am twenty-four—I live without a word for myself for eight-ninths of my life.

The wait staff of the Korean restaurant I frequent looks puzzled whenever I stop by. I know they think I am just any White girl. I wait for them to verbalize their confusion. One day one of them asks, "Do you have a Korean friend?" which I understand to mean, "Where did a girl like you develop a taste for Korean food?" "My father is Korean," I explain. "Oh," they nod and smile. It suddenly makes sense.

At the same time, a bespectacled East Asian stranger stops me at work. "I think you are Korean but I'm not sure," he tells me. I tell him that I am half Korean but that I cannot talk to strangers while I am working. I resent that he has presumed some sort of connection between us. But then, I am bothered when other Koreans do not.

When people ask it is always in the form of a question rather than an accusation or a recognition. *They* don't know either.

"You're obviously *something*," my friend Heekyu says.

"I've been meaning to ask you what you are," the bank teller says. I know immediately what she is asking, but wonder how almost any other person would respond to this question. She is half Korean, too, she says when I answer, but people tend to think she's Filipina. She has lived in Japan and I look Japanese—and especially in my driver's license photo.

At the dyke bar, I am recruited for the local queer Asian group twice but not before I am asked: *"Are you Asian?"* Jenny, the red-haired British doctoral student, asks: "Are you Chinese or Japanese or something?" Desi, newly arrived from Peru, asks: "Are you Asian?" (Her ex-girlfriend is Japanese.) The Black butch woman in flannel asks: "Are you Asian? I'm not Asian, you know what I'm saying, but will you dance with me?" This exchange suggests to me the highly impractical social possibility of consenting to dance only with ethnically like partners.

Baltimore. My friends and I are seated on the patio of a bar. We walk inside to find an ATM. Immediately, a (Chinese?) man wraps his arm around mine and says, "Excuse me. Are you Asian? My friend and I are arguing about whether or not you're Asian. He says you are and I say you're not." I tell him that my father is from Korea. "Oh, and your mother's from here?" he asks. He thanks me and returns to his friend. I wonder who has won the argument.

After he seats us, the waiter at Applebee's asks me where I am from. I tell him that I am from Maryland but that I was actually *born* in D.C. He pauses a moment and shakes his head. "Man, I never saw an Asian chick with red hair before." I do not bother to tell him my hair color is not natural, but that somewhere I have a lot of red-haired Irish aunts.

I show Kate a photograph of a woman from the Asian film festival catalog. For the first time, I have found an image of someone who resembles me—or so I think. "Do I look like her?" I ask. "Not really," she says. "Is it you?"

At work my co-workers are discussing the experience of anti-Asian racism in America. I begin to say something but Mark cuts me off. "You? You can't talk. *You look White.*"

Manhattan. The men at the next table want to know where I am from. They have been glancing over at me throughout the evening. I dumbly and deliberately insist that I am from "here." They are from Nepal, but one of them, the younger one, lived in Japan for ten years. Do I know that I look Japanese? In a city of 6+ million people and doubtless thousands of actual Japanese women, I am mystified that they have chosen me to admire.

On our first sort-of-date, my former significant other tells me I have an interesting face. "What do you mean?" I ask. "You have Asian eyes but that's the only one of your features that's Asian," he explains. But my father tells me I have a perfect Japanese mouth.

Paris. The Vietnamese shopkeeper asks: "Vous etês Japonaise?" When I hesitate, she adds, "ou Corénne?" At Gare du Nord the smoker loitering outside the entrance tries to speak to me in Mandarin (or was it Cantonese?).

The Italian word for "Korean" is "Koreano." From Napoli to Palermo and back, each successive passenger who shares our compartment nods toward me and asks my Italian-speaking companion, "Lei es Japonais?" After the fourth or fifth such exchange, she begins to understand my exasperation—exasperation at this misidentification, at being a subject of inquiry in the first place. Later, with the knowledge that I can pass for Japanese, I pretend to comprehend neither English nor Italian and communicate with people only by pointing and nodding. The novelty soon wears off.

Food for Thought, Dupont Circle. I spot her in the crowd before the show starts. She is wearing orange, not a color I usually wear, and has her hair in pigtails. "Does she look like me?" I ask my companions pointedly. Kati will admit to only a broad resemblance, but Erin, whom I have only just met, gasps, "It's uncanny!" Transfixed, I lose track of the performers and watch her throughout the evening. She is gone before I have the chance to approach her—but what would I have said?

We have not been in touch for years, but a chance meeting leads to an exchange, his announcement that he is getting married, and an invitation to view his personally authored wedding Web site. My semirecognition of his bride (and my old haircut) bring amazement, (private) laughter, and vindication. But I realize that my judgment may be biased and so I seek other opinions. And Megan agrees, "She does look like you. It's uncanny!" Paula thinks not—she is a bit heavier. Fearing I will not be able to get quite the right self-mocking tone of voice, I resist observing that not everyone has my figure.

My father has three sons with his White wife. From the back, with my hair cut short, I look just like Mark, the youngest. "Mark's the best-looking—he has round eyes." I don't know if he is conflating the two things—round eyes and attractiveness. I do not have round eyes, and it is this more than anything else that marks me as his daughter. The first (and last) time I visit my father's house, I see photographs of his grandchildren—my nieces. My father has spoken with regret of his choice of a non-Korean wife. His sons, too, have chosen non-Korean partners. His grandchildren have his Korean surname but bear no physical resemblance to him. They would not look out of place in a Norman Rockwell painting. And I think I know that this is never what he would have wanted.

They have just returned from Hawaii. "Lots of girls like you there . . ." I do not know what he is going to say next, but I know that I would rather he did not continue. "Yeah, lots of *Japanese* girls." For the first time in my nearly thirty years, my adoptive father has acknowledged that I am not White—but he has incomprehensibly mistaken me for someone Japanese.

7. "BROWN LIKE ME"
Explorations of a Shifting Self

Stefanie Dunning

My old man's a white old man
And my old mother's black ...

* * * * * * * * * * * * *

I wonder where I'm gonna die,
Being neither white nor black?

—Langston Hughes, "Cross" [1]

Rebecca Walker, in her recent book *Black, White, and Jewish: Autobiography of a Shifting Self*, references the poem excerpted above by saying, "I'm the one in the Langston Hughes poem with the white daddy and the black mama who doesn't know where she'll rest her head when she's dead" (13). Walker's engagement with the poem suggests that the same issues that characterized discussions about biracial identity in the 1960s, when this poem was written, remain relevant for the biracial person today. And while I understand the history that produces many of the feelings explored in the poem, I do not wonder where I will rest my head when I am dead. This is an essay not about the space between blackness and whiteness, as this poem seems to be; instead, it is an exploration of the spaces between feeling like the biracial person who is "neither white nor black" and feeling "brown like me."

In this essay, I examine discussions about biracial identity and relate them to my own experiences as a biracial person. Furthermore, I analyze the tendency in theories of biracial identity to argue that the biracial person subverts or upsets the racial hegemony simply by his or her existence. The implication of much biracial discourse, particularly in the work of Naomi Zack and Maria P. P. Root, is that the biracial person is essentially different from other racially marked persons. Both Zack and Root have written copiously on the question of mixed-race identity, and I find many of their ideas intriguing and important springboards for continuing work on biraciality. In this essay, however, I seek to explore and critique their construction of an "essential" biracial identity. I will not attempt to offer a theory of biracial subjectivity, or an "answer" to whatever problems one might assume attend the biracial individual. My focus here follows from what I see as an unwillingness in biracial studies to recognize that the biracial person shares with the "monoracial" person the same relationship to White supremacist discourses *and*, importantly, that the biracial person might have privileges that other racially marked people do not. Despite these criticisms, it is not my intention to disavow the experiences particular to the biracial person. What I hope to accomplish, in my own life and in this essay, is a careful and open-ended mediation between two extremes that argue, on the one hand, that biracial identity is so different from other raced identities that it can "undo" race or, on the other hand, that there is no significant distinction between biracial and "monoracial" experience, and that the biracial person must "choose" one identity over another.

Like the title of Walker's autobiography suggests, this is an essay of my "shifting" self. As a biracial person I do not live in an "in-between" space, but rather in a constantly shifting one. Walker's autobiography enacts this complicated shifting of perspective and identity. Her work is also instructive in the use of personal narrative, and in this, her work is connected to many other explorations of biracial identity.[2] This essay is no exception; it exposes my own academic and intimate thinking about biraciality. I use personal narrative because by grounding the assertions I make here in the experiential, I expose myself instead of hiding behind an insufficient and disingenuous "objectivity."[3] Furthermore, doing so particularizes my ideas about biracial identity, rather than proposes a theory of being for an amazingly heterogeneous group of people. Through the use of personal narrative, I seek not to reproduce and transmit "knowledge said to be arrived at through experience"; instead I seek to "analy[ze] the production of that knowledge itself" (Scott, 37). I divulge my personal experiences in order to highlight the ways in which the theoretical arguments I make, and the experiences I relate, are constantly constitutive of each other. In other words, my experiences do not function as "proof" of an unquestionable authority as a biracial person; rather, they function as glimpses into the perpetual metamorphosis, the incessant shifting, of myself as a biracial person.

My use of personal narrative here is a tacit recognition that there is no *essential* biracial identity one can speak of; the biracial person who is perceived in the world as Asian will have a vastly different experience than my own, for example. This multiplicity of experience should be looked upon as a strength that destabilizes any essentializing narrative of "the" biracial experience. The problem with these narratives is that they have the power to define and therefore exclude, as is the case in so many other "essentialized" racial narratives.[4] I weave my experience into these pages because I know that there will be many readers who identify with the assertions I make and, more importantly perhaps, there will be many who do not. The nonidentifying reader is as important as the identifying one, because she ensures that I can never speak for everyone who is both Black and White like myself, and she relieves me of the task of having to do so.

THE RIGHT TO OTHERIZE

It has been said that "no one is free when others are oppressed." As much as things may seem to have changed for the biracial person in the United States, questions of identity, cultural authenticity, and group belonging still dog the biracial individual.[5] This became abundantly clear to me when an African American male friend asked me how it felt being in an interracial relationship. This was such a jarring question for me because interracial relationships have always characterized my family life. It also caught me off guard because his question was informed by an assumption that I identified racially in a particular way, which is something I do not consistently do. Within the context of my immediate family, I am *recognized* as biracial, and there is no shame in this recognition, as we are an extremely multiracial family: one of my brothers is married to a Filipina woman and my other brother is engaged to a White woman. My partner is South Asian. My friend's comment made real to me a fact that I had known theoretically but not in actuality: that most people do not have the ability to identify differently at different times and locations. For him, it is unimaginable that one might identify differently in different spaces, because as a Black man in American society, he has never had this option. I told him that, for me, a relationship with anyone—regardless of his or her race—would be an interracial relationship. Therefore, it never occurred to me to "feel" differently about my partner's race. This configuration of identity, that I am somehow always already different from everyone else (even other biracial people), had not occurred to him because the way race is constituted in his world does not allow for multiple racial identifications.

This idea of racial mobility versus racial predetermination goes directly to the heart of my discussion of Maria P. P. Root's "Bill of Rights for Racially Mixed People." This text, while short, is representative of

Root's arguments about mixed-race identity and concerns. It nicely condenses and gathers together a range of Root's writing on mixed-race identity into a manageable document, and the discourse it invokes—that of "rights"—is indicative of Root's understanding of mixed-race experience. At stake for Root is a rejection of the ways in which she feels she has had to "fragment and fractionalize" (3) herself as a multiracial person. Her claim that "It took me over 30 years to realize that fragmenting myself seldom served a purpose other than to preserve the delusions this country has created around race" (3) succinctly speaks to the need for an articulation of a mixed-race discourse that at once addresses the imposition of always having to explain one's self, and aptly personalizes the set of rights she proposes. I am sympathetic to the issues at stake in Root's article, particularly her emphasis on naming and recognition. It seems to me, however, that her view of the "oppressive squeeze" (5) that racially mixed persons have been subject to is skewed, because while she seeks "revolution, resistance and change" (6), by re-creating a racial dichotomy (monoracial versus multiracial) she reestablishes the very paradigm she claims the racially mixed person's existence undoes. While Root aptly grounds her criticism of America's racist system and its inability to recognize racial multiplicity, she problematically collapses monoracial communities into one category. She begins her discussion in this essay by talking about monoracial individuals in power as racially oppressive, but then moves on to include other presumably monoracial groups—many of whom have been oppressed at the hands of those in power—in the same category. She writes,

> Although the mechanics of racism seem to start with those in power, the system is also maintained by the oppressed's internalization of the mechanics; for example, an insistence on singular ethnic or racial loyalties, colorism, and discrimination against multiracial people across all ethnic and racial groups in this country. (5)

This construction of multiracial versus monoracial is not attentive to the differences in monoracial communities nor what might be at stake, historically and politically, in various communities' responses to the mixed-race individual. While Root's deconstruction of the ways in which the multiracial person suffers in American society is an important contribution to how we understand race in this society, it seems equally important that in our attempts to recognize racial multiplicity we do not ignore the specificities of various and heterogeneous monoracial groups.

The first set of rights Root argues for on behalf of racially mixed people are the rights "not to justify my existence in this world; not to keep the races separate within me; not to be responsible for people's discomfort with my physical ambiguity; not to justify my ethnic legitimacy" (7). In these concerns, Root addresses an important and significant set of problems experienced by many biracial people, who must constantly defend their ethnic heritage and explain their bodies. Root argues that "when race is constructed through the mechanics of racism, oppression chokes multiracial people from all sides" (5). Nowhere does the dichotomy of monoracial versus multiracial break down more than in this way. I have been told on more than one occasion by biracial people and "monoracial" people, "Oh, I thought you were a regular old Black girl," or, "You don't look mixed to me." Racial confusion is also an element of biracial people's response to other biracial people. Injuries of misrecognition or exclusion are not solely the product of a monoracial perspective. We cannot simply construct a "them" versus "us" dichotomy in which the "them" is always a monoracial individual probing into the biracial person's background. What I am arguing here is not that Root's contention that multiracial people not be asked to "explain" themselves is problematic, rather I suggest a shift in the paradigm so that the criticisms offered by Root can be reflected back to the self, not simply onto a monoracial "other."

In the second set of rights, Root claims "the right to identify myself differently than strangers expect me to identify, to identify myself differently than how my parents identify me, to identify myself differently than my brothers and sisters, to identify myself differently in different situations" (7). At stake in this set of concerns is the biracial's prerogative to be all, or as much as, he or she wants to be racially at any given moment. Here Root simplifies the process of racial identification as an entirely personal matter. The racial schema in which we in the United States live, whether we are Latino, Asian, Black, or biracial (or all of the above), does not allow us to choose how we will identify. An Asian American woman does not have the "right" to tell strangers that she is not Asian American, nor does she have the "right" to identify differently in different situations. I am thinking here specifically of a friend of mine, Keisha, who was born in China, but was adopted by African American parents in infancy and so identifies as African American, despite the fact that most people in the world "see" her as Chinese American, including other Chinese Americans. Recently, she called me in a state of emotional distress because she applied for a fellowship for graduate school for African American students and was scrutinized intensely about her ethnic background. She asked me, a previous recipient of this scholarship, how she should handle the situation. I called the fellowship office and asked them what their policy was on "cases" such as hers. The fellowship office told me, "As long as she identifies as Black, that is fine. But she must be willing to represent the group in public." This statement affirmed for my friend and me, yet again, the difficulties of occupying a racially liminal space in American society, and the ways in which one is penalized for claiming an identity one does not "look" like. Keisha is a perfect example of a person who has invoked her "right" to identify differently than strangers expect her to identify, but who suffers because her personal identification does not "match" the identity assigned her by society.

Keisha's experience raises the question, who is of mixed race? She might by some people be called "monoracial," yet her experiences are similar to those people who identify as biracial. Do Root's rights apply to her? Race is not something we are born with or that we simply "have." Rather, race is constructed for us through a complex interplay of history and phenotypic visibility, which defines in large part how racial identity is constructed by society. One's right to "identify differently in different situations" (7) is enabled by a community that will *recognize* one as differently raced in different situations. In other words, my ability to move from African American to biracial, a shift I frequently make, is predicated on my inclusion in a social and familial community that recognizes my claims to biraciality. And while I may choose to identify differently in different situations (sometimes, for example, referring to myself as Black biracial, biracial, or African American), I am rarely acknowledged or recognized by people who do not know me as anything other than a light-skinned African American. Note, too, that the American system of racial classification completely disallows the possibility that I might identify as White. The same is true for Keisha; she is African American in those communities that recognize her as such, but in the world she is read as, and mistaken for, a Chinese American woman.

Therefore, for those biracial individuals who bear the mark of "otherness" upon their bodies, the question of how one will identify is not entirely up to them. This is not some special restriction meted out only to biracial people; it is a particular feature of our society that we do not choose our race, *it chooses* us. If we are to see racism undone, *we must all*—biracial, monoracial, or multiracial—have the right to identify as we wish. What is required, if Root's demands are to actually undo racism, is that we all operate from an assumption that no one we see is "raced" in a particular way until and unless that person identifies as such.

Root's third set of rights contends that as a racially mixed person I have the right to "create a vocabulary to communicate about being multiracial; to change my identity over my lifetime—and more than once; to have loyalties to and identify with more than one group of people; to freely choose whom I befriend and love" (7). This right responds to a lack of an official category on the United States Census form that acknowledges the existence of mixed-race individuals. The creation of a biracial, or multiracial, category on the United States Census form is a hotly debated issue. I at once understand and am sympathetic to this desire, and yet I am suspicious about what the creation of such a "box" might engender.[6] It is, however, beyond the scope of my discussion here to argue about the efficacy of a multiracial category. Instead, I consider here the theoretical implications of the rights stipulated by Root. The first demand, to "create a vocabulary to communicate about being multiracial," is a vexed issue. There has always been a vocabulary, though not a legally recognized vocabulary, for talking about the racially mixed figure, even if that vocabulary has been flawed. Most "race" vocabulary in the United States has been oppressive. The term nigger in its racist effect is not unlike the terms used to describe biracial people: mulatto, half-breed, quadroon, and octoroon. This aspect of Root's "Bill of Rights" builds on the contention of many biracial people that they should not have to name which one race they are, but instead they should be allowed to name who they are in their entirety. I can recall, still quite vividly, a television talk show I saw when I was fifteen years old about biracial children. There was an African American "expert" there who argued that for their own emotional health, biracial children should look in the mirror and pick the race they most look like and affirm that aspect of their identity and leave the rest to the wayside, like so much discarded chaff. The right to create a vocabulary to communicate about one's self is intimately and importantly tied to Root's second right, the right "to change my identity over my lifetime" (7). I am sympathetic to the first right, since I can remember applying to a historically Black college as a senior in high school and feeling so relieved and acknowledged to see a biracial "box" to check. It was wonderful not to have to choose and not to have to participate in the "passing" that checking the African American box has always felt like to me.[7] The second right—to change one's identity more than once over a lifetime—raises certain questions. For example, some biracial individuals "claim" their ethnic heritage only when it serves them. Kathleen Odell Korgen addresses this problem: "There is a danger . . . that mixed racial Americans may be the first to fill positions set aside for monoracial minorities. Because they may appear 'whiter,' biracial employees may be more palatable for an employer under pressure to hire racial minorities" (104). The biracial individual can exploit race in ways that are unethical and that separate him or her from other racial minorities who cannot manipulate their identity to their advantage in the way that the racially mixed and ambiguously marked person can. This does not mean that we must *all* be conscripted into narrow racial categories. It simply means that these rights that Root wants to see extended to racially mixed people should be granted to *all* people. Why cannot an African American man be Black when he fills out his affirmative action form, but White when the Los Angeles, New York, or Cincinnati police pull him over and begin to brutalize him? Is it not also his right to use and exploit a method of racial shifting for his own benefit?

The *Random House Dictionary* defines the word "right" as "that which is due to anyone by just claim, legal guarantees, moral principles, etc." (Urdang, 1008). In the *Oxford American Desk Thesaurus* "right," however, is also synonymous with the words "prerogative," "privilege," "authority," "power," "license," "permission," "warrant," "sanction," and "entitlement" (Lindberg, 379). The word "right" not only refers to what is legally and morally due one, but it is also aligned with—and oftentimes elided with—power, privilege, and entitlement. When invoking such terminology, then, one must always be attentive to the ways in which rights have so often been, and can so easily be, aligned with supremacy and advantage.

The rights Root imagines all racially mixed people should have are not, in and of themselves, problematic. I believe, however, that they are rights that *everyone* should have. Root's "Bill of Rights" suggests, as I pointed out above, that the racially mixed person has been oppressed by all segments of society, and by couching them in terms of "A Bill of Rights *for Racially Mixed People*" (7, emphasis added), she implies that everyone except the biracial individual holds these rights. This simply is not the case. Most people of color do not have these rights. Black people, for example, *become* "Black"[8] through a complicated and painful process involving slavery, Jim Crow, and segregation. White people, it has been argued, also become White through the elaborate practice of assimilation required in America.[9] And while many White and Black people embrace, and even exalt, the categories that name them as such, this does not change the compulsory application of those labels. And while being forced to be called "Black" *is not the same* as being forced to be called "White," the fact remains, most people do not choose their racial designation. There is no reason why Root's rights should not belong to all people.

Some people would argue that, historically, mixed-race people have oppressed those who are not of mixed race or who do not appear to be so.[10] Korgen argues that this oppression of the darker-skinned person continues today: "Light-complected blacks dominate the middle and professional classes of African Americans. Evidence indicates that 'dark-skinned' blacks suffer much the same disadvantages relative to light-skinned blacks that blacks, in general, suffer relative to whites" (105). There does not seem to be space in Root's argument for the ways in which mixed-race individuals, in racial economies that privilege whiteness, might *benefit* from their ambiguous phenotype and mixed racial heritage. This is a realization I was slow to acknowledge myself. In a women's studies course in college, I noticed there was one woman who never spoke in class. One day when this student was absent, our teacher asked if we knew why this particular student was not participating in discussion. After others ventured several guesses, a friend of this woman told the class that her friend felt intimidated talking in class because we were all light-skinned (including our teacher). As a dark-skinned woman she did not feel "authorized" to speak in front of so many light-skinned people. She felt intimidated by our "physical brightness." I had never, up until that point, thought about the ways in which I may be empowered by my light skin or the ways in which I may be privileged through my relationship to whiteness. And usually when it is pointed out to me, I respond negatively.

Recently, at a new job, I noticed that some of my African American colleagues were finding it difficult to bond with our White colleagues and were generally feeling isolated. I conveyed to a friend the discomfort of my African American colleagues, my sympathy with their unhappiness, and my bafflement at why I had been able to make good friends with several of my White colleagues and they had not. My friend, who is African Caribbean, said to my dismay and incredulity: "Well, Stefanie, you are half White." At first I could not concede that I might get along more "easily" with White people because of this; later, however, I had to acknowledge that I might have some physical and cultural privilege accruing from my biraciality. It never occurred to me to think that my lighter skin might put my White colleagues more at ease with me than with my darker-skinned peers. Nor did it occur to me that my lifetime of experience with White culture might make me more at ease with my White colleagues.

Root offers explication alongside each of her rights. For the first right, the right not to justify one's existence, she writes, "Questions such as . . . 'Are your parents married?' indicate the stereotypes that make up the schema by which the *other* attempts to make meaning of the multiracial person's experiences" (7). She emphasizes the term "other" by italicizing it, drawing attention to her otherizing of those not of mixed race, and therefore problematically aligns herself against all those whom she terms monoracial, or *other*. By doing so, she reinscribes the us/them dichotomy she argues that multiracial people undercut. If it is true, as Root argues, that "Multiracial people blur the boundaries between the 'us' and 'them,'" then why re-create an "us" (as racially mixed) and "them" (as monoracial) binary that risks reproducing all of the other troubling constructions which arise from such a division? My vision of revolution, and of resistance, is one in which *no one* is otherized. I do not want the right to otherize, nor do I want to shake off the shackles of racism (nor can I) while *other others* continue to suffer.

MIXED AND MIGHTY

Could I be just another child stepping out into some unknown destiny?

—Rebecca Walker[11]

I am mixed blood, it is true, but I differ from the party line in that I consider it neither an honor nor a shame.

—Zora Neale Hurston[12]

Root contends in her "Bill of Rights" that "the multiracial person's existence challenges the rigidity of racial lines that are a prerequisite for maintaining the delusion that race is a scientific fact" (7), thereby investing the very *existence* of the biracial person with an inherent subversion of the hegemonic and oppressive racial order. Rainier Spencer makes a similar argument in his essay "Race and Mixed Race":

> Race thought is safe thought, uncomplicated and familiar, while mestizaje [thought] is a disruptive, subversive threat to turn the whole universe upside down. . . . The absolute strength of mestizaje is the power it has by its even being able to be thought of dissolving race and everything associated with it, ultimately dissolving even itself. (136)

Mestizaje, or mixed-race identity, is imagined here as an "acid" that can dissolve race and then destroy all traces of itself. Spencer imbues *mestizaje* with the power to "turn the whole universe upside down" (136). This is a responsibility no one group should, or can, have. The dissolving of racial categories, and of racism, will not occur as a result of one particular exalted racial category or group. The undoing of racial hegemony is the work of all people. The notion that a combination of perceived racial polarities can somehow erase its antecedent categories assumes that the racial hegemony under which we all live does not have a mechanism for explaining and reconciling those persons who are biracial. The fact is that the biracial person has often been used not to challenge the rigidity of racial lines, but rather to demonstrate the necessity of maintaining these lines. That is, the biracial person's existence only challenges racist paradigms if one constructs and interprets biracial existence as subversive. Via the one-drop rule, for example, mixed-race persons were divested of their threatening potential because the law simply rendered them "Black," regardless of phenotype, parental history, or personal identification. The biracial person is immediately absorbed into traditional monoracial categories.[13]

The fantasy that biracial subjectivity offers a way out of the old problematic constructions of race is a common feature of works that seek to explore the idea of mixed-race identity. In the introduction to *As We Are Now*, William S. Penn promises "to offer a new vision of race and identity" (3). Similarly, Judy Scales-Trent argues in her book *Notes of a White Black Woman* that

> There is something about living on the margins of race that gives me a unique view of the categories of black and white, that presents a different picture. . . . I understand race as a socially created metaphor, for my very existence unsettles expectations of race. (7)

Positing that mixed-race ideology is a cultural force capable of defeating American racism, Naomi Zack writes, "What was lost during the [Harlem Renaissance] was the concept of mixed race as a theoretical wedge against racism and the concept of physical race" (97). This is a tempting and almost irresistible idea to have about one's self in a society that constantly questions one about the "difficulty" of being biracial. I, too, at one time believed that as a biracial person I could disarm the racism of White and Black friends alike, showing them the error of their thinking. Because I lived with and grew up with knowledge of whiteness and blackness, I thought I could trace the breakdown in logic and communication, which so often characterizes racism, better than my Black or White counterparts could. I was disabused of this notion during my senior year in high school. Driving home from school one day with a friend, a White girl named Jennifer, we saw a Black man in the road repairing a telephone pole. He was in the way of the car, and she had to slow the car down quickly. She said, loud enough for me to hear, "Damn nigger needs to get out of the road." She then looked at my shocked face and apologized. She went on to explain, "Mixed people are different, you know? Black people, to me, look and act just like animals. But mixed people are the most beautiful people because they have the best of both worlds. They can dance and think." And she actually laughed. As we drove up to my house, I said finally, "Do you know that my mother is Black?" This had never occurred to her while she was explaining her thinking on race, nor did it seem to affect her after I had pointed it out. My mere existence did nothing to "unsettle" her racial expectations; she did not look at me and see evidence for rethinking her racist ideology. Her racism was easily able to accommodate the "blurring of the boundaries between the races" (7) that, according to Root, I am supposed to represent.

Though I could see how acutely wrong she was in her privileging of me as biracial over Black people, my own mother had told me some variation of this, too. My mother always reminded my brothers and me that we were "special." And when we asked her why she married our father, she would sometimes say, "Because I didn't want to have children with nappy hair." My mother never explicitly said that because we were mixed we were better than other people. But the implication was there that other children were not as "special" as we were. I am aware, too, that it may also have been her way of helping us combat the negative messages we received from both Black and White children at school. I know that she told us we were "special" precisely because of experiences like the time an African American classmate told me when I was thirteen years old that because I had a White father I was "half-devil." She and her family were in the Nation of Islam, and she believed that all White people were "devils." This comment was painful primarily because I had already internalized scores of assumptions about Black and White people and, as a result, I had a distorted notion of my own subjectivity. I tried throughout my life to reconcile this notion of the fundamental racial difference between my parents with my own sense of myself as "mixed." It is not surprising, then, that as a biracial child I grew up with as much learned racism as my friend Jennifer did. I simply believed not that White people were superior to Black people, or that White people were devils; I believed, because of my biraciality, that I could save them all because in my mixed-ness, I was superior to both groups. This is a kind of racism.

Being biracial made race visible in a way that disallowed the perception that racism was something that occurred in the outside world, in society, as something that happens to one; as a biracial individual I realized that racism was inside one's thoughts and actions. This particular awareness of my racial position and its relationship to a larger racial hegemony did not provide built-in or obvious answers about how to subvert the racial order. My experiences often produced ideas within me that were just as troubling as the ones I could identify as racist.

"I STAND WITH THOSE WHO STAND WITH ME"

I have experienced the frustration of feeling as if I did not "fit" in any racial group. This gave rise to my own biracial elitism; I became exclusive primarily because I had been excluded. As a middle school student, I became friends with another biracial girl. We felt particularly marginalized by the White and Black students at school, and in each other we found a sympathetic ear for the problems we experienced as a result of our mediated racial status. We formed our own biracial "club," where we collected posters of our biracial icons (Lisa Bonet, Prince, Sade), and we would not let anyone join who was not also biracial. We felt at once superior in our difference from everyone else, but this was not a difference we had chosen. It was one that was enforced through the policing of racial boundaries by those who saw us as racially different from themselves. Accordingly, we felt it necessary to turn that negative difference into a personal positive difference. We turned the realization that the Black and White kids did not want to associate with us into a decision of ours rather than a compulsory exclusion. It was our way of protecting ourselves from the severity of the racism we experienced; we created a refuge for each other within the rigid Black-White economy of the 1980s South. We had to "make a way out of no way" if we wanted to survive emotionally and socially. We, therefore, mimicked the behavior of our classmates and created a different and separate category of difference; in essence, we created ourselves as different from everyone else and reified our undesired and forced status as "other."

We did not understand, at that time, that our club was participating in the same cultural and social practices that we hated because it had kept us from finding our place within that particular school system. This anecdote suggests that we needed our own group because we had been excluded from others. Racial exclusion, however, should not necessarily be "answered" by a cordoning off of one's self from other racial groups and presuming that one has the answer to the race problem and those on the "outside" do not. At the same time I do not mean to suggest that the biracial person must seek approval and acceptance from those who seek to reject her on the basis of her biraciality.

Instead, I propose we recognize multiplicity in form and content

rather than running away from or toward essentialism, rather than attempting to understand "mixed-race identity" as a "thing" which can be
dissected, deconstructed, explained, and codified into one fixed ideology
or experience. What I suggest is not an erasure of racial identity (racelessness) or an endorsement of racial identity (group or race pride). This
means that I have no overarching theory of biracial identity, nor do I have
any suggestion about what the "best" term might be for describing the
biracial individual. Most of all, I do not have the answer for how to dismantle centuries-old practices of oppression that took more than one
person to build and will certainly take many more to disband. I can say de-
finitively that I am willing to dialogue about oppression, and I am willing,
through my life and my actions and in my beliefs to work with a community of all kinds of people—however they define themselves and even if
they do not define themselves—for our common liberation.

I have no way of restraining myself, or this piece, into a single argument or methodological strain. I resist this tendency to indulge in the creation of a grand narrative or ideology and instead offer instances of my
personal experiences and reactions to various writings on biracial subjectivity. What I want most from any article or book that seeks to discuss
biracial identity is the exploratory rather than the definitive; I want to see
a willingness of the ideology to be permeable, flexible, and mutating; I
want to see variety and diversity, rather than essentialism, gatekeeping,
and a return to cultural and historical sites in which our oppression has
often been founded and perpetuated.

I want a theory that can account for the ways in which I am Black *and*
the ways in which I am biracial, without those distinctions functioning as
evidence that my existence explodes the racial paradigm. I want theories
about liberation to be ones that take into account both the material and
philosophical dilemmas of race. So while race still exists as a material condition in the lives of the racially marked, we might proceed from an idea of
biracial subjectivity as another of many identities in a great community of
identifications and experiences, all of which have some overlap and diver-
gence. As a college student at a historically Black college for women, I understood and identified with the feelings of anger many of my colleagues
expressed about the racism we experienced, without any sense of distinction between them and myself. But the experience of solidarity and group
identification I experienced there does not invalidate this incident I leave
you with, an incident that highlights the complexity of these questions
about identity, belonging, and recognition. One of my friends from college, Marjorie, has a mixed-race niece named Tanya. She has very light

skin, blonde hair, and blue eyes. In almost every way, she is phenotypically different from Marjorie and me. On one of the many occasions I spent time with Marjorie and Tanya, we got into a conversation about race. Tanya said to Marjorie, who is only a few shades darker than me, "You're Black." Then pointing at me and smiling, Tanya said, "Stefanie is brown like me."

I end with this story because it was a powerful moment of naming and recognition for me as a biracial person. I felt at once claimed by Marjorie, who does not identify as biracial, and by Tanya, who does. I was not between two places, nor was any hierarchy being imposed in that moment. This experience demonstrates Walker's idea that "I stand with those who stand with me. I am tired of claiming for claiming's sake, hiding behind masks of culture, creed, religion. My blood is made from water and so it is bloodwater that I am made of, and so it is a constant empathic link with others which claims me, not only carefully drawn lines of relation" (320). This idea is poignant for me; it emphasizes that I am with those, and one of those, who choose to create community not only based on ethnic history and (self-)identification but also through empathic solidarity, through blood as well as water, and through a recognition of the risks we all share in this, our racist society.

Notes

1. See Langston Hughes, "Cross," in *Selected Poems* (New York: Vintage Press, 1963), p. 158, for the entire text of the poem.

2. A review of the major anthologies and works that discuss biracial identity will clearly demonstrate the use of personal narrative as a common device in the exploration of biraciality. Some relevant examples are: Maria P. P. Root, ed., *The Multiracial Experience: Racial Borders as the New Frontier* (Thousand Oaks, Calif.: Sage Publications, 1996); Carol Camper, ed., *Miscegenation Blues: Voices of Mixed Race Women* (Toronto: Sister Vision Press, 1994); Ishmael Reed, ed., *MultiAmerica: Essays on Cultural Wars and Cultural Peace* (New York: Viking Press, 1997); Lise Funderburg, ed., *Black, White, Other: Biracial Americans Talk about Race and Identity* (New York: Morrow and Co., 1994).

3. Joan Scott has argued that too often the relating of personal experience "reproduces rather than contests given ideological systems" (25). This is due, she argues, to the idea that personal experience can stand as "facts of history [that] speak for themselves" (25). Scott later problematizes her critique of the use of personal experience by recognizing the ways it has been used as a de-essentializing tool and asks, "How can we write about identity without essentializing it?" (33). One way, in my view, of resisting the tendency to essentialize racial experience is through the use of personal narrative. As Scott points out, there is a connection—whether we want to acknowledge it or not—between our theoretical assertions and our personal experiences.

4. I am thinking here about the critiques that have been made in the area of African American Studies of the notion of a "Black" experience as that which can be easily and readily defined, or which speaks to some monolithic and "knowable" experience. The book *Who Is Black?*, by F. James Davis, is a good example of a work that seeks to interrogate the essentialism of the term "Black" in cultural, legal, and societal terms.

5. Kathleen Odell Korgen, in *From Black to Biracial: Transforming Racial Identity among Americans* (Westport, Conn.: Praeger, 1998), demonstrates that despite the fact that many biracial people, after the Civil Rights Movement, feel free to identify as biracial, they still face many difficult issues of belonging and recognition in society. See the chapter "Marginality and the Biracial American."

6. Korgen discusses the implications of creating a biracial category on the U.S. Census forms in her chapter "Public Policy Implications" in the previously cited book. She analyzes the goals of Project RACE and its advocacy of "official recognition of multiracial persons through legal and legislative channels" (105). Korgen argues for the creation of a multiracial category in the census: "It is time for the Census to mirror truly the population it attempts to measure—complications and all" (106). Ostensibly, the goal of such a category is to "resist replacing today's racial hierarchy with another" (117). As I stated above, and through the relation of my experience and feeling at having a biracial "box" to check, I am entirely sympathetic to the desire for a category that recognizes my biracial background. I do not think, however, that the creation of such a category will do one iota of good in dismantling racism or challenging its logic. A good correlative in this case would be South Africa, which has an intermediate category—that of "colored"— in which nonblack and nonwhite South Africans belong; this group consists mostly of East Indians and biracial people. We can clearly see, in that national context, that this long-standing category that acknowledged those who are neither Black nor White did absolutely nothing to undo the virulent racism of apartheid. For more on the racial distinctions in South Africa see Frederick Johnstone, *Class, Race and Gold: A Study of Class Relations and Racial Discrimination in South Africa* (London: Routledge and K. Paul, 1976). Also see Anthony Marx, *Making Race and Nation: A Comparison of South Africa, the United States and Brazil* (Cambridge: Cambridge University Press, 1998).

7. I often comment to people that I pass for/am Black. I do this to upset their notions of who they think I am, as well as to highlight the ways in which my passing through the world and being recognized as a monoracial Black woman is the same as the white-skinned person, with a Black parent, walking through the world and passing, whether willingly or unwillingly, for White. The only difference between my passing and a white-skinned person's passing is that we live in a society where one cannot pass for Black, since if you have a Black parent, U.S. society understands you to be Black. I began to understand, when I was an exchange student to Brazil in 1989, that how I thought about race was defined largely by my national context. While there I noticed that everyone seemed to be of mixed race and that it was the rule, rather than the exception, that the Brazilian people were an extremely heterogeneous mix of cultures. It was the first place where I looked more like everyone than not. I was told that I looked like a "typical" Brasilera and was often mistaken for a local. This was especially clear when I ordered a pizza one

evening and the delivery boy interrogated me, after hearing my broken Portuguese, about my national identity. When I told him I was an American, he did not believe me and instead thought I was a rich Brasilera putting on airs. I had passed so well in that national-racial context that my own identity was not believed, even when I asserted it (and performed it through my horrible Portuguese). Passing, then, can also be read not only as a shield behind which to hide the evidence of racial difference and as a device invoked only by the (guilty) deceiving passer. Instead, passing can also be understood as a membrane over the eye of the racial voyeur, who looks for particular kinds of racial proofs and, thinking he has found them, is upset to discover that he has deceived himself. We live in a society that at once condemns and yet requires passing, since how we define race does not allow for the possibility that a person may not be what *we* think he or she looks like. It is this conundrum, in my view, that biracial studies is also wrestling with.

8. I do not mean to suggest here that Black identity is constituted solely through oppression. Rather, I am referring here to the ways in which "blackness," and not particular cultural identity—i.e., various aspects of African culture—is constructed in American society as inferior.

9. Much critical race theory takes as its project the question of how "blackness" and "whiteness" come to exist in an American context. These theories seek to expose the ways in which race is constructed, highlighting the fact that while many people now accept the labels "Black" and "White," and in some cases, even exult in those labels, these ways of naming racial identity are far from naturalized, inherent identities. See Noel Ignatiev, *How the Irish Became White* (New York: Routledge, 1995). Also see Jewelle Taylor Gibbs, "The Social Construction of Race, Ethnicity and Culture," in *Souls Looking Back: Life Stories of Growing Up Black*, ed. Andrew Garrod, pp. 75–85 (New York: Routledge, 1999).

10. Naomi Zack, among others, argues that there was a "mulatto" elite during the Harlem Renaissance that maintained an aloof attitude toward the Black community. This is evidenced during that time with the rise of such organizations as the Blue Vein Society, which only allowed people with skin light enough to show blue veins to join. See Naomi Zack, *Race and Mixed Race* (Philadelphia: Temple University Press, 1993). See also Joel Williamson, *New People: Miscegenation and Mulattoes in the United States* (New York: Free Press, 1980).

11. Walker, 13.

12. Zora Neale Hurston, *Dust Tracks on a Road*, 242–243.

13. It was also theorized by eugenicists that the "offspring" of interracial unions would yield everything from "torturous and complicated coronal suture," to various "disharmonies of constitution," such as "nervousness," mental anguish, and even psychosis (351). See S. J. Holmes, *Human Genetics and Its Social Imports* (New York: McGraw-Hill, 1936).

Works Cited

Camper, Carol, ed. *Miscegenation Blues: Voices of Mixed Race Women.* Toronto: Sister Vision Press, 1994.

Davis, F. James. *Who Is Black? One Nation's Definition.* University Park: Pennsylvania State University Press, 1991.

Funderburg, Lise, ed. *Black, White, Other: Biracial Americans Talk about Race and Identity.* New York: Morrow and Co., 1994.

Gibbs, Jewelle Taylor. "The Social Construction of Race, Ethnicity and Culture." In *Souls Looking Back: Life Stories of Growing Up Black,* ed. Andrew Garrod, pp. 75–85. New York: Routledge, 1999.

Holmes, S. J. *Human Genetics and Its Social Imports.* New York: McGraw-Hill, 1936.

Hughes, Langston. "Cross." In *Selected Poems,* p. 158. New York: Vintage Press, 1963.

Hurston, Zora Neale. *Dust Tracks on a Road.* New York: HarperPerennial, 1996.

Ignatiev, Noel. *How the Irish Became White.* New York: Routledge, 1995.

Johnstone, Frederick. *Class, Race and Gold: A Study of Class Relations and Racial Discrimination in South Africa.* London: Routledge and K. Paul, 1976.

Korgen, Kathleen Odell. *From Black to Biracial: Transforming Racial Identity among Americans.* Westport, Conn.: Praeger, 1998.

Lindberg, Christine A., ed. *The Oxford American Desk Thesaurus.* New York and Oxford: Oxford University Press, 1998.

Marx, Anthony. *Making Race and Nation: A Comparison of South Africa, the United States and Brazil.* Cambridge: Cambridge University Press, 1998.

Penn, William S., ed. *As We Are Now: Mixblood Essays on Race and Identity.* Berkeley: University of California Press, 1998.

Reed, Ishmael, ed. *MultiAmerica: Essays on Cultural Wars and Cultural Peace.* New York: Viking Press, 1997.

Root, Maria P. P. "Bill of Rights for Racially Mixed People." In *The Multiracial Experience,* ed. Maria P. P. Root, pp. 3–14. Thousand Oaks, Calif.: Sage Publications, 1996.

———, ed. *The Multiracial Experience: Racial Borders as the New Frontier.* Thousand Oaks, Calif.: Sage Publications, 1996.

Scales-Trent, Judy. *Notes of a White Black Woman: Race, Color, Community.* University Park: Pennsylvania State University Press, 1995.

Scott, Joan. "Experience." In *Feminists Theorize the Political,* ed. Judith Butler and Joan W. Scott, pp. 22–40. New York and London: Routledge, 1992.

Spencer, Rainier. "Race and Mixed Race: A Personal Tour." In *As We Are Now: Mixblood Essays on Race and Identity,* ed. William S. Penn, pp. 126–139. Berkeley and Los Angeles: University of California Press, 1998.

Urdang, Laurence, ed. *The Random House Dictionary of the English Language.* New York: Random House, 1968.

Walker, Rebecca. *Black, White, and Jewish: Autobiography of a Shifting Self.* New York: Riverhead Books, 2001.

Williamson, Joel. *New People: Miscegenation and Mulattoes in the United States.* New York: Free Press, 1980.

Zack, Naomi. *Race and Mixed Race.* Philadelphia: Temple University Press, 1993.

8. TOWARD A MULTIETHNIC CARTOGRAPHY

Multiethnic Identity, Monoracial Cultural
Logic, and Popular Culture

Evelyn Alsultany

These incidents and others like them had a peculiar cognitive feel to them, as though the individuals involved felt driven to make special efforts to situate me in their conceptual mapping of the world, [...] to locate me within the rigid confines of [their] stereotype of black people.

—Adrian Piper, "Passing for White, Passing for Black"[1]

Ethnicity in such a world needs to be recast so that our moving selves can be acknowledged [...] Who am I? When am I? The questions that are asked in the street, of my identity, mold me. Appearing in the flesh, I am cast afresh, a female of color—skin color, hair texture, clothing, speech, all marking me in ways that I could scarcely have conceived of.

—Meena Alexander, *The Shock of Arrival*[2]

NARROW CARTOGRAPHIES[3]

I am in a graduate class at the New School in New York City. A White woman sits next to me and we begin "friendly" conversation. She asks me where I am from. I reply that I was born and raised in New York City and return the question. She tells me that she is from Ohio and has lived in New York for several years. She continues her inquiry: "Oh, . . . well, how about your parents?" I feel her trying to map me onto her narrow cartography; New York City is not a sufficient answer. A seemingly "friendly" question turns into a claim to land and belonging. "My father is Iraqi and my mother Cuban," I answer. "How exotic! Are you a U.S. citizen?"

I am waiting for the New York City subway. A man also waiting asks me if I, too, am Pakistani. I reply that I am part Iraqi and part Cuban. He asks if I am Muslim, and I reply that I am. He asks me if I am married, and

I tell him I am not. In cultural camaraderie he leans over and says that he has cousins in Pakistan available for an arranged marriage if my family so desires. I tell him that I am not interested in marriage but thank him for his kindness. I accept how he has situated me within his narrow cartography and respond accordingly, avoiding an awkward situation in which he realizes that I am not who he assumes I am.

I am in a New York City deli waiting for my bagel to toast. The man behind the counter asks if I am an Arab Muslim (he, too, is Arab and Muslim). I reply that yes, my father is. He asks my name, I say, "Evelyn," and his appearance sours. In utter disdain, he tells me that I could not possibly be Muslim, for if I were truly Muslim I would have a Muslim name. What was I doing with such a name? Although painfully aware of how questions of my identity mark me in unexpected ways and resisting the impulse to get upset, I reply that my Cuban mother named me and that I honor her choice. His eyes now scour my appearance; he quickly points out the lipstick that I am wearing and says that I am a reflection of the decay of the Arab Muslim in America.

I am on an airplane flying from Miami to New York City, sitting next to an Ecuadorian man. He asks me where I am from. I tell him. He asks me if I am more Arab, Latina, or American, and I state that I am all of the above. He says that it is impossible; I must be more of one ethnicity than another. He determines that I am not really Arab, that I am more Latina because of the solidarity he feels in our speaking Spanish.

I am in Costa Rica. I walk the streets, and my brown skin and dark hair blend in with the multiple shades of brown around me. I love this first-time experience of blending in! I walk into a coffee shop, order *café con leche*, and my fantasy of belonging is shattered when the woman preparing the coffee asks me where I am from. I tell her that my mother is Cuban, my father is Arab, and that I was born and raised in New York City. She replies, "*Que eres una gringa.*"

MISRECOGNITION, DISPLACEMENT, AND THE MULTIETHNIC DILEMMA

These experiences illuminate the commonness of the question "Where are you from?" They also reveal that the "correct" answer to these questions changes depending on the context. In the United States, when I answer, "I am from New York City," my answer is "incorrect," since it does not respond to the assumptions behind the question. In other words, it does not help the questioner to place me adequately within his/her narrow conceptual mapping of racial identities, for in the United States, nonwhite appearance is assumed to signify non-American identity. The White American has been constructed as "naturally" having roots in the United States (unless he/she displays other markers, such as an accent), erasing the place of Native Americans as indigenous. While Native Americans are erased and replaced through this ideology, people of color are assumed to be from another nation.[4] Race and nationality have come to be equated, such that "whiteness" signifies "Americanness" and non-whiteness implies a primary attachment to a nation or community other than the United States. Meanwhile, as my experience in Costa Rica demonstrates, the relationship between race and nationality depends on context; despite my brown skin and Latino/Arab descent, I am at times read as a White American! In either location, the seemingly innocent question of national or ethnic affiliation begs to map identity in accordance with already established constructions of racial identities and thereby situate each identity "in its place."

My stories also demonstrate the difficulty in conceptualizing multi-ethnic identity.[5] Multiethnic identity is either understood as "exotic"[6] or ignored and translated to monoracial through the submerging of one identification and the privileging of another. When Latinos or Arabs discover that I am multiethnic, I risk exclusion from those communities for not being "authentic" enough.

This pervasive inability to conceptualize multiethnicity results in mis-recognition and displacement as a defining experience for multiethnic people. I would characterize the multiethnic experience as an unmappable space. To inhabit more than one ethnicity is to go against the monoracial cultural logic.[7] Thus, many multiethnics must choose a monoracial identification in order to be rendered visible. Identities that make sense within the cultural logic (monoracial) are rewarded with belonging, while those posited as "illogical" (multiethnic) are denied community belonging. In most cases, monoracial identification is dictated by appearance—if you look White, then you can either pass as White or struggle to be acknowledged as nonwhite, and, similarly, if you do not look White, then you are automatically designated nonwhite. As Camille Hernandez-Ramdwar has stated: "There is no camp for us to fit easily into, there never has been, and we are always asked to choose, but by reason of our appearance the choice is often made for us" (7).

I use the terms "multiethnic" and "monoracial cultural logic" intentionally. My choice of terms is influenced in part by the United States Census's problematic framing of race and ethnicity and by Stephen

Cornell and Douglas Hartmann's useful definition of race and ethnicity. Cornell and Hartmann define ethnicity as a group of people with a shared history, culture, and symbolism—such as language, spiritual belief, geographical region, etc. Race, in contrast, is defined as a social construct, based on physical characteristics. Race, unlike ethnicity, is not based on history, culture, or symbolism, but on a hierarchy of power, having been invented out of a Eurocentric ideology to distribute power in favor of Whites. Ethnicity, in comparison, is not necessarily infused with power structures and is often a self-conscious identification, while race is an imposed identification. The term "monoracial cultural logic" is based on this definition of race. It acknowledges the Eurocentric hegemonic ideology that still operates today in the United States and imposes monoracial identities onto the population. The term "multiethnic" seeks to embody the history, culture, and symbolism of a group of people as a self-conscious identification. It seeks to move toward locating agency in self-definition within a multiethnic cartography. I use the term "multiethnicity" in the same way as Cornell and Hartmann, to refer to "the mixing of ethnic and racial identities and ancestries in single persons, the offspring of interethnic and interracial unions" (238).

My conception of monoraciality and multiethnicity is also influenced by the 2000 Census, which reflects the "official" understanding of race and ethnicity in the United States. The 2000 Census classified five racial categories: (1) White, (2) Black or African American, (3) American Indian and Alaska Native, (4) Asian, and (5) Native Hawaiian and Other Pacific Islander; and one ethnic category: Hispanic or Latino. Apart from the fact that Arabs are not even acknowledged by the Census, the cases of both Arabs and Latinos in the United States point to the inadequacies of the Census definitions of race. Neither is considered a racial group, since both groups are phenotypically diverse, spanning the "racial" spectrum, yet both groups have nonetheless been "racialized" as nonwhite. Though some light-skinned Arabs and Latinos do pass for White, particularly if they are Christian and of high economic status, those who are Muslim, or who speak Arabic or Spanish, or display any "difference" from the White American standard, are racialized as nonwhite.[8]

Race, as it is currently conceived, provides us with an inadequate framework through which to understand identity. To begin with, it fails to account for many individuals, such as Middle Easterners, Latinos, and multiethnics. It also fails to register the nuances that people experience as part of their identity, whether identifying, for example, as White and Jewish; White, Muslim, and Arab; or Ghanaian-American. Racial discourse increases the discrepancy between how we internally experience our identities and the externally imposed frameworks on our identities. At the same time, however, this inadequate monoracial ideology pervades our culture, and as a result, I use the term "monoracial cultural logic" to point to the mechanisms of racialization that operate to produce the multi-ethnic as monoracial. I use the term "multiethnic," as opposed to "inter-racial" or "mixed race," to be inclusive of those identities, such as my own as Arab-Latina, that are not acknowledged by racial categories, yet which nonetheless undergo a process of racialization in the United States.

Remaining unmapped as a multiethnic within the monoracial cultural logic results in being treated as suspect by all parties for not being mono-racial enough, in other words, "catching it from all sides." For example, for some Whites, the multiethnic represents the pollution of the White race; for some African Americans, the multiethnic represents an attempt to escape blackness; and for other ethnicities, such as South Asians, Lati-nos, or Arabs, the multiethnic can be seen as ill-equipped to perpetuate cultural traditions and therefore represents the dilution of that particular culture. Such suspicion of the multiethnic often leads to a variety of sur-vival tactics. The most common response to "catching it from all sides" is to embrace monoraciality and to become as identifiably monoracial as possible. The alternative—to claim a multiethnic identity—often leads to accusations of betrayal, weakness, or escapism. The desire to be viewed in accordance with one's self-perception becomes criminalized, seen as a cop-out and meriting community ostracization. To compound the prob-lem, as multiethnics move into different public spaces, they are frequently misread because existing frameworks cannot appropriately map or con-ceptualize them.

SOCIAL INTERACTION AND EXPANDED CARTOGRAPHIES

The problem with such a narrow cartography of ethnic identity is that it leads to ethnic misrecognition in a variety of contexts and consequently to displacement in social interactions. Social interactions tend to be rid-dled with misidentifications of possible relatedness. The social organiza-tion of interaction is such that relatedness is a privilege granted only to those who are, or appear to be, monoracial and who conform to the stan-dards of identity set forth by a particular unified ethnicity. Not fully of one ethnicity or another, the multiethnic body is displaced not only from the dominant culture, but also by those groups to which it "partially" be-longs. To move toward a multiethnic cartography, as I will suggest, is to move away from our current, narrow conceptualizations of identity.

Social psychology has demonstrated that in order to coordinate with others one must have a definition of self and other that will map out certain modes of behavior and response in a given situation. Most cultures have two to four salient categories of identity that operate in all social interactions. According to Marilynn B. Brewer and Layton N. Lui, race, gender, and age are the top three interactionally relevant categories in the United States; these provide crucial information that is most often visually accessible, and virtually determinable. (I would add class and sexuality to this list of interactionally relevant categories in the United States.) Within this automatic process of categorization, in-group members are identified and favored, while out-group members are judged and marginalized more frequently (Fiske, 2:367). Categorization is central to human interaction, occurring automatically. Categorization is considered functional in preserving cognitive resources and socially useful in helping people interact more easily. People in social interaction "normally engage in cognitive shortcuts, unless motivated to go beyond them," tactically deciding which interactions require additional effort depending on the goals of the interaction (Fiske, 2:363).

The primary motive in interaction is belonging. Racial categories are automatically applied within initial interactions to anticipate another's views to negotiate the potential for conflict, camaraderie, or understanding. Trust is another motive in social interaction; one is more likely to trust someone in the in-group than the out-group. Social interaction is also driven by a desire for understanding and control. Order and predictability are preferred over ambiguity. These behavioral patterns are problematic when acted out within the narrow cartography previously discussed. For example, monoraciality is assumed predictable and multiethnicity is ambiguous, unfamiliar, and therefore assumed to be unpredictable, causing discomfort. A psychological study has shown that the difference between high- and low-prejudiced people is not the activation of a stereotype that occurs automatically during interaction, but the ability to control that activation (Devine, 12). However, both high- and low-prejudiced people tend to rely on stereotypes in the case of ambiguous racial identities. In other words, even if a person consciously monitors his/her stereotypes to prohibit them from taking over in an interaction, in the case of ambiguous identities, such as multiethnicity, stereotypes are activated and used to navigate through the ambiguity caused by the narrow cartography, as demonstrated by my personal experiences.

In other words, the goals of social interaction as outlined above are often closed off to the multiethnic within our monoracial cultural logic. Without a multiethnic conception of identity, multiethnics, if visually identified as part of the in-group, can be seen as traitors and rejected when discovered to be part of the out-group as well (e.g., not having a Muslim first name). In the case of the multiethnic, categorization leads to distancing as opposed to belonging, understanding, control, or trust.

Successful interaction hinges upon the classification of one's race, gender, and age. Ambiguity causes confusion, complicates the interaction, and activates stereotypes. A common case in point from popular culture is the *Saturday Night Live* character Pat. Pat is sexually ambiguous and no one knows if he/she is male or female. The comedic skit revolves around those who interact with him/her going to great lengths to get Pat to reveal his/her sex, often relying on stereotypes of masculinity and femininity as determining factors. The skit demonstrates how people are unable to relate to Pat unless the ambiguity around his/her sex is resolved. Similarly, multiethnics often find that the ambiguity around their ethnicity needs to be resolved for social interaction to proceed. Sociological theory posits that categories enable understanding even if they are restrictive or reductive, since they produce collective understandings. However, the monoracial logic and accompanying categories that prevail in our culture produce collective misunderstandings. The narrow ethnic cartography that we currently draw on to interact with each other does not accurately account for multiethnic identities and also renders multiethnics illegible, costing multiethnics belonging within their communities.

Rather than accepting this narrow cartography as simply a part of societal functioning, I would like to consider how we could revise our ethnic cartography to be inclusive of multiethnic identities. In our rapidly changing transnational world, we need to revise our conceptualization of ethnic identity to allow for a more accurate and richer understanding of multiethnic identity and ultimately of all identities; we need to find ways to bridge the gap between how we see and experience our identities and how we are socially seen and categorically reduced. Echoing Alexander's words in the epigraph, ethnicity needs to be recast so that our moving selves can be acknowledged.

Racial cartographies are not static but clearly change over time. A ready example of a changing racial cartography is the caste system that operated in eighteenth-century colonial Mexico. This elaborately conceived caste system distinguished among numerous permutations of racial mixing and was used to uphold White power and privilege. When Mexico achieved independence in 1810, the caste system was eventually replaced through the creation of a single category—mestizo—that came to be equated with the prototypical "Mexican."[9] Similar revisions and expansions in the way race is conceived occurred in Cuba, Puerto Rico, and Brazil. In these countries Spanish, African, Native, and Asian peoples, among others, came to be categorized as "Cuban," "Puerto Rican," and "Brazilian"— pan-ethnic identity categories that corresponded to nationality.

Another important example of a racial cartography that has changed over time is reflected in the historical changes to the United States Census. Clara E. Rodriguez charts how categorization has changed since the first Census in 1790, which distinguished between free White males, females of various age groups, and (Black) slaves. The 1850 Census counted Whites, free Blacks, free mulattoes, slave Blacks, and slave mulattoes. In subsequent years, the Census expanded to include Chinese, Japanese, and the category "other." The most recent United States Census in 2000 is evidence of a changing racial cartography, particularly for multiethnics, who for the first time had the opportunity to identify with more than one category. This leads me to wonder how we might imagine a future conceptual framework of our identities. How might we effect greater change in the monoracial cultural logic that leaves me, and other multiethnics like me, unmapped and displaced?

I want to suggest one resource that might aid efforts to revise and expand the prevailing ethnic cartography. Popular culture—and more specifically for my purposes, the lives of multiethnic pop figures such as Mariah Carey, Paula Abdul, Tiger Woods, and Melissa Howard—has helped to bring about a significant shift in public discourse on multiethnicity. I will examine how Mariah Carey and Paula Abdul's multiethnic identities were reinscribed as monoracial and how Tiger Woods and Melissa Howard's insistence on being represented as multiethnic poses a challenge to monoracial cultural logic and as a result might introduce the possibility of a multiethnic conceptualization into our narrow ethnic cartography.

POPULAR CULTURE AND THE REINSCRIPTION OF MONORACIAL CULTURAL LOGIC: MARIAH CAREY AND PAULA ABDUL

Popular culture plays a crucial role in reinforcing the monoracial cultural logic. The media are a powerful operative within popular culture, working to refract reality and infuse it with ideological meaning. In the words of Stuart Hall, "the media play a part in the formation, in the constitution, of the things that they reflect [. . .] The reality of race in any society is 'media-mediated'" (1996, 340). How do the media mediate multiethnicity? In line with my earlier claims that multiethnicity is understood either through the category of "the exotic" or through the reinscription of monoraciality, the media reinforce these limiting conceptual options. Multiethnic persons who appear to be monoracial are accordingly categorized, such as Halle Berry (categorized as Black though she has a White parent), Cameron Diaz (categorized as White though she is part Cuban), and Linda Carter (categorized as White though she is part Mexican). However, for multiethnic persons whose ethnic appearance is ambiguous, their identity is a question to be discussed and resolved. Mariah Carey and Paula Abdul are examples of ambiguous-looking women in popular culture, and the way they have been written about in popular magazines reveals that multiethnicity is often debated and reinscribed as monoraciality.

When Mariah Carey became famous, there was some confusion around her racial identity, best captured on the March 1991 cover of *Jet* magazine, which featured a picture of her and a headline that read, "Mariah Carey Tells Why She Looks White but Sings Black." This article sought to resolve the confusion through legitimizing her blackness, not only by featuring her on the cover of the magazine, but also by explaining to the Black community that it is valid for her to be embraced by them, since her father is African-Venezuelan.

> Like former Rick James sidekick Teena Marie and the popular members of New Kids on the Block, songstress Mariah Carey finds herself on the receiving end of routine remarks insisting she's another White singer trying to sound Black.
>
> But this frivolous accusation is w-a-a-a-a-y over the fence in the ballpark of reality for the 20-year-old rising New York starlet whose fair complexion and fine sandy-colored mane clearly result from the genetic fusion of a Black, Venezuelan father—Washington, D.C., aeronautical engineer Alfred Roy Carey—and Irish mother—N.Y. voice coach Patricia Carey.
>
> Saying she's a combination of all three nationalities during the March *Ebony* interview in Manhattan, Ms. Carey asserted: "I can't help the way I look, because it's me. I don't try to look a certain way or sing a certain way." (56)

The article addresses Carey's dilemma as she is scrutinized by the Black community. The article also helps her out of the bind by declaring her Black despite her light skin tone. Though Carey is acknowledged as multiethnic, the article settles this confusion by affirming to the public that she is not a traitor or a Black wannabe, but is in fact Black and can be treated and regarded as monoracially Black.

Paula Abdul is another example of a physically ambiguous multiethnic celebrity who became monoracially Black through the media's attempts to clarify confusion. In March of 1990, *Ebony* featured an article entitled "Who's Black?" that identified Black-biracial and multiracial celebrities, how the Black community perceives them, how they identify, and their actual racial makeup. The article stated that when Paula Abdul's *Forever Your Girl* album came out, Black fans bought her album, believing that she was Black. This information is presented as though posing a question of allegiance and authenticity: have her fans been fooled into believing she is Black?

> It turns out to be a bit more complicated than that, for Abdul says she is not Black, but adds that she does not consider herself White either. "I am Third World," says the former Los Angeles "Laker Girl" cheerleader; who says her mother is French-Canadian and her father is Brazilian-Syrian. An Abdul associate says: "I can't say that this is a Black woman totally, but the major part of her early success came from the Black community, and her identity is definitely with Blacks." (136)

This article claims that Abdul is not Black or White, but is allied with African Americans. Her Brazilian-Syrian-French-Canadian identity is confusing to the monoracial-logic-minded. Two months later, Paula Abdul was featured in the May 1990 edition of *Ebony* in the article "The Many Talents of Paula Abdul: Sassy Entertainer Gives Expanded Definition to the Term 'Multiple.'" Although such articles acknowledge her multiethnicity, they effectively position her as monoracially Black.

Abdul and Carey are both perfect examples of how the media translate multiethnicity and frame it as monoraciality. But it is important to acknowledge that both Carey and Adbul were complicit in portraying themselves as monoracially Black. As Hall's influential theory of encoding/decoding demonstrates, although the media contribute to the construction and maintenance of social reality through mediating—that is, through presenting certain frameworks (monoraciality) for the interpretation of events and issues (multiethnicity)—the power of the media as definers of social reality is limited by the way in which the produced/encoded message is received/decoded. The process of mass communication involves production, circulation, consumption, and reproduction. Producers construct/encode the message, the broadcast or other means of dissemination circulates the message, the consumer decodes the message, and reproduction begins the process all over again. This can be seen as a circular process subject to confirmation and modification. As Hall points out, "If no 'meaning' is taken, there can be no 'consumption.' If the meaning is not articulated in practice, it has no effect" (1980, 128).

Hall understands broadcast television as yielding an encoded meaning that reinforces the status quo of the dominant culture. Within this process of mass communications, production and consumption are not necessarily identical, but related and mutually influential. Hall states that there must be some reciprocity for effective communicative exchange to take place between the mass media and the public. There are instances, however, of equivalent reciprocity between the production and consumption of meaning, which have the effect of constructing naturalized codes. Monoraciality is an example of a naturalized code. As with other naturalized codes, naturalization occurred through, to borrow Louis Althusser's term, various ideological state apparatuses, such as the census, and also through the repetition of the encoded and decoded meanings over time. As Hall states,

> What naturalized codes demonstrate is the degree of habituation produced when there is a fundamental alignment and reciprocity—an achieved equivalence—between the encoding and decoding sides of an exchange of meanings. The functioning of the codes on the decoding side will frequently assume the status of naturalized perceptions. (1980, 132)

Through the achieved equivalence between the production and consumption of the meaning of multiethnicity, and through habituation, monoracial cultural logic has become naturalized.

Carey and Abdul have been active agents in the naturalization of monoracial cultural logic through their complicity with media representations of themselves and through their own self-presentation as monoracially Black. Since their ambiguous ethnic appearance defies easy categorization, other criteria, such as cultural codes and personal associations, have been employed to successfully align themselves with monoraciality. Carey, for example, as we are told by *Ebony*, "sings black," and Abdul popularized the Black vernacular saying "straight-up" through one of her hit songs. In addition, they have both worked with many famous African American artists and producers (Carey has worked with Whitney Houston, Ol' Dirty Bastard, Da Brat, Brian McKnight, Jermaine Dupri, Boyz II Men, Bone Thugs N' Harmony, Missy "Misdemeanor" Elliot, Dru Hill, Prince, and Sean "P. Diddy" Combs, and Adbul has worked with Janet Jackson, the Family Stand, and Prince, among other African Americans). Not only have the media played a role in reinscribing Carey's and Abdul's multiethnic identities as monoracial, but they, too, have participated in their monoracialization through public displays of their personal associations and through their performances of "blackness." [10]

In the next section, I will consider two examples of multiethnic celebrities who problematize the naturalized equivalence between the production and consumption of monoraciality in place of multiethnicity by refusing and resisting monoracialization.

TOWARD A MULTIETHNIC CARTOGRAPHY:
TIGER WOODS AND MELISSA HOWARD

How can we move away from understanding multiethnic identity through monoraciality and exoticism and create alternate cartographies through which to understand multiethnicity? Popular culture can play a role in shifting public understanding of multiethnicity and move us toward a multiethnic cartography if the signifying chain of encoding/ decoding is disrupted and resignified. Ella Shohat and Robert Stam have argued that just as the media have marginalized cultures, they also have the power to represent and promote the multifaceted world (7). José Esteban Muñoz, in his study of performances by queers of color, examines moments in which the dominant logic is challenged:

> I am interested here in unveiling moments in which the majoritarian
> public sphere's publicity—its public discourse and reproduction of
> that discourse—is challenged by performances of counterpublicity
> that defy its discriminatory ideology. Counterpublicity is disseminated
> through acts that are representational *and* political interventions in the
> service of subaltern counterpublics. (147)

I would like to examine several recent multiethnic interventions in popular culture that have disrupted the dominant monoracial logic and created the possibility for multiethnic understanding and representation. The two cases I will examine are golfer Tiger Woods and *Real World New Orleans* cast member Melissa Howard. I would like to consider how these multiethnic public figures break the chain of monoracial signification and thereby its effect on the monoracial cultural logic.

Tiger Woods's multiethnic identity has been controversial and publicly debated. Woods is not only the youngest player in golf history to win the Masters, but also the first major championship winner of African or Asian descent. Regarded by the general public, and represented by the media, as monoracially Black, the truth is that Woods is multiethnic: his father is half Black, a quarter American Indian, and a quarter Chinese, and his mother is half Thai, a quarter Chinese, and a quarter White. He has

jokingly referred to himself as "Cablinasian"[11]—Caucasian, Black, Indian, and Asian—but has simplified his identity to African American and
Asian for the media, insisting that he be recognized accordingly. In a formal statement issued to the media, Woods attempts to map for himself a
new position:

> The purpose of this statement is to explain my heritage for the
> benefit of members of the media, who may be seeing me play for the
> first time. It is the final and only comment I will make regarding the is-
> sue. My parents have taught me to always be proud of my ethnic back-
> ground. Please rest assured that is, and will be, the case. . . . The vari-
> ous media have portrayed me as African-American, sometimes Asian.
> In fact, I am both.
>
> Yes, I am the product of two great cultures. . . . On my father's side
> I am African-American, on my mother's side, I am Thai. . . . I feel very
> fortunate, and equally proud, to be both African-American and Asian!
> (Strege, 115)

Woods's insistence on being acknowledged as multiethnic has been met
with a great deal of resistance. Gary Kamiya, writing for *Salon* in
April 1997, reports that,

> According to *Time* magazine, Woods' coming out as a Cablinasian
> caused "a mini-racial firestorm. . . . Woods' remarks infuriated many
> African Americans who . . . see him as a traitor. . . . Some blacks saw
> Woods' assertion of a multiracial identity as a sellout that could touch
> off an epidemic of 'passing.'" Light-skinned Colin Powell, responding
> to Woods' comments, "In America, which I love from the depths of my
> heart and soul, when you look like me, you're black." (par. 4)

Woods's resolve that his multiethnic identity be represented as such
has disrupted the equivalent reciprocity between the encoding and decoding of multiethnicity as monoraciality. As a result, we witness a shift
in the encoding of multiethnicity, that is, in the production and framing
of discourses on multiethnicity. In an article from the *Washington Post*, for
example, Woods states that

> My mother is from Thailand. . . . My father is part black, Chinese and
> American Indian. So I am all of those. It's an injustice to all my her-
> itages to single me out as black." [. . .] These were not the words of a
> young man trying to "pass," to deny his heritage, to reject the shade
> of melanin that would have categorized him as "Negro" under not-so-

ancient race laws. This was a voice of a new generation of Americans who resist the cultural pressure to make one choice, who say I am the sum and the son of many parts. (Goodman)

This piece suggests a shift in public discourse. Woods's choice to be represented as multiethnic is defended, and he is framed, along with other multiethnics, as "a new generation of Americans," thus engendering a new identity within the ethnic cartography of the United States.

On *The News Hour with Jim Lehrer*, Woods is positioned as a racial hero:

Perhaps Tiger Woods is showing us the way, upsetting the tyranny of group identity to reassert himself as an individual and to add a new twist to the American notion of freedom. Proud, jolly, and confident, he shows old masters new tricks. He also shows us Americans how much we have been prisoners of our past, even as our future is overtaking us. He's a credit to his races—every one of them. (Page transcript, 3)

Not only is Woods acknowledged as multiethnic here, but his multiethnic identification is defended and multiethnicity is presented as the wave of the future. Such discourses present multiethnicity as enriching instead of escapist, illustrating a shift in the process of encoding multiethnicity.

The positioning of Woods as part of "a new generation of Americans" and as "adding a new twist to the American notion of freedom" invokes a nationalist discourse, particularly the rhetoric of the "melting pot" and "multiculturalism" so frequently circulated throughout the history of the United States. What is important to remember is that such nationalist discourses often function either to create an illusion and mask a reality or to stand in for an imagined possibility. Although such discourses provide the opportunity for multiethnic identity to be represented, the positioning of multiethnics as "the new face of America," or as the culmination of the American promise of multiculturalism, is premature and misleading. As I mentioned earlier, whiteness and Americanness have come to be equated, despite discourses of melting pots and multiculturalism. Discourses of multiethnicity, as examples of American notions of freedom, can mask the firm place of whiteness at the center of American citizenship. Although the idea of multiethnic faces of color dethroning whiteness as the signifier of American identity and opening the gates for all ethnicities to be equally encoded as American is an appealing possibility, it is nonetheless important to be wary of the history of misleading nationalist discourses on multiethnicity.

Despite the shift from monoracial discourses on multiethnicity to heroic and nationalist discourses in popular media, Woods's intervention has provided alternative ways to conceptualize and decode multiethnicity, partly through visual means. Muñoz, writing about Marga Gomez, a Cuban–Puerto Rican performance artist, claims that

> [h]er performance permits the spectator, often a queer who has been locked out of the halls of representation or rendered a static caricature there, to imagine a world where queer lives, politics, and possibilities are representable in their complexity. The importance of such public and semipublic enactments of the hybrid self cannot be undervalued in relation to the formation of counterpublics that contest the hegemonic supremacy of the majoritarian public sphere. (1)

According to Muñoz, Marga Gomez's performance constitutes a "counterpublic" because it is a public expression contrary to the dominant hegemonic discourse, and works to create a new space in which the spectator can imagine a queer world that is not static or homogeneous, but complex and heterogeneous.[12] Similarly, I perceive Tiger Woods as having created counterpublic moments. One way Woods does this is by being in the public eye with his parents. The sight of Tiger standing, on and off the golf course, with his Asian-looking mother and African American–looking father, is by now familiar. These images allow the public to begin to conceive of a relationship to ethnicity other than monoraciality. Hall has stated that the "televisual sign is a complex one. It is itself constituted by the combination of two types of discourse, visual and aural" (1980, 131). In seeing Woods with his parents, it becomes apparent that he stands in relation to both Asian and African American cultures, and the visual component of the televisual sign is accordingly encoded. The possibility that both parents and their respective cultures have shaped his identity and identifications is made visible, thereby producing and circulating a new encoded message around multiethnicity. The possibility that one can be affiliated with, feel at home in, relate to, or identify with aspects of two cultures is created as a concept that holds the potential of shifting our narrow monoracial cartography.

Melissa Howard, cast member of the 2000 New Orleans edition of MTV's *The Real World*, a popular television program among sixteen- to twenty-five-year-olds, presents other moments of multiethnic public disruption by insisting on being recognized as both Asian and African American. On *The Real World*, she often addresses the dilemma she frequently finds herself in as a multiethnic in a monoracial world. She talks about how African Americans do not think she is Black enough because she is Asian, and Asians do not think she is Asian enough because she is Black. In the show she is portrayed as confused, distressed, frustrated, and having problems fitting in, particularly where men are concerned. She tends to date White men who lack any understanding of her identity and are drawn to her for her "exoticism." While some might think that her portrayal on *The Real World* reinforces stereotypes of the "confused multiethnic," I think she inserts an alternative encoding of multiethnicity that disrupts the naturalized monoracial codes.

Howard is known for her comedic imitations of her mother and father, and it is through such imitations that the public is provided a glimpse into both growing up in a household with multiple ethnicities and the ways such ethnicities might influence her own multiethnic identity. In an interview on *BET Live*, the host asks Howard to imitate her parents:

> Well, let's see. [. . .] My parents watch the show sometimes, when I am out on the road and I'll call and I'll be like, "Tell me what happened on the show." And my mom will be like [strong Asian accent], "Well, what happen is, Danny, he is the gay one, did you know that?" "Yeah, I knew that." "So Danny he go and his parent come and then he say that he is gay." "Yeah, okay, what happened on the show?" "Then Danny, he is gay and then he climb this tree." And I am like "What?" And sure enough I turn on the show and Danny is gay and climbing a tree. And then my dad's like, "Let me tell you what happened." And then Shorty's [her father's name] take on the show is like, what you didn't see. And he's like, "I ain't see you and David [the other African American on the cast], right? So I thought maybe y'all was at the store." And I am like, "What?" "Y'all was at the store talkin' it out, right? They ain't really show that because they already fill they Black quota for the day." And I am like, "What?" So like every time I am not on the show, my dad thinks it's some sort of Black conspiracy. It's hilarious. (*BET Live*)

Howard's imitation of her parents allows the public to see her identity in relation to her parents' different ethnicities and to imagine her resulting complex multiethnic experience. Similar to Woods encoding multiethnicity visually for the public, Howard provides imaginative aural depictions of her multiethnic experience through comedic dialogue. Later on the show, Howard is asked to pick a question to answer out of a bucket:

What would your last meal consist of? Let's see. See I am half Black and half Filipino and I will eat some pigs' feet with some rice and soy sauce [audience laughs]. I do! I will eat some lumpia with some collard greens. *(BET Live)*

In what seems like an insignificant commentary on food, Howard illustrates her simultaneous relationship to two cultures, two cultures that she identifies with and that make her who she is. Howard disrupts and modifies the naturalized chain of mass communication (production, circulation, consumption, reproduction) by producing an alternate encoded message.

The examples of Mariah Carey and Paula Abdul suggest that these public figures serve as agents in the confirmation of the monoracial dominant logic. In contrast, the experiences of Tiger Woods and Melissa Howard demonstrate the ways in which they actively resist the monoracial narration of their identities and alter the predominant production/encoding process. Of course, Woods and Howard do not have absolute control over how this modified multiethnic encoded message is received/consumed/decoded. Ien Ang and Purnima Mankekar have demonstrated that audiences are not passive receivers of media, but actually decode, interpret, and often resist information they receive through the media. The alternate discourses produced by Woods and Howard are left to the consuming public, who must sort through which discourse is more meaningful to them. Some will agree with and some will resist the multiethnic cartography, depending on the consumer's subject position.

Studies have shown that reinforcement, as opposed to persuasion, is the main effect of mass communications. As we have seen, discourses on monoraciality in the media have served to reinforce the monoracial cultural logic. In contrast, discourses on multiethnicity, operating against the dominant logic, could be seen as working to persuade. As Jay G. Blumler and Michael Gurevitch have written on audience psychology: "Where overt persuasion is recognized, audience members may be on their guard. But media contents may be received in a less skeptical spirit if people perceive them as information, i.e., as if they have no specific axe to grind" (248). Therefore, the ways in which the news, a political campaign, and popular culture are received could be different depending on their presentation and content, and on the various possible subjectivities of media consumers. Similarly, a challenge to naturalized codes might be seen as an attempt toward persuasion as opposed to information. After receiving the same monoracial message habitually over time, receiving multiethnicity encoded as such could be cause for resistance, as exemplified in the case of Tiger Woods, in which he was seen as having a "specific axe to grind"—namely, climbing up the racial hierarchy away from blackness and toward multiethnicity.

We are still far from a paradigm shift in our ethnic cartography, and I do not mean to suggest that a multiethnic cartography now exists as a result of Tiger Woods and Melissa Howard's disruptions. However, we are one step closer to a multiethnic cartography as a result of their resistance to monoracial cultural logic. Just as monoracial cultural logic is naturalized through the habituation of encoded and decoded meanings in the media, it is possible for a more inclusive cartography to become naturalized through these same mechanisms. The long-term effects of the change in the 2000 Census, which portends official recognition of multiethnicity, and the disruptions to the chain of media signification exemplified by Woods and Howard stand as examples of such a possibility. This new chain of signification holds the possibility of better representing multiethnics and others who experience a discrepancy between how they are culturally framed and how they experience themselves. As Mankekar has stated regarding hegemonic narratives, "they seek to create unitary subject positions by denying men and women a complex subjectivity" (38). Disrupting the signifying chain of monoraciality might move us toward better representation of more complex subjectivities.

In closing, I would like to recount a recent and very unusual personal experience, keeping in mind Hall's claim that if the encoded meaning is not articulated in practice, then it has no effect. Recently, I met Carmelita Tropicana, a Cuban-American comedienne and performance artist. I was introduced to her as an Iraqi-Cuban, and later in our conversation she asked me what I was studying in graduate school. I told her that my focus was on Latino Studies and Arab-American Studies. She replied, very much in line with her comedic personality, "Yes, of course. Because you . . . you can go both ways. You know what I mean?"

Notes

Author's Note: I would like to thank those who participated in the Modern Thought and Literature Symposium (May 2001) and the Comparative Studies in Race and Ethnicity Graduate Seminar Presentation Forum (January 2002) at Stanford University for engaging with my paper. I would particularly like to thank Renato Rosaldo, Yvonne Yarbro-Bejarano, Benefo Ofosu-Benefo, Julia Carpenter, Ebony Chatman, Flavio Paniagua, Mireille Abelin, Shana Bernstein, Mona El-Ghobashy, Phil Goff, Linda Lin, Inger Petterson, Cecilia Ridgeway, Simon Weffer, and Michelle Zamora for their insights, bringing sources to my attention, and support. I would like to extend my sincere gratitude to SanSan Kwan and Kenneth Speirs for their thoughtful and detailed feedback.

1. Piper, 83.

2. Alexander, 66.

3. A version of this section appears in Ana Louise Keating and Gloria Anzaldúa, eds., *This Bridge We Call Home: Radical Visions for Transformations* (New York: Routledge, 2002).

4. I am currently writing about how this might have momentarily shifted as a result of the events of September 11, 2001, particularly how people of color were suddenly able to claim "American" as a primary identity, defined against the Arab Muslim "Other."

5. When speaking of multiethnicity in the United States, I am excluding a discussion of Hawaii, which is a unique case with a complicated history of racial mixing.

6. Although the primary focus of this paper is not the exoticization of the multiethnic, it is important to acknowledge that the multiethnic is often encoded through the trope of the "exotic." As Ella Shohat and Robert Stam have illustrated in *Unthinking Eurocentrism*, discourses of exoticism are expressions of Eurocentrism; exoticism is racism masked in romanticized and eroticized language. The "exotic," in this case the multiethnic, is produced from the perspective and for the pleasure of the colonizer. Discourses of the exotic multiethnic position multiethnicity as the exotic "other" and, like discourses on monoraciality, fail to adequately account for multiethnic identity. Examples drawn from popular culture reflect this phenomenon. For instance, actress Cameron Diaz is usually portrayed as monoracial (White), unless reference is made to her "exotic beauty." *Rolling Stone* magazine's Web page claims that "[H]er unusual beauty—the result of her Cuban-American and Anglo--German–Native American parentage—helped to ensure that she would not be soon forgotten" (http://www.rollingstone.com/mv_people/bio.asp?oid=72712).

Multiethnic men are also exoticized and in their case "hunkified." Keanu Reeves, for example, whose mother is White and father half Hawaiian and half Chinese, and Benjamin Bratt, whose mother is Quechua Indian from Peru and father is European American, have gained popularity for their "exotic" good looks and have been cast in some "nonethnic" or "hunk" roles. (Reeves has played "nonethnic" roles for most of his career, such as in *Speed* and *The Matrix*, and Bratt only recently achieved "hunk status" and as a result can be seen as Madonna's love interest in *The Next Best Thing* and opposite Sandra Bullock in *Miss Congeniality.*) In both cases, Bratt and Reeves are granted "nonethnic" status because they have achieved popular "hunk" status and are therefore moneymaking assets to Hollywood. Hollywood's depoliticizing mechanisms replace their multiethnic identity with an exotic hunk identity. In the end, whether monoracialized or exoticized, multiethnicity remains outside of conventional ethnic cartographies.

7. The term "monoracial cultural logic" is modified from José Esteban Muñoz's book *Disidentifications: Queers of Color and the Performance of Politics*, in which he refers to heteronormative, White supremacist, and misogynist "cultural logic" (5).

8. For more on the racialization of Islam, see Nadine Naber, "Ambiguous Insiders: An Investigation of Arab American Invisibility," *Ethnic and Racial Studies* 23, no. 1 (2000): 37–61.

9. In eighteenth-century colonial Mexico, multiethnicity functioned to uphold White supremacy and was elaborately categorized in the following way:

1. *Español con india, mestizo:* Spanish with Indian = Mestizo
2. *Mestiza con español, castizo:* Mestizo with Spanish = Castizo
3. *Castizo con española, español:* Castizo with Spanish = Spanish
4. *Español con negra, mulatto:* Spanish with Black = Mulatto
5. *Mulata con español, morisco:* Mulatto with Spanish = Morisco
6. *Morisco con española, chino:* Morisco with Spanish = Chinese
7. *Chino con india, salta atrás:* Chinese with Indian = A Jump Backwards
8. *Salta atrás con mulata, lobo:* A Jump Backwards with Mulatto = Wolf
9. *Lobo con china, gibara:* Wolf with Chinese = Gibara
10. *Gibaro con mulata, albarazado:* Gibaro with Mulata = Albarazado
11. *Albarazado con negra, cambujo:* Albarazado with Black = Cambujo
12. *Cambujo con india, zambaigo:* Cambujo with Indian = Zambaigo
13. *Zambaigo con loba, calpa mulatto:* Zambaigo with Wolf = Calpa Mulatto
14. *Calpa mulatto con cambuja, tente en el aire:* Calpa Mulatto with Cambuja = Suspended in the Air
15. *Tente en el aire con mulata, no te entiendo:* Suspended in the Air with Mulatto = I Don't Understand You
16. *No te entiendo con india, torna atrás:* I Don't Understand You with Indian = Turn Back

See Gonzalo Aguirre Beltrán, *La Poblacion Negra de México* (México: Fondo de Cultura Económica, 1972), 176–177. Also see Pedro Alonso O'Crouley, *A Description of the Kingdom of New Spain*, trans. Seán Galvin (John Howell Books, 1774), 17–21.

10. The role that *Ebony* and *Jet* magazines play in defining the boundaries of blackness is notable. It reflects the Black community's investment in identifying blackness. Since the civil rights movement, identifying as Black has become a political strategy and a political force, including identifying who is Black regardless of mixture. The division of the multiethnic person from the monoracially Black category is actively resisted because such divisions were historically used to strengthen the hegemonic discourse of whiteness. While I understand the importance of resisting the reinscription of racial hierarchies based on skin tone, mixture, and proximity to whiteness, I would like to encourage us to move ourselves into new discursive and ideological spaces and to avoid what Helen Safa has cautioned against: the reification of the binary model of racial hegemony through the affirmation of monoracial Black culture and identity (15).

11. Cablinasian is the term Tiger Woods used to describe his racial identity when asked to by Oprah Winfrey on her show after he won his first Masters tournament.

12. Muñoz's use, and subsequently my use, of counterpublics comes from Nancy Fraser's essay "Rethinking the Public Sphere," in *The Phantom Public Sphere*, ed. Bruce Robbins (Minneapolis: University of Minnesota Press, 1993).

Works Cited

Alexander, Meena. *The Shock of Arrival: Reflections on Postcolonial Experience.* Boston: South End Press, 1996.

Althusser, Louis. "Ideology and Ideological State Apparatuses." In *Lenin and Philosophy, and Other Essays*, pp. 85–126. New York: Monthly Review Press, 2001.

Ang, Ien. *Living Room Wars: Rethinking Media Audiences for a Postmodern World.* New York: Routledge, 1996.

BET Live. Black Entertainment Television, January 4, 2001.

Blumler, Jay G., and Michael Gurevitch. "The Political Effects of Mass Communication." In *Culture, Society and the Media*, ed. Michael Gurevitch, Tony Bennett, James Curran, and Janet Woollacott, pp. 236–267. New York: Routledge, 1982.

Brewer, Marilynn B., and Layton N. Lui. "The Primacy of Age and Sex in the Structure of Person Categories." *Social Cognition* 2, no. 3 (Fall 1989): 262–274.

Cornell, Stephen, and Douglas Hartmann. *Ethnicity and Race: Making Identities in a Changing World.* Thousand Oaks, Calif.: Pine Forge Press, 1998.

Devine, Patricia G. "Stereotypes and Prejudice: Their Automatic and Controlled Components." *Journal of Personality and Social Psychology* 56, no. 1 (1989): 5–18.

Fiske, Susan T. "Stereotyping, Prejudice, and Discrimination." In *The Handbook of Social Psychology*, 4th ed., ed. Susan T. Fiske, Daniel T. Gilbert, and Gardner Lindsey, pp. 357–411. Boston: McGraw-Hill, 1988.

Goodman, Ellen. "Black (White, Asian, Indian) Like Me," *Washington Post*, April 15, 1995.

Hall, Stuart. "Encoding/Decoding." In *Culture, Media, Language: Working Papers in Cultural Studies, 1972–79*, ed. Stuart Hall, Dorothy Hobson, Andrew Lowe, and Paul Willis, pp. 128–138. London: Hutchinson/The Centre for Contemporary Cultural Studies, University of Birmingham, 1980.

———. "Race, Culture, and Communications: Looking Backward and Forward at Cultural Studies." In *What Is Cultural Studies?*, ed. John Storey, pp. 336–343. New York: Arnold, 1996.

Hernandez-Ramdwar, Camille. "Ms. Edge Innate." In *Miscegenation Blues: Voices of Mixed Race Women*, ed. Carol Camper, pp. 2–7. Toronto: Sister Vision, 1994.

Kamiya, Gary. "Cablinasian Like Me: Tiger Woods' Rejection of Orthodox Racial Classifications Points the Way to a Future Where Race Will No Longer Define Us." *Salon*, April 1997 (http://www.salon.com/april97/tiger 970430.html).

Mankekar, Purnima. *Screening Culture, Viewing Politics: An Ethnography of Television, Womanhood, and Nation in Postcolonial India.* Durham, N.C.: Duke University Press, 1999.

"The Many Talents of Paula Abdul: Sassy Entertainer Gives Expanded Definition to the Term 'Multiple.'" *Ebony*, May 1990, 118–122.

"Mariah Carey Tells Why She Looks White but Sings Black." *Jet*, March 4, 1991, p. 56.

Muñoz, José Esteban. *Disidentifications: Queers of Color and the Performance of Politics*. Minneapolis: University of Minnesota Press, 1999.

Page, Clarence. "A Credit to His Races." *News Hour with Jim Lehrer*, Public Broadcasting Service, May 1, 1997. Transcript.

Piper, Adrian. "Passing for White, Passing for Black." In *Talking Visions: Multicultural Feminism in a Transnational Age*, ed. Ella Shohat, pp. 79–97. New York and Cambridge: New Museum and the MIT Press, 1998.

Rodriguez, Clara E. *Changing Race: Latinos, the Census, and the History of Ethnicity in the United States*. New York: New York University Press, 2000.

Safa, Helen I. "Introduction: Race and National Identity in the Americas." *Latin American Perspectives* 25, no. 3 (1998): 3–20.

Shohat, Ella, and Robert Stam. *Unthinking Eurocentrism: Multiculturalism and the Media*. New York: Routledge, 1995.

Strege, John. *Tiger: A Biography of Tiger Woods*. New York: Broadway Books, 1997.

"Who's Black?" *Ebony*, March 1990, pp. 134–139.

9. KEEPING UP APPEARANCES
Ethnic Alien-Nation in Female Solo Performance

Cathy Irwin and Sean Metzger

The closest thing that we have to a national theater, our network of regional theaters, remains the "bastion of white male representation."

—Velina Hasu Houston (xvii)

In terms of demographics, the major regional theater scene has shifted very little over the course of the last decade. Ethnic tokenism continues to govern season selection policies, perhaps to a greater extent than ever with the success of shows like *Angels in America* (featuring one Black role) and *Rent* (a diverse cast with two White men at its core). Asian American communities, in particular, remain in the wings, seeing but not participating in the action as scene after scene passes in America's major houses.

Although the occasional play by an established figure like David Henry Hwang or Velina Hasu Houston reaches the mainstage, Asian American drama finds its greatest promoter in the ethnic theater circuit and other small performance venues. In recognition of this fact, various institutions have established community development programs like the Asian American Theatre Workshop at the Mark Taper Forum in Los Angeles. These programs feature one night or perhaps two weeks of Asian American performances to balance seasons that might otherwise find themselves devoid of any Asian American representation. Unfortunately, such facile solutions generate another set of problems; they often fail to allow for diversity within racial and cultural groups. Thus, the ethnic allotment creates a situation in which differences among the heterogeneous constituencies of the "Asian American community" must, from time to time, remain offstage in order to shine the spotlight on commonality. To perform under the auspices of "Asian American," in other words, usually requires an aspiring artist to justify his or her inclusion within that rubric.[1]

In response to such representational practices, another performance movement has begun to blossom outside of the house. Liberating themselves from the cost of major stage productions, Asian American actors are increasingly going on the road . . . by themselves. Solo performers now abound, and include such diverse names as Noel Alumit, Dan Bacalzo, Daryl Chin, Margaret Cho, Dan Kwong, Sandra Tsing Loh, Alec Mapa, Hung Nguyen, Lane Nishikawa, Dawn Saito, Paula Westin Solano, Denise Uyehara, and Byron Yee. What Holly Hughes and David Roman have said about solo queer performance might also apply to this loosely bound group: solo performance is "one of the few forms of artistic expression that registers as democratic: nearly anyone can do it and nearly everyone does" (1).

But what are the effects of this proliferation of solo performances? Our essay explores Asian American solo performance as a genre that foregrounds the problematic aspects of identity, one that potentially disrupts and destabilizes representations that produce and perpetuate dominant (i.e., White, heterosexual, male) positions of privilege.[2] In *Straight White Male*, Michael Peterson contends that these challenges to dominant discourse produce a "crisis of identity" (6) for straight White men and render the stage a battleground of racial, gender, and class representation. Following Peterson's assertion, we look at how two female mixed-race performers negotiate their work in a market that ostensibly supports diversity. However, we find that this inclusiveness supports only specific kinds of difference that are both marketable and politically noncontentious.

Recall that the early nineties witnessed tremendous debate over this same issue of who has the artistic right to tell stories. The debates culminated in the gutting of the National Endowment for the Arts (NEA). Right-wing political discourse contended that "[t]he NEA was bleeding the American people so that artists could show off their privates, smear themselves with chocolate, cross-dress, and splatter the audience with HIV-positive blood" (Hughes and Roman, 8). Such allegations mark the provocative allure of the corporeal and remind us how performance constructs bodies that matter. Moreover, the material nature of live performance, Josephine Lee has written, "suggests an immediate, visceral response to the physicality of race" (7).

These qualities of performance having been noted, the remainder of this essay enacts a kind of dialogue between two biracial observers of two different mixed-race solo productions. Our pleasure in seeing Sandra Tsing Loh and Paula Weston Solano, each of whom foregrounds mixed-race issues, is tempered by other feelings that run the gamut from awe to envy to disappointment. By engaging our personal investments in these performances, we hope better to illustrate what each performing body signifies for particular kinds of audiences. We interrogate the ways in which our own Asian affiliations impinge on our reading of these artists as ethnic representatives. And we ask ourselves what strategies of co-optation and intervention these stage productions reveal in the context of multiple communal allegiances. Perhaps most importantly, we examine class and gender considerations that complicate the seen (scene) of the racial body, and how viewing and enjoying a performance implicates us in particular kinds of politics.

LIVING THE LOH LIFE
Sean Metzger

I had my life all worked out in the fall of 1996. I had just arrived in Los Angeles. I was young, I was ambitious, and I was stupid. You see, I wanted to become a gay, biracial solo phenomenon—not just a star—a phenomenon. I told myself that I did not have any aspirations to become another dumb actor, waiting on tables while I was waiting for a break. Instead, I was going to perform an ethnically oriented show about life, my life, as a Chinese, German queer . . . and I was going to attempt graduate school, all at the same time. I would become a public icon. Call me "the diva with the doctorate," I thought.

But my dream ended (as nightmares usually do). I realized two things about Los Angeles: firstly, a few hours in the gym can earn you thousands more dollars than many hours reading books, and, secondly, Los Angeles already had its German, Chinese muse, writing in the pages of 'zines, resounding through the radio waves, and, in a coup de grace, acting on the stage.

No, it was not Sigrid Nunez and her novel *A Feather on the Breath of God* that took away my dream. It was not the witty words of Jennifer Tseng, who fictionalized East-West family narratives for our shared generation of twenty-somethings. It was not even the fact that John Travolta was developing a Hollywood formula that would steal my title: *Phenomenon*. It was instead a specific multiracial body on the stage that preempted my debut. The stage performance that involved this body presented and simultaneously disowned cultural difference. Thus, it was, in three words, Sandra Tsing Loh who spoiled my dream. Loh constructed her unique body as the cipher through which every-body in Los Angeles, if we believe critics such as Daryl Miller of the *Los Angeles Daily News*, could understand her or his own Americanness.

How did this woman with a Chinese father and a German mother become the spokesperson for humanity in Southern California? What accounts for the phenomenal success of this lady, lauded by the *Los Angeles Times*, *LA Weekly*, and Los Angeles's elite theatergoing public? I pursue these questions through an analysis of Loh's one-woman show, *Aliens in America*.

The *Los Angeles Daily News* has described this work as "deeply personal and broadly universal" (Miller). The *New York Times* finds a similar oxymoron appropriate: "both exceptional and very familiar" (Brantley). Indeed, *Time Out New York* goes so far as to assure an audience that we "need not possess Loh's unique gene structure to clearly see all our families in her wonderfully observant performance piece."[3]

What I will contend is that Loh achieves such praise only by "Americanizing" herself in relation to her parents, whose status as immigrants marks them as "other" in contrast to their American-born daughters. Loh describes the difference produced by her mother and particularly her father in primarily ethnic, as opposed to generational, terms. These ethnic descriptions suggest the tacit requirements of American citizenship, for, as Toni Morrison has pointed out, to be "American means [to be] white" (47). Loh thus participates in and appeals to what Ruth Frankenburg calls "whiteness masquerading as universal" (3); the perceived commonality that Loh offers her audience has everything to do with rendering her body as an unfortunate accident of cultural meeting. In other words, Loh has sufficient distance from her family roots to claim affiliation with the "White" American majority. If Loh's autobiographical piece does more than elicit laughs, I want to suggest that it helps us to understand what it means to be White . . . excuse me, almost White, during the 1990s in a place like Los Angeles.

Loh initiates her appeal to a transcendent Americanness with the program. On the cover, Loh stands wrapped in an American flag. She thus cloaks her physical difference under the international sign of the United States, the stars and stripes. Explicating this symbology, Loh dedicates this show, as the inside of the pamphlet reveals, to "all mixed-ethnicity—i.e., all AMERICAN—families" (Loh 1999).

Loh thus prepares her audience to receive the simultaneous registers of difference and sameness that inform her work before the performance begins. The mise-en-scène continues this effort. On both sides of the stage, forming two sloping walls, sit stacks of Chinese take-out boxes. At center stage, we see a screen on which appears the title "My Father's Chinese Wives," written in a bamboo-shaped script. This screen forms part of a larger structure that looks something like a telephone booth. Popular American music from the fifties and sixties fills the theater. Then, a gong sounds; a red light flashes. The booth turns, and Sandra crashes through a screen of butcher paper.

Aliens in America opens with a section entitled "1992 Adulthood: My Father's Chinese Wives . . . My Father, the Alien." In calling her father an "alien," Loh reinscribes the prejudice that immigrants are "foreigners" who should not reside here. Loh explores this particular prejudice early on in the piece. "At age seventy, my father—a retired Chinese aerospace engineer—is starting to look more and more like somebody's gardener" (1997, 4). The stereotypical gardener in California is the Mexican immigrant, whom, legal citizen or not, American cultural discourse always already identifies as the illegal alien.

The fact that Dr. Loh does not belong in the United States becomes more explicit when Loh states that "'Crazy old Chinese father' is actually a kind of code word for the fact that . . . [my] father has always had a hard time . . . spending money" (1997, 5). His lack of desire to participate in the capitalist machine further marks him as (hopelessly) Chinese in the eyes of his progeny, as someone who does not fit into the middle-class-consumer mold of the United States. The narrator's mention of her Chevrolet Geo, her education at USC, and her clothes codes her as circulating well within the flows of capital. In stark contrast to even modest displays of wealth, Loh's father wears a Speedo taken from a dumpster, uses a cereal box for a briefcase, and takes paper towels from public bathrooms. Loh spends a large portion of the first section of the performance commenting on the excessively thrifty behavior of her dad, deemed un-American because of his spending habits. Performing the voice of her older sister Kaitlin, Loh laments, "This is a man who has $300,000 in mutual funds alone! Can't he liberate fifty of it to spend on a throw rug?" (1997, 22). A moment later, she adds, "I mean, I know things were really, really, really difficult in Shanghai, but he hasn't lived there now for forty years, has he? Will it never end? Will it never end?" (1997, 22).

Loh further distinguishes herself from her Chinese father in ethnic terms. Through the voice of Kaitlin, Loh erects a divide between father and daughters based on the lack of cross-cultural communication. In describing the failure of his first marriage to a German woman, Kaitlin surmises, "To him, it will have been that rebellious Aryan strain that's the problem" (1997, 7). Kaitlin advances this distinction further, clearly marking her father as Chinese and her sister and herself as something quite different. When his second marriage, to a Chinese woman, fails, for example, she says, "Isn't it interesting how he seems to repell [sic] even his own kind?" (1997, 16). On the one hand, this line registers the fact that Dr. Loh, his wife, and their daughters occupied one household, which all the women have left. On the other hand, these same words imply that even other Chinese people, with whom Kaitlin does not identify, cannot tolerate Dr. Loh. The father has erred in bringing over financial practices that create a lifestyle the daughters do not desire. The experiences of the past belong, it would seem, locked away in Shanghai.

In light of this context, Loh's earlier observation speaks volumes. "In describing this potential new wife, my father had used one word: Chinese. He has not said: 'I'm looking for a smart wife,' or even 'a fat wife.' He has said 'Chinese.' That word is meant to stand for so much" (1997, 7). Indeed, nothing could be more accurate. "Chinese" stands as the figure of difference, the almost insurmountable wall that separates Dr. Loh from his (almost) American girls (recall that this wall is literally erected on stage through the set design).

Nothing substantiates this claim more than the fact that the father's second wife, Liu Tzun, adapts to the United States far more quickly than her new husband, who has lived in the States forty years longer. Loh tells us, "Although she speaks no English, she [Liu Tzun] seems to be an expert on American culture" (1997, 13). That she has "ambitions in the entertainment business" and "wants to drive the car" (1997, 16) are the signs of separation between the spouses. Liu Tzun maintains some belief in an American dream. In order to pursue it, she leaves her husband a note: "I have left you, Dr. Loh, and taken the Toyota—so there!" (1997, 15).

But Dr. Loh is only momentarily set back in pursuit of a much younger partner. With a few more letters, he procures yet a third wife: Zhou Ping. But Zhou Ping differs from the previous spouses. She has had China etched into her psyche. "She worked in a coal mine in Manchuria until she was twenty-five years old. . . . Then she worked on a farming collective" (1997, 17). At dinner, she cooks an "authentic Chinese meal." Although Loh questions Zhou's ability to adapt to Los Angeles, the new woman surprises her. She even encourages Dr. Loh to buy a CD player. In the brief narrative describing this latest addition to the family, Loh portrays Zhou Ping as the immigrant who successfully balances Chinese traditions and her new American lifestyle. Kaitlin, for example, receives a Hallmark birthday card with mooncakes from her father's new wife. While she convinces her husband to buy new things, Zhou Ping also recycles; she has, for instance, salvaged a rug from the dumpster. When the recently wed couple converses "quietly in Mandarin" and "eat[s] deftly with chop-sticks," the youngest daughter realizes that "it's not Zhou Ping who's the stranger at this table. It's Kaitlin and I. They are the same culture. We are not" (1997, 23). Loh implies that Zhou Ping and her father find a com-mon denominator in China. Thus, in this first section, Loh describes her dad as a displaced Chinese man whose status as such marks him as differ-ent from his daughters. This assertion becomes possible, however, only through the disavowal of the diversity within that category (Chinese) that Loh herself represents and in fact acknowledges in discussing each of her father's very different Chinese brides. To link Zhou Ping and Dr. Loh based on cultural affiliation and country of origin is to ignore the fact that Liu Tzun also emigrated from China yet had very little in common with the man. The ethnic difference of which Loh speaks is an over-simplification of complicated cultural and generational conflicts that can occur within families. Loh's performance insists on reading these family tensions through the lens of ethnicity. From this perspective, Dr. Loh becomes a Chinese man living in the United States, while his daughters are Americans. Loh enacts a removal from the term of "Chinese" into an-other space, a space her performance then moves on to explore.

Separated so much from her father, Loh takes the logical next step and examines potential connections to her mother. Enter section two: "1969 Childhood: Ethiopian Vacation . . . My Mother, the Alien." What is strik-ing about this discussion is the fact that the action it describes occurs largely outside of the United States. Whereas Loh's father is an alien in the country in which he currently lives, her mother becomes an alien in large measure because she married a Chinese man and because her narra-tive in the show occurs, for the most part, in a foreign locale, with the added exoticism of both tourists and terrorists. Because Loh describes so much of her mother's behavior as reacting to that of Dr. Loh, Loh's mother occupies a position similar to that of her daughters: she also does not identify with the Chinese man. Loh ponders what could have brought this odd couple together, stating, "I blame it on Buick. . . . I guess a man looks better than he ought, in a Buick" (1997, 34). The "anomaly" of his life, the new car that first helped Dad attract Mom's notice, creates paral-lels among the Loh women. The women aspire to exhibit the trappings of middle-class life. They all desire material things in which their father ex-presses no interest, since the acquisition of products requires the spend-ing of money. Sandra and her mother, not surprisingly, also agree on their first choice for vacation: Hawaii.

Mother's second choice for vacation, a compromise between her own desire for the beach and her husband's desire for an educational and inexpensive trip, is Malawa. When terrorists intercept the bus to Malawa, Loh notes that her father, "with his small body, dark coloring, and worn rag sweater," manages to "blend in" (1997, 47) with the locals and escape capture. Reinscribing her father's difference in a simultaneously positive (he survives) and problematic (all dark people are the same) way, the adventure provides the audience with yet another opportunity to understand the Chinese man as a marker of difference from the performer's own position.

This vacation also provides an opportunity in the narrative for the mother to meet with other German tourists; an increase in the amount of German dialogue follows. In this respect, the descriptions of the parents differ markedly, for while the father never says anything to the children in Chinese in spite of being so ingrained in the culture, the mother constantly chatters in German. One justification for this split is the need to mark both of the parents as aliens, not only in terms of generation, which is what the last section of the monologue, in part, accomplishes, but also in terms of cultural difference. To signify a cultural gap, however, proves a bit of a challenge. The spectator understands the mother's Germanness because of her language, her predilection for schnapps, and the fact that the daughters are "hustled off to kindergarten in Heidi of the Alps–type dirndls and clogs" (1997, 36–37). In other respects, however, Mom is like her daughter: in American society both are culturally unmarked.

The primary difference in this story is between the Chinese alien and the others. That Dr. Loh is the patriarch ensures that Chineseness becomes the dominant cultural index in the family, thus swallowing up the more minor differences between Germany and the United States. The performance phrases this power dynamic as follows: "So while my mother left her WWII behind, he could not forget his Shanghai. He has brought it with him, and this is where they live" (1997, 51). Thus, the mother remains "a foreign person ... always ... in a foreign land" (1997, 51) in spite of the fact that she seems to have adapted to Los Angeles far better than her husband.

It would be somewhat misleading to suggest that all Dr. Loh represents to Loh is otherness. Loh writes that she, too, is an alien, as is revealed by the title of section three: "1981 Adolescence: Musk . . . I, the Alien." She is an alien in the sense of not fitting in with other White youth, as well as being alienated from her parents' ethnic heritages. The former assertion is made through Loh's description of the humiliation she suffers while trying to be like the White kids that surround her. The latter point is made apparent in her depiction of her parents' nonstandard English, which stands against her own unaccented speech.

The salient image in the Epilogue, that is, of "a small Chinese man, two Hispanic-looking girls with Heidi of the Alps braids, and a tall German brunette in Jackie O. sunglasses trying to look very elegant" (1997, 72), leaves ambiguous what kind of ethnic signifier might best describe Loh. I contend that this ambiguity is reconstituted as a space of generic middle-class whiteness. In this space the father's position is radically othered and thus helps to explain the women's varying degrees of difference. Without the language, the nostalgia for certain clothes, cordials, and comrades, Loh's mother also whitens in the narrative; she becomes indistinguishable from the assumed mass. Similarly, Loh suggests that her own alienation is a result of having grown up with her parents. Even when she reminisces about splashing fully clothed into a hot tub filled with four naked peers, she attributes this action to her lineage: "What could I do? It was my DNA. I was a jackalope in dirndl and clogs, raised by . . . Venusians" (1997, 68). To materialize the alien-nation that she feels, she refers to herself as "Hispanic-looking" (1997, 72).

Cleverly titled, Loh's performance points to the constructed division between citizen and illegal immigrant in this country, especially in Southern California. The marked illegal alien, the Mexican immigrant, what I believe Loh terms the Hispanic, is the figure with whom Loh claims physical resemblance. The assertion that shared physical characteristics can have multiple racial classifications might be an enlightened perspective on the formation of race. However, as Lisa Lowe argues,

> Narratives of Multiculturalism which do not make . . . connections between historically differentiated forms of disempowerment or which do not make space for oppositional critiques risk denuding racial and ethnic groups of their specificity. Subject to the leveling operations of both post-modern pastiche and pluralism, African, Asian and Latino cultures all become equally other, are metaphorized as equally different and whole without contradiction. (96)

In performing Americanness by distancing herself from her own roots, yet simultaneously claiming an obscure affiliation with other American ethnic groups, Sandra Tsing Loh reduces the facets of diverse communities to a generic condition of alienation. Her own body comes to stand for human. And it is this universal humanity, unarticulated as a specifically dominant White racial formation and linked to specific practices of consumption and appropriation, that lurks behind the sign of Loh's America.

BEHIND THE COVER GIRL:
PAULA WESTON SOLANO'S *APPEARANCES*
Cathy Irwin

After living for more than twenty-five years in Los Angeles, a miracle has happened: I am considered cool! I have the "look" that Hollywood wants! My brown hair with natural red and golden highlights is a hot hair color in beauty salons! And my face . . . okay, so I'm not Miss Cover Girl, but skimming through fashion magazines, I have found models and artists— Keanu Reeves (Hawaiian, Chinese, White), Mariah Carey (Black, Venezuelan, White), Johnny Depp (Cherokee, White), to name a few—with features that suggest their mixed-race heritages. People with ambiguous racial features are hot commodities!

Yet people of mixed race also unsettle mainstream American culture— *if* they use their voices and bodies to speak against systems of classification that pigeonhole them into monoracial categories. The leveling of racial differences by the mainstream media, as well as performances like Sandra Tsing Loh's solo act, indicates society's need to contain the differences potentially posed by a multiracial identity. In the fall of 1993, for example, *Time* magazine published a special issue entitled "The New Face of America: How Immigrants Are Shaping the World's First Multicultural Society." On the cover, created by *Time* imaging specialist and cyber-geneticist Kin Wah Lam, is a woman's face: 15 percent Anglo-Saxon, 17.5 percent Middle Eastern, 17.5 percent African, 7.5 percent Asian, 35 percent South European, and 7.5 percent Hispanic. Writing about their invention of such a face via the computer, *Time*'s editors ignore America's history of miscegenation and colonialism, writing that "The woman on the cover of this special issue of *Time* does not exist— except metaphysically" (2). However, this metaphysical ideal produced material consequences: "As the onlookers watched the image of our new Eve begin to appear on our computer screen, several staff members promptly fell in love. Said one, 'It really breaks my heart that she doesn't exist'" (2). *Time*'s use of a cyber-face in lieu of an actual person with mixed-race features for its cover reveals a desire to control the discourse of multiraciality. That the magazine named its cover girl "the new Eve" suggests that mixed-race bodies are marked by the biblical Fall and its connotations of sin, temptation, and ultimate banishment.

Such a performance on the page underscores the kinds of investments that different communities have in regulating the bodies and voices of multiracial people. Solo performance is a genre that allows an individual to speak without interruption, and audiences usually follow the conventions of performance art that allow the artist to test the limits of cultural acceptability. But who can afford to negotiate their mixed-race identity on stage? How artists are positioned once they address and mark themselves as "mixed" suggests the economic and professional costs of marking one's self outside acceptable racial categories. In comparing Paula Weston Solano's solo performance with Sandra Tsing Loh's, I will argue that because Solano's monologues expose racial, class, and gender differences within the Asian American community, her work potentially threatens monoracial categories and communities. Unlike Loh, who disavows her ethnic heritage by marking her parents as other, Solano tries to resist such binaries by continually shifting the racial, class, and gender positions of both her characters and her audiences. As a result of not appealing to Loh's universal whiteness, Solano has been invited to perform primarily in all-Asian-American festivals, where her body is always juxtaposed against the monoracial solo performer. Such juxtapositions provide a form of control, a way to create a binary that maintains existing categories and communities by marking neither White nor Asian American bodies as alien; instead the mixed-race body serves as the "other."

Nineteen ninety-eight. Halloween night. I have just sat down to watch a lineup of five Asian American solo performers at the annual *Treasure in the House*, an Asian Pacific American Performance and Visual Arts Festival that has been hosted by Highways Performance Space in Santa Monica for the past eight years. The second artist to perform is an actress new to the solo genre and the Asian American theater circuit: Paula Weston Solano.

On stage, Solano wears a red cotton-knit sweater and black pants. Like Sandra Tsing Loh, Solano is tall and slender, with dark hair and light skin. Unlike Loh's array of cultural memorabilia, Solano's only props are a chair and a large screen, which flashes a title that includes the character's name before each monologue. Given that she is part of an all-Asian-American lineup of people such as Ivy Yee, Jill Yip, Alex Luu, and Rodney Kageyama, Solano's name and multiracial body mark her as different. Moreover, unlike the other soloists, Solano has chosen not to perform autobiographical pieces of her family experience that explicitly suggest her part Chinese American, part Russian Jewish heritage. Instead, Solano creates characters that fail to place her in one racial category or ethnic community, even while they emphasize the intersections of race, class, and gender oppression that characterize different positions of power within Asian American populations.

Solano also attempts to position the audience in relationship to the character she is performing. In her first monologue, "Jenny Meets Her Husband's Boss," Solano, as Jenny, looks out at her audience, who assume the role of the boss because she addresses them as such. In this tragicomic situation, Solano as Jenny innocently recalls how her spouse has struggled to keep jobs while she looks after her "10,000 employees" and travels the globe selling chairs. With her accent, Jenny is easy to mark as Chinese. But at the end of this monologue, Solano quickly switches to a character named Kicks, who is more difficult to identify. Kicks is a tough-talking female gang member with a boyfriend named Silence, who tells of having to "duel it out on the dance floor" with another girl for "sole rights to her name." From Jenny's narrative of workplace and commerce, audiences are suddenly transported to Kicks's low-income, multiracial neighborhood along Los Angeles's Glendale Boulevard. The juxtaposition of Jenny and Kicks provides a way for Solano to roam across class and racial lines and to gesture toward her own mixed-race heritage. Because Solano's multiracial body is the site of representation for these different characters, she disturbs dominant stereotypical images of the Asian American female. Solano interrogates the notion of Asian for her mostly Asian American audiences.

By playing different characters, Solano asks the spectator to examine some of the consequences of racial and economic inequality. While Jenny talks about her immigrant husband to his boss, audiences must experience the disparity between Jenny and her husband's economic productivity. As Jenny chatters on about her husband using the money she earns to vacation in faraway places and forget about his wife and son, audiences confront the different positions of men and women of color. In the monologue in which Solano as Jenny visits her son Jeremy in juvenile hall, she addresses the audience as if she were talking to her son. When Jenny inquires why her son has to steal, rationalizes to him why his father is not around, and cheers him up by promising to refurbish all the chairs in juvenile hall, the spectator is challenged to identify with the oppression of Asian American male youth. Interspersed between these two monologues is Kicks's own story about her relationship with Silence, and how he is forcing her to have an abortion because of her addiction to smack, which Silence, a drug dealer, sold to her in the first place. By constantly moving across class lines, Solano encourages audiences to acknowledge and identify with diverse positions of power. By the end of her show, audiences have "played" the role of someone's boss, a young Asian American male named Jeremy, and a young female gang member's confidante. Both through the ways she attempts to character-ize her audience and through her own embodiment of distinct people, Solano emphasizes the fluidity of identities. Racial identity, in Solano's world, becomes a performance dependent on not just culturally coded accents and physical gestures, but on Solano's position of power in relationship to her audience and the other performers. At the same time, because Solano's body is itself an ambiguous racial referent, her work potentially challenges the idea of a monoracial community.

How challenging and radical is Solano's performance, especially in Los Angeles, where interracial dating is quite frequent and people of mixed race are Hollywood commodities? In following Solano's rise in the theater scene in Los Angeles over the past two years, I have noticed that she has almost always been billed with Asian American performers who categorize themselves as strictly Asian American.[4] Even for the world premiere of *Appearances* at the David Henry Hwang Theater, monoracial performers preceded and followed her show, which seems to raise questions not only about her marketability but also the desire to contain her within the Asian American community. When she first started doing solo performances, Solano was only invited to write and stage her own work if she wrote about her Asian American experiences (personal interview). Unlike Loh, whose work has been consumed and appropriated by the larger community of Los Angeles, Solano has been supported and consumed primarily by the Asian American theater community. However, that Solano's works are staged and produced by the Asian American community only if she writes about the Asian American experience suggests the investment that the community has in marking her as Asian American. Perhaps Solano's female characters mirror her own complicated position within the Asian American community: her desire to "duel it out on the dance floor" for sole rights to her name and identity, while understanding that there are voices that she can bring on stage so that they can be heard and acknowledged by different "bosses."

Solano's use of different characters to interrogate and question the borders of what is Asian American makes emphatic the political force of mixed-race artists who are developing performance styles that display a liberating fluidity that refuses easy categorization or communal affiliation. By looking at how Solano has been positioned within the Asian American community, I have been forced to look at my own place and investment in that same grouping. By writing about Solano in relationship to a racial label, I find myself reproducing the same discourses and binaries that lead to simplistic racial categorization. This discussion of a mixed-race performer who is *included* in an Asian American lineup, however, reproduces these discourses with a difference. By including mixed-race performers in scholarly and artistic works about Asian Americans, scholars, curators, and artist-activists participate in the process of producing new cultural ideas about what is considered "Asian American." The continuing presence of mixed-race performers in Asian American theater and festivals depends on these kinds of decisions that question cultural notions of racial affiliation and community.

Few performance opportunities exist for Asian Americans of mixed-race heritage because of cultural ideals about "Asianness." In spite of this, mixed-race performers, who put their bodies and careers on the line by continually finding ways to test the boundaries of rigid racial and gender categories, have begun to show us what is really behind Eve, *Time*'s Cover Girl. "Live" racially mixed Eves, who can materialize into endless combinations of distinct ethnic identities, are such a threat to the status quo that computer technology is one of the ways that the cultural apparatus can mimic and therefore control those bodies that challenge dominant racial formations. Solano's own position within Asian American theater and the performance art world also underscores the need to control bodies that trouble the binary. At the same time, her performance reminds me that people like me exist—and not just metaphysically.

KEEPING UP APPEARANCES

The September 18, 2000, issue of *Newsweek* featured on its cover a "Special Report" entitled "Redefining Race in America." The lead article by Jon Meacham offers a perspective on "the new face of race" and includes captioned pictures of various people of mixed ancestry, including a Trinidadian-Sicilian male, a German Jewish–Korean female, and two children of Polish, African American, and Puerto Rican descent. Supplementing the text with these images, *Newsweek* attempts to move beyond the Black/White binary. The article asserts that "We are now in an Age of Color in which the nuances of brown and yellow and red are as important, if not more so, than the ancient divisions of Black and white" (40). Praising its own "pioneering race coverage," *Newsweek* provides a brief history of its own journalistic accounts of race, as well as a more general historical context. Meacham informs us that, "In 1860, just before Fort Sumter, there were only three Census categories—white, black and 'quadroon.' This year there are 30, from Asian Indian to Other Pacific Islander, and there are 11 subcategories under 'Hispanic ethnicity'" (40).

What is interesting about this particular *Newsweek* piece is the language it uses to describe people of color. Although Meacham admits that "[l]anguage can't keep up with the changing calculus" of racial composition, the prose invokes stereotypical racial descriptions by referring to "the nuances of brown and yellow and red" to draw this conclusion (38). Many of the people that the article itself depicts do not readily seem to fall into these historically reified color categories—nuanced or not. Expanding the discourse by merely adding shades to previous color groups is a weak effort to create a more appropriate language for the complications introduced by changing racial demographics. We do not want to maintain a racial discourse that promotes the status quo, yet we find it difficult to address "race" without some reference to old, very limiting terms of racial categorization. This dilemma generates a backlash. The appeal to a universal "we," as opposed to specific ethnic constituencies, reflects a political discourse that is struggling to replace the ever more complicated realities of race with a more generic universalism. Mixed-race performance, we believe, creates a space for performers and audience members to rethink such facile attempts to apprehend the dissolution of the old racial categories of White, Black, yellow, red, and brown in hopes of creating new dialogues.

More specifically, the performances that we have examined participate in this same political drive. Loh has become "The Multi-Cult Semi-Celeb," as the cover of the April 9, 2000, issue of the *Los Angeles Times Magazine* attests. "She has put a unique stamp on a prime piece of socio-geography" (Glionna, 16), the story states before revealing Loh's own take on the matter: "Oh, no, I'm white, what does this mean, that the tribe I most relate to is the tribe of the middle class?" (17). White, in Loh's words, becomes at once an empty signifier and/or a place-holder for the largest economic group in the country. Her ability to masquerade as either White or ethnic as the need arises (she is, in addition to being a writer and solo performer, also the voice of Mrs. Duong, the Vietnamese neighbor in Disney's animated series *Weekenders)* marks her as a kind of opportunist, what the *Los Angeles Times Magazine* calls a "savvy social chameleon who slips between disparate orbs—hanging out in greasy spoons, then jetting off to be a judge at Sundance" (Glionna, 14).

Paula Weston Solano, on the other hand, remains in relative obscurity. While the different reputations of these two women undoubtedly have a variety of causes, we contend that Loh's broader appeal rests, in part, on her posing mixed race as the condition of American identity. Indeed, Loh's success seems to rest on her marketing of difference as—of all things—sameness. While this particular strategy may not have gained her unlimited access to Hollywood ("Not only can Loh not produce her show, the shot-callers say, but she can't have any acting roles, not even a cameo" [Lacher]), it has enabled her to move from niche market performance spaces like those of the David Henry Hwang Theater and Highways Performance Space to the Tiffany Theater on Los Angeles's Sunset Strip. While Loh "footed the bill to stage a reprise run of 'Aliens' at West Hollywood's Tiffany Theater" (Glionna, 36), she could at least convince the theater owners that they should allot her a slot. That venue also seems to have justified ticket prices of $20+, enough for Loh to benefit significantly from her investment. This admission fee is more than double that charged for a multiple-artist performance (including Solano and others) in another venue. Watching Loh and Solano at different venues that are themselves coded by race and class as a result of their geographic locations, we begin to understand that these artists paid for their visibility within different communities. The ways each artist negotiates her representation through solo performance, in specifically coded venues, impact the kinds of interventions in racial discourse that they can enact within those communities to which they belong.

If Loh's performance serves as any index, ethnic difference sells when it is equated with the general feeling of difference everyone occasionally experiences. But leveling all difference and forgetting the uneven power dynamics accorded by categories of race and ethnicity, gender and class, can leave some very unsettling impressions. The images of Chinese people that Loh's performance offers us provide some striking examples. In fact, Loh's father kept up his appearance quite well—for better or for worse: "At last year's 'Aliens' opening in L.A. . . . [Loh's father] came dressed in a floor-length blue satin Mandarin robe and sat in the front row, snapping pictures and turning heads" (Glionna, 16). On the other hand, Solano's *Appearances* unsettles audiences by reminding us of the unequal race, class, and gender dynamics within different communities. Solano's own position as a performer in the Asian American and theater communities shows how difficult it is to perform a racial identity that complicates the discourse of race and difference. However, perhaps this is what compels Solano and other mixed-race artists to create performances that expose the way communities alienate and incorporate those rendered other based on appearances.

Notes

1. Recent scholarship has attended to the increasing difficulty of using "Asian American" to categorize a very diverse group of travelers, immigrants, and sojourners from Asia and the Pacific islands. See, for example, King-Kok Cheung's *An Interethnic Companion to Asian American Literature* and Sau-Ling Wong's essay "Denationalization Reconsidered." We retain such a label in order to examine and problematize its function in the context of mixed-race, female solo performance.

2. Here we mean to invoke "unmarked whiteness," as Richard Dyer has elaborated the term, as "the natural, inevitable, ordinary way of being human" in *Screen* 29, no. 4 (1983): 44. Ruth Frankenberg has shown the ways in which this construction supports racist structures of thought, and we mean to use the term here in all of its contradiction, that is, as a term that embodies a racial disavowal.

3. This quotation appears on the book jacket of Loh's *Aliens in America*. Neither I nor the current staff of *Time Out New York* has been able to locate the original source of the quotation. My attempt to contact the publicist for Riverhead Books was also to no avail.

4. From 1997 to 1999, Solano appeared with other Asian American solo performers in the Mark Taper Forum's *Wing Festival*, which showcased new works written by Taper's Asian American Theatre Workshop; in Highways Performance Space's *Treasure in the House*, a month-long Asian American performance and visual arts festival; in the Japanese American Cultural Center's *Fresh Tracks* series, a weekend festival of Asian American solo performances; in the Mark Taper Forum's *Word-Up!*, a festival introducing Asian American performers; and in California State University, Los Angeles's *Radiant Colors: Close and Affectionate Encounters*, performances with Solano, Jude Narita, and Denise Uyehara.

Works Cited

Brantley, Ben. "Theater Review: Ever Wincing at Her Roots Yet Unwilling to Let Go." *New York Times*, July 20, 1996, late ed. Final, 11.

Cheung, King-Kok, ed. *An Interethnic Companion to Asian American Literature.* New York: Cambridge University Press, 1997.

Dyer, Richard. "White." *Screen* 29, no. 4 (1983): 44.

Frankenberg, Ruth. "Introduction: Local Whitenesses, Localizing Whiteness." In *Displacing Whiteness: Essays in Social and Cultural Criticism*, ed. Ruth Frankenberg, pp. 1–33. Durham, N.C.: Duke University Press, 1997.

Glionna, John M. "The Multi-Cult Semi-Celeb." *Los Angeles Times Magazine*, April 9, 2000, pp. 14–17, 35–36.

Houston, Velina, ed. *But Still, Like Air, I'll Rise: New Asian American Plays.* Philadelphia: Temple University Press, 1997.

Hughes, Holly, and David Roman. *O Solo Homo: The New Queer Performance.* New York: Grove Press, 1998.

Lacher, Irene. "In Search of the Real Valley: In Sandra Tsing Loh's Neighborhood, Hot Dog Stands and Swimming Pools Rule." *Los Angeles Times*, May 23, 1996.

Lee, Josephine. *Performing Asian America: Race and Ethnicity on the Contemporary Stage*. Philadelphia: Temple University Press, 1997.

Loh, Sandra Tsing. *Aliens in America*. New York: Riverhead Books, 1997.

———. *Aliens in America*. Program. Tiffany Theater, Hollywood, California. August 21, 1999.

Lowe, Lisa. *Immigrant Acts: On Asian American Cultural Politics*. Durham, N.C.: Duke University Press, 1996.

Meacham, Jon. "The New Face of Race." *Newsweek*, September 18, 2000, pp. 38–41.

Miller, Daryl H. "Aliens in America Captures the Spirit of Solo/LA." *Daily News of Los Angeles*, April 20, 1995.

Morrison, Toni. *Playing in the Dark: Whiteness and the American Literary Imagination*. New York: Vintage Books, 1993.

Nunez, Sigrid. *A Feather on the Breath of God*. New York: HarperPerennial, 1996.

Peterson, Michael. *Straight White Male: Performance Art Monologues*. Jackson: University of Mississippi Press, 1997.

Solano, Paula Weston. Personal interview. July 27, 1999.

Time. "Special Issue. The New Face of America: How Immigrants Are Shaping the World's First Multicultural Society." Fall 1993.

Wong, Sau-ling Cynthia. "Denationalization Reconsidered: Asian American Cultural Criticism at a Theoretical Crossroads." *Amerasia Journal* 21, nos. 1–2: 1–27.

10. AGAINST ERASURE

The Multiracial Voice in Cherríe Moraga's Loving in the War Years

Carole DeSouza

Though it has been said a thousand times, it is because I felt alone that I became a writer. And a common motivation of all fledgling writers, I suppose, is to be published in order to make that necessary connection with the reader. One desires to move through the text as a mode of expression and, ultimately, a means of existence.

Then the day came when I realized that I was just another writer with plenty to proclaim and—in typically tragic fledgling form—no voice of my own to say it. The "know thyself" prescription of writing workshops soon failed when I realized that my problems in writing were problems with being. Compared to those I came across in my travels, I did not "know myself" in the ways that they knew themselves; I did not write with the confidence of those writers who have an audience that receives their personal account with universal acceptance. Why was it that I could not pin down on paper an authorial self that felt whole or fully accessible? Why did I feel, as Adrienne Rich has described, "split at the root" (Rich, 36)?

And though it had been posed a thousand times, the "What are you?" question finally sparked my realization that it is my racial identity that had blocked my development as a writer. As a multiracial, I had failed to formulate on paper what I could not answer in social reality: "What am I?"

The answer to the "What are you?" question, experientially, was "alone." In the American South of my childhood, one was either Black or White, and there were never any gray areas—which precluded being both Black *and* White. The Black-White "mixed" kids we knew fought to the teeth every day on the ride to school to prove that they were *only* Black. If it had not been for the dozens of "army brats" of my generation, whose fathers, like mine, settled in the civilian outskirts of Fort Jackson, South Carolina—a family here and there that provoked as many stares as did mine, in restaurants and movie theaters and parks—then I would have thought for sure that my existence was freakish by nature, and for this reason never reflected in the media or in public except for the occasional "mutt" and "half-breed" references hurled here and there.

I invested much energy into researching multiraciality, only to find that multiracial experience means marginalization. My experiences as a multiracial have resulted from a pervasive American sociopolitical agenda against racial convergence of any kind. Discussing this phenomenon with anyone who claims a singular racial identity—which is almost everyone I know, including those whose parents are different races—has proved highly emotional and, for the multiracials whom I approach, personally compromising even to address.

To articulate mixed-race or multiracial existence is to open dialogue where it has traditionally been silenced or diverted (Spaulding, 100). Too much of our everyday lives in America is invested in racial difference to accept the overlapping inherent in multiracial existence. The denial of the right to racially self-describe, or to act as a member of multiple races at once, is indicative of institutionalized monoraciality as the naturalized norm; to assert "multiraciality" or suggest it through an interracial sexual relationship has been traditionally perceived as deviant, isolationist, and antisocial behavior. Its scientific founding largely refuted, "race" nonetheless retains its institutionalized force, as well as functioning as a primary agent of socialization via compulsory monoraciality. Though American Whites and non-Whites may disagree as to the extent to which they are "raced" as social beings, many would agree that to not claim a single racial identity, or to act without recognized racial identity, is to suffer from an identity crisis (Ferber, 164).

In the first section of this essay, I discuss how the American racial classification system denies legitimacy to individuals whose racial ambiguity threatens to overthrow it. The ultimate "absorption" of multiracials into monoracial communities, coupled with the historical erasure of the multiracial, is symptomatic of the greater refusal within the United States to recognize multiraciality, an expense paid for the preservation of our current racial paradigms. In sum, the historical manipulations of "race" have divided the American population and isolated those who refuse to take a monoracially drawn side.

The second section of this essay examines American literature as an example of dominant discourse that reflects sociopolitical investments in "race." Here I focus on the literary "tragic mulatto/a" character: the supposedly continual "war between the races" is traditionally personified by a naturally flawed, because "mixed," character. Further evidence that the representation of multiracial identity has not been forged by multiracial people, multiraciality has either been visibly suppressed or pathologized into negatively imagined representations. Historical erasure and negative media portrayal together posit the problematic existence of the multiracial within the American social arena.

Considering the suppression of multiracial identification both privately and publicly, within almost every community across the country, surely I am not "alone." As American "raced" beings we have been collectively ordered according to monoracial socialization. And yet— against silence and misrepresentation—what does the multiracial voice sound like? My task as a multiracial author is to decide: *If not "alone," then what does it mean to be "multiracial"?*

Cherríe Moraga's response is an expression of self through the literary mapping of her multiracial consciousness, a multifaceted consciousness, complex and seemingly contradictory as a site of converging racial and cultural meanings. Moraga's dialogue broadens our understanding of "race" and offers possibilities for how we may apply a new conceptualization to the human body. The autobiographical collection, *Loving in the War Years*, is, I believe, a successful expression of multiracial existence.

In *Loving in the War Years*, Moraga speaks from a racial "no man's land" where she herself is at stake. The subtitle, "Lo que nunca pasó por sus labios," or "That which has never passed though their lips," signals— because of its challenge to English language supremacy—that Moraga means to confront, through bilingualism, the traditional dominance of monoracial representational practices. And though the White reader may not or will never identify as a "raced subject," against Moraga's polyvocal personal account he/she is provoked to identify as a "monoracialized subject." The voice rendered in the Spanish subtitle represents the voice of the collective; it is not a lone multiracial/racial Other who speaks.

Moraga articulates a challenge to compulsory monoraciality through *la conciencia de la mestiza*, what Gloria Anzaldúa calls a "new multiracial consciousness" (377). It is in the schoolyard where Moraga learns that— unlike the harmonious heterogeneity of her home life—greater society requires the assumption of a monoracial identity. The pale skin that marks her as "la güera" has enabled Moraga to "pass" as White; yet it is the articulation of her multiracial inheritance *(la conciencia)* that she must continually reinscribe upon her body so that others may read it as an expression of multiraciality. Moraga introduces herself, and the challenge she faces as a multiracial:

I am the daughter of a Chicana and an anglo. I think most days I am an embarrassment to both groups. I sometimes hate the white in me so viciously that I long to forget the commitment my skin has imposed upon my life. To speak two tongues . . . I must. But I will not double-talk and I refuse to let *anybody's* movement determine for me what is safe and fair to say. (vi)

In autobiographical form, Moraga addresses specific incidents from her past that present a series of "choices" she is coerced to make in a society that frames identity as an exclusionary mode of being. In critique of the Whitewashing socialization of her childhood, *Loving in the War Years* charts Moraga's "coming-out" as a multiracial. The Spanish word for the ethnically/culturally "mixed" individual, "*mestiza*" acts as a metaphor for the multiracial person. In the Introducción, Moraga writes:

I have been translating my experience out of fear of aloneness too great to bear. I have learned analysis as a mode to communicate what I feel the experience itself already speaks for. The combining of poetry and essays in this book is the compromise I make in the effort to be understood. In Spanish, "compromiso" means obligation or commitment. And I guess, in fact, I write as I do because I am committed to communicating with both sides of myself. (vi)

For years denied the free exercise of multilingualism, Moraga's present articulation of mestiza consciousness marks the unification of her multiple racial identities, the coming together of an expression, word by word, that represents her true multiracial self. *La conciencia* formulates racial hybridity as the alternative to a monoracial identity. That is, the new shaping of "race" recognizes racial diversity within the individual.

I devote section three of this essay to Moraga's multiracial expression via her hybridized language use, language innovation, and unconventional poetic imagery. The mestiza author reimagines the tragic mulatto/a in a poetic rebirth of the multiracial. She assumes authority over the tropes that traditionally define "race" as a measure of "racial purity," thus transforming the literary multiracial from an eternally damaged and damned half-being to the harmonic balance of multiple racial identities. By reshaping the human body on paper, and extending the fluidity of that image via *la conciencia* into the reader's mind, Moraga successfully translates the body as the site of multiple racial and cultural meanings.

The multiracial is prevented from entering dominant discourse, as current racial paradigms interpret "race" to signify an essentialist and exclusionary mode of being. The definition of "race," then, must be challenged and changed, because multiracials do indeed exist, while the American multiracial population (despite the denial of its political legitimacy) is increasing dramatically by the decade. Through dialogue, racial hybridity must be extended into the understanding of those who believe they are racially pure, for only when the monoracially identified broaden their binary vision can we collectively reinterpret the human body as capable of exhibiting multiple racial identities at one time.

A BRIEF HISTORY OF THE AMERICAN MULTIRACIAL

The history of American state and federal legislation supporting the rule of *hypodescent*, or the "one-drop rule," testifies to how "race" has been deliberately manipulated and qualified by specific sets of signifiers to codify society while stratifying it. Categories, based on difference, that maintain a power structure are naturalized by dominant discourse in order to preserve that structure. As race theorist Naomi Zack points out, it would mean "little, if anything, in biological terms to say that I am 'one-quarter black'" (quoted in Root, xvi). At the same time, however, governmental promotion of "blood quantum," the idea that blood inheritance is the vehicle for racial identity, was used in the eighteenth and nineteenth centuries to forge the social signifiers "quadroon" and "octoroon" and thereby help enforce racial stratification (Root, xvi).

The scientific basis of race has been refuted in the biological sciences in part by the widespread emergence and confirmation of the idea that real difference is greater *within* racial groups than *between* them. Though "race" has largely lost its claim to a scientific foundation, the superstructure established on its naturalization has inflated its role in the construction and destruction of community. The institutionalization of Jim Crowist "separate but equal" discourse, and the failure of legal challenges to the racial absolutism exemplified in such cases as *Plessy v. Ferguson* (at the heart of which was the defense of multiracial existence), promoted the conditioning of anyone with an African ancestor to—rather than cast off Black identity—organize on the basis of shared oppression (Nakashima, 174). Despite the efforts of the civil rights movement to equalize the privilege denoted by racial hierarchies, marginalization for multiracial individuals still prevails. "Diversity," a euphemism for "racial difference," has ripened into a call to celebrate monoracial identity (Zack, ix). As multiracial scholar Linda Alcoff summarily states, "No proponent of the melting pot ideology ever promoted miscegenation" (263).

Thus the United States segregates its population along racial lines, drawing the markers of "difference" into distinct, obdurate borders. While African Americans are born into "blackness," cultural populations that have recently entered the country offer a direct challenge to the binary classification system. Those called "Mexicans" are actually a mélange of Spanish, Indian/indigenous, and Black African cultures and peoples. In Latin America, these racial hybrids are called mestizos, translating to a literal mix, who celebrate *El Dia de la Raza* (the Day of the [New Mixed] Race) in commemoration of their colonial-era birth as the hybridized mestizo peoples (Anzaldúa, 377).[1] The birth of the mestizos resulted from the Spanish-Indian alliance that solidified mutually agreeable social and political conditions via intermarriage between Spanish soldiery and noble Indian women. Products of these marriages inherited the social esteem of their forefathers and were recognized as "Spanish" or "Creole" rather than judged as a separate class or race. They were recorded as a new generation whose existence was considered continuous from their forebears, both paternal and maternal. The "hybrid degeneracy theory" was not put into effect in that these mestizos were not considered naturally inferior to either parental group because of their racial hybridity (Goldberg, 245).[2]

Mexican nationals transport their mestizo/a sensibility, which includes the valuing of Indian ancestry and tradition, in their emigration to the United States, only to encounter American discomfort with both multiracial and Native American existence. The North American "one-drop rule" runs counter to a mestizo consciousness, especially since mestizo identity is already established as historically multicultural before it is monoracially socialized in the United States. And though Black Americans are read visually along a rainbow of possible racial traits while still included and identified as "Black," Latin Americans are resistant to such "racial amnesia" and cognizant of their individual mixture of parental races.[3] That some Americans have been content with reading mestizos/as as "Mexicans" ignores the question of racial ambiguity. However, considering that the United States Census Bureau recently released data reporting that in the next five to ten years "Hispanics" will supersede Black Americans as the largest non-White racial group in the country (currently, Hispanics represent 9.0 percent and Blacks 12.3 percent of the population), and that Mexican mestizos/as currently constitute the majority of those "Hispanics," the United States must deal with an increasing number of citizens whose interracial mixture upsets the rigid Black/White dichotomy.

Because ambiguity disrupts current racial stratification, the United

States tends to "racialize the body count" by attempting to group, however superficially, all Latin Americans as a single racial population. Multiracial researcher David Theo Goldberg claims that the United States government's shifting label for Latin Americans in the Census that, until 2000, prescribed "check one box only" monoraciality indicates greater political and social resistance to granting multiracial identity. Goldberg notes that "Hispanic" as a category has been

> manufactured as "black" was from its inception. Although "black" was created initially in the name of the project of racial purity, "Hispanic" was crafted to cut across racial designations, to reflect [admixture]. In its generality, however, "Hispanic" has served and serves silently to reify a new racial category, to extend the project of purity, even as it is a product of mixture. (245)

Currently most Americans are ignorant of the cultural and racial mix of Mexicans mainly because the United States, as Goldberg explains, attempts to resolve the visually and racially ambiguous with an equally ambiguous racial name. The designation "Hispanic" does not fully represent the heterogeneous racial background of Mexicans. Until 1980, persons of Latin American origin were included in the United States Census as "Whites"; subsequently they were grouped together, despite a continent's worth of disparate ethnicities, ancestral records, colonial histories, and nationalities, as persons "of Hispanic origin." The term "Hispanic," signifying a postcolonial Spanish-speaking population, was no improvement, considering its illogical application to Brazil and multiple other South American countries whose previous colonial rulers were Portugal, England, France, or Holland. Further, its application to postcolonial Spanish-speaking South Americans disregards the indigenous heritage; "Hispanic" monoracializes semantically as well.[4]

Our dialogue here is crucial because multiracial people exist throughout American society, among all racial communities, only to live out their lives enshrouded by silence. The silence of the stigma lies in the capacity of the body as an exclusive site for reading sociopolitical loyalties to permit *only one racial identity per person.* The privileged signifier "race," and the benefits claimed by a monolithic racial identity, restrain many people from "coming out" in assertion of a multiracial identity. Consider Maria P. P. Root's conservative estimate that currently 30–70 percent of the Black community has some White ancestry, while F. James Davis surmises that this is true of from 75 percent to more than 90 percent. Davis claims that the "Black" community is overwhelmingly composed of individuals who sacrifice personal freedom of racial/cultural expression for the increased cohesion and attractiveness of one group identity (124). In addition, Omi and Winant have found in their studies that

> we utilize race to provide clues about *who* a person is. This fact is made painfully obvious when we encounter someone whom we cannot conveniently racially categorize. . . . Such an encounter becomes a source of discomfort and momentarily a crisis of racial meaning. (Quoted in Ferber, 164)

In effect, without a racial identity, one is in danger of having no identity at all. Ambiguity may "momentarily" cause discomfort for the onlooker, but multiracials are burdened for as long as racial meaning remains indeterminable, an identity crisis that may run the length of their lives.

Contemporary discourse that normalizes monoracial identification was founded upon the "hybrid degeneracy theory," which emerged around the end of the Civil War and continued as a fact of science until the mid-1930s. The theory holds that the multiracial child is genetically inferior to both (and all) of his or her parental races, the consequent logic inciting a fear of intermarriage as the surest form of cultural genocide. The multiracial offspring was dubbed "mulatto" and, like the mule, was marked as a reproductive dead end; underscoring the postulation was the dominant cultural view that such a union was both bestial and yet unnatural (Spickard, 19–20). The lengthy history of the "racial degenerate" has been written by those invested in the rigidity of racial classifications, from French psychologist Gustave Lebon, who in 1912 claimed that "mixed breeds are ungovernable" (quoted in Spickard, 20), to American sociologist Edward Reuter, who in 1939 insisted that "the mixed blood is [by definition] an unadjusted person" (quoted in Spickard, 20). Linda Alcoff theorizes that

> a self that is internally heterogeneous beyond repair or resolution becomes a candidate for pathology in a society where the integration of self is taken to be necessary for mental health. (261)

Because "race" registers as a measure of purity, being "mixed" problematizes "being." What has been considered a pathology of the body— multiracial inheritance—is read as psychologically and mentally pathological. As a multiracial herself who recalls victimization as a "half-breed," Alcoff speaks out against the implications of wholeness reserved for the monoracial:

We need to reflect upon this premium put on internal coherence and racial purity and how this is manifested in Western concepts and practices of identity as a public persona as well as subjectivity as a foundational understanding of the self. (261)

Those who may suffer estrangement the most in America under the dividing forces of "race" are perhaps those who, because pathologized, are refused the right to be heard.

Ultimately, for the individual to assert an American social identity requires the assumption of an exclusive racial identity in a confirmation of the myth of monoraciality. Each of us must "pass" in this exercise, since the phenomenon of "passing," generally the process by which members of "racial minority" communities are able to visibly and socially "pass" as White in America, at bottom means to pass as a member of a single race and not any other(s).[5] Whites, then, are subject to Whitewashing just as the boundaries are manufactured for Other monolithic identities. As Alcoff asserts,

> Discourses and institutions implicitly invoke selves that have specific racial identities, which are correlated to those selves' specific legal status, discursive authority, epistemic credibility, and social standing. (261)

"White" is de-Europeanized, "Black" is one-drop-ruled. Just as "Hispanic" results from monoracialist discourse, other races are homogenized while distinguished from each other. The individual passes as the American (mono)raced being. Ironically, and despite its inclusivity, "multiracial" experientially means "alone."

THE MULTIRACIAL IN AMERICAN LITERATURE

Compulsory monoraciality and the social resistance to and condemnation of multiraciality are manifested within American literature as a matter of tradition. In an extension of the "one-drop rule" to the realm of literary representation, multiracial authors, as well as multiracial main characters, are organized under Other monoracial categories. Despite their assertions of a multiracial voice, authors Langston Hughes and Nella Larsen, among a multitude of multiracials, "belong" to African American literature, just as they "belong" to the Black community. The "mulatto/a" character is bound within the category of African American literature, the "Eurasian" confined to Asian American, and the "half-blood" (half-evolved from "half-breed") to Native American literature. Further, there is no comparable record of a "Hispanic" or mestizo/a literary model. Despite their pejorative connotations, the terms "mulatto/a," "Eurasian," and "half-blood" are employed within literary criticisms synonymously with "multiracial" to a degree to which most (monoracially identifying) critics are insensitive.

As Carol Roh Spaulding explains, "racial and ethnic formations have had and continue to have great authority in the reading of race" within various discourses, particularly in how we read individual character (100). Rendered most often by the hands of dominant culture, the tragic mulatto/a character type that permeates American literature

> could be identified with and pitied as the victim of the miscegenation taboo while at the same time be feared as the despised Other lurking within who had to be punished, either for trying to sneak into the white world as an imposter or for reminding the black world of the mark of the oppressor. (Giles, 64)[6]

As prescribed by the "hybrid degeneracy theory," the tragic mulatto/a character reflects the pathology of the real life multiracial. Because of its specificity to American history, this recurring tragic mulatto/a portrayal illustrates an American preoccupation with measuring "race" and the relentless fixation on "blood quantum," the idea that race runs within one's blood. Toni Morrison has written that the Euro-American literary imagining of blood is "a pervasive fetish":

> . . . black blood, white blood, the purity of blood; the purity of white female sexuality, the pollution of African blood and sex. Fetishization is a strategy often used to assert the categorical absolutism of civilization and savagery. (68)

Blood inheritance determines the traditionally tragic fate of the literary character in dramatic illustration of the limitations that American multiracials and Blacks face as real "raced" beings. Blood as pure or polluted has been engineered by traditional authors to reflect real social division, while working as propaganda for keeping the races apart. The reader (him/herself "raced" in social reality) witnesses through the life experiences of the tragic mulatto/a how a lone "drop" of Other blood redirects an otherwise perfectly "normal" (read White) life. The seemingly innocuous, pseudoscientific statement "I am one-quarter Black" comes at a high social and psychological price after all.

Freda Scott Giles applies Morrison's notion of the fetishization of blood as a metaphor for race in her claim that the "flaw" of the tragic mulatto/a lies in the perceived immiscibility of blood: "The consciousness remains ever divided, because the blood is always at war" (65). While bloodlines polarize the human population, the force of mixed blood *within* the individual is catastrophically divisive. The mulatto/a, who is damaged through no fault of his/her own, must suffer a disastrous demise much like the destruction of a "bad egg" in miscarriage—an event to be mourned, and yet considered natural to the human life cycle.

Films like *An Imitation of Life*, as well as countless works of literature, like Nella Larsen's "Passing" or Mark Twain's *Pudd'nhead Wilson*, showcase the tragic mulatto/a's frayed sense of self. His/her fragmentation is a metaphor for greater world division, rendering the character's efforts to assimilate via assertion of a monoracial (White) identity futile at best, and ultimately damning. Giles holds that the tragic mulatto/a is usually depicted as female to amplify her vulnerability and sexual powerlessness. Misogyny conflates the mulatta's body as a site of natural weakness and inferiority with the juxtaposed standard of White male, while the interracial sex act is cast within literature as the rape of the Black slave woman by the White master (Giles, 64). The "family," then, represents no positive resort for the tragic mulatto/a, but is (like other symbols of unity) consistently denied. The atomic building blocks of society—blood and the family—are toxic and absent as applied to the life of the multiracial character in literature. The tragic mulatto/a character exemplifies just how effectively literature reflects American sociopolitical investments in race. These representations in turn manipulate multiracials against embracing such a denigrated designation in social reality.

How does the multiracial person resist a marginalization that is considered inherent in multiraciality? How does he/she resist absorption, denying the proposed benefits incurred in the assertion of a monoracial identity? Why does the potential harmony of the mixing of races continue to be overshadowed by tragedy? Are multiracials not products of human (racial) convergence?

Solutions to these inquiries first require a foundational discourse that would render such a positive multiracial representation possible; for the multiracial is written about in a language that denies it real meaning or conceptual existence. Philosopher Naomi Zack, editor of *American Mixed Race: The Culture of Microdiversity*, contends that "the life of the mind" and its extension, the invention of authorship, are at this time the only sites of resistance and counterproduction to the existent (monoracialized) discourse (297). Zack states that

> To write about one's mixed-race identity is as much to invent oneself
> or one's racial group, as to describe them. One invents oneself, on pa-
> per, as part of a theoretical inquiry, because outside of one's activities
> as an intellectual, that is, outside of the life of the mind, one has no se-
> cure racial existence. Mixed race is not recognized as an identity or
> form of culture by those individuals—the majority—who believe that
> they are racially pure. And, predictably, the self-invention of mixed-
> race identity is precarious. (298)

Here Zack confirms the fortitude required of the multiracial author to
break the silence and establish a multiracial identity. Despite the "precarious" nature of self-invention, surely multiracials can find ways to represent their experiences for the developing comprehension of "the monoracial majority." To form the bridge to human understanding, the reason
that most writers seek to write, is the aim of the multiracial author. It is
the same goal that Zack exhibits in her own dialogue: to create for the
reader a new awareness that he/she may extend to others. This new
awareness or consciousness—indicative of the conceptual shifting of
"race" in the mind—then shifts how we collectively read race.

CHERRÍE MORAGA'S ASSERTION OF RACIAL HYBRIDITY

Cherríe Moraga employs the space of writing as the platform for ideological change. In *Loving in the War Years*, she shapes her suffering into a
voice that provokes the reader to identify as the "monoracialized subject"
and recognize compulsory monoraciality as the basis for racial division
and subjugation. Writing is the means by which the multiracial author,
like any other, may acquire a sense of safety, community, and freedom to
fully express what she feels internally. It is the integrity of the personal essay that grants the humanity of the multiracial author and displaces the
pathologized tragic mulatto persona, so that the multiracial identity may
solidify in social reality. Finally, through her writing, Moraga as multiracial author may articulate the unsaid and there establish the racially/
culturally multiplicit being that is consistent with her life experiences.

   In the Introducción of *Loving in the War Years*, Moraga voices fear for
the integrity of her hybridized textual existence, yet envisions writing as
the proper vehicle for social change. As Naomi Zack has anticipated, the
mestiza's authorship is problematic because her multiracial existence is
"precarious." In this way, Moraga's anxiety surfaces: if the multiracial author "truly follows her own voice, she may depict a world so specific, so

privately ours, so full of 'foreign' language to the anglo reader, there will be no publisher" (vi). Her concern characterizes the dilemma of the multiracial, as well as the writer, who strives to face down the fear that no "readership" signals true alienation from the rest of the world. Moraga first suggests here that perhaps her articulation will introduce new tropes or historical allusions too specific to the cultural/racial crossings of mestizo/a existence. She fears that academia will reject or resist her writing before it may reshape academic discursive conceptualizations of "race." At the same time, the author worries that other multiracials and mestizos/as will lack access to her multiracial expression because, historically, discourse has shut them out as an audience (vi).

Moraga confirms, however, that writing is the place where anything— especially multiracial expression—is possible. As recorded in the short story "A Long Line of Vendidas," a friend on a train reminds Moraga that writing speaks to the human connection, to the ultimate experience, thereby nullifying perceived manifestations of "difference" (vi). Considering that monoracial identity is drawn along lines of presumed "racial difference," the author reflects that the rigidity of racial classification has been enforced upon everyone who claims an American identity; and it is a fabricated monoracial identity that we have in common. Rather than eliciting no publisher or audience, Moraga discovers an expansive reception *because* of her unflinching approach to the topic of compulsory monoraciality. Both the academic and marginalized reader may unite in a new reading of "race" as she writes it. In sum, the details of Moraga's autobiographical accounts enable *Loving in the War Years* to strike so personally that the reader must reflect upon his/her own racial identity, as well as the process through which that identity has been produced.

The human connection between the reader and the multiracial author in *Loving in the War Years* is the shared experience of (mono)racial identity formation. This connection is crucial because it initiates the reader's reconceptualization of "race." In *Chicano Poetics*, Alfred Arteaga writes,

> Moraga names herself as the subject agent, [mestiza] writer. She rejects silent acquiescence and nameless identity. She articulates, therefore she is; she speaks differently, therefore things are different. (43)

Moraga introduces "race" as a categorical cell we are born into—not by approaching the topic as an objective outsider to American racial identity, but rather as a protesting product of American social identity formation. Born of a Mexican mother and Euro-American father, Moraga recounts personally damaging experiences resulting from the monoracialization efforts of a Southern California school system, in the years before that state's educational institutions began to sponsor multilingualism or promote multiculturalism.

Pushed toward White identification at school because of her pale skin and her intelligence, Moraga as an early writer was versed within (and only within) dominant discursive modes of thinking and interpreting. This voice was not her own, for her academic authorship ran as an extension of the Whitewashed identity she assumed as a child. Moraga concedes that her first writings set her off from her less educated, less "White" family:

> I know with my family that even as my writing functioned to separate me from them . . . it has freed me to love them from places in myself that had before been mired in unexpressed pain. Writing has ultimately brought me back to them. They don't need this book. They have me. (v)

Moraga began life as a mestiza whose existence—once rooted in the haven of interracial family life—yielded to hegemonic Whiteness in order to succeed outside of the home, specifically within academia. Dominant discursive existence "functioned to separate" the mestiza author from a literary expression of multiracial consciousness (v). However, it is the scrutiny of self required by writing that has brought the true Moraga to life; that is, Moraga has "come out" as a multiracial via writing her existence as one.

Its author "freed" from "unexpressed pain," *Loving in the War Years* represents Moraga's act of self-expression as the multiracial's modus operandi (v). She moves through the text, existing, as Naomi Zack claims, as a presence where dominant discourse has failed. In the poem "It's the Poverty," Moraga literally portrays writing as a vehicle for self-determined meaning through the image of a typewriter ribbon.

> Understand.
> My family is poor.
> Poor. I can't afford a new ribbon. The risk
> of this one
> is enough
> to keep me moving
> through it, accountable. (63)

The "risk" of the ribbon, the very one that has forged the written word we read, translates to the high cultural cost of conforming to the standards and expectations of the academic/anglo writing space. Moraga calls on the reader, presumably the "monoracial subject," to understand the urgent need for her authorship, for her writing produces meaning against erasure. The simple image of Moraga's overused typewriter ribbon displays the tired overuse and insufficiency of the literary and linguistic tools of anglo-academia. The title "It's the Poverty" signals, first, financial worry, and, more significantly, Moraga opens an address of the unsaid without yet determining it. The multiracial author calls to attention the lack of language, despite the lack.

The "lack" results from the withheld: the right and writing space to signify the multiplicity inherent in language mixture. Norma Alarcón asserts that the silence and silencing of multiracials, here the mestiza, "begins with the dominating enforcement of linguistic conventions, the resistance to relational dialogues, as well as the disenablement of people by outlawing their forms of speech" (362). Historically, the authoring of American history and discourse

> valorizes English and suppresses expression both in and about Spanish. English is elevated from the status of one language among languages, albeit the dominant one, to that of sole and pervasive language in general. This is coupled with the simultaneous erasure of Spanish through the restriction of its use and the interdiction of dialogue. (Arteaga, 72)

Moraga claims that she would have spoken Spanish with her darker-skinned mestiza friends at school, "if [those in charge] had let me," concluding that Spanish was promoted as a lesser language in order to segregate "*a difernt claz o' people*" (20). While the mestiza speaks Spanish as a legacy of colonial rule, Moraga makes clear that the European language is perceived as a mark of Otherness within the de-Europeanized, Euro-American sociopolitical context; consequently, Spanish signifies racial difference in the United States. "Hispanic" Spanish evokes stereotyped imaginings of brown skin, lower-class status, and eternal colonization. It is systematically and tacitly suppressed first on the playground and later in academic or "American" writing. The denial of the hybridized language of her home is a first step toward Moraga's monoracial identification as White.

To challenge the naturalization of English as the lone linguistic option, Moraga demonstrates how American society stagnates when monolingualism prevents the familial transmission of cultural and historical knowledge. In "It's the Poverty," after being confronted by a White friend/fellow writer's hegemonic prejudice, Moraga deliberately does not use Spanish, while pointing to its absence:

> Yes, we both agree. I could use
> a new ribbon. But it's the poverty
> the poverty of my imagination, we agree.
> *I lack imagination* you say.
>
> *No.* I lack language. (62)

Drawing solely upon a bank of American English, Moraga is limited not only in language but in the ability to speak from her multiracial inheritance. This poverty permeates American literature; for if the author lacks, so does the reader. The complexity of the author's condition surfaces as she presents her defense, which is, ultimately, a defense of racial hybridity.

> The language to clarify
> my resistance to the literate.
>
> Words are a war to me.
> They threaten my family.
>
> To gain the word to describe the loss,
> I risk losing everything.
> I may create a monster,
> the word's length and body
> swelling up colorful and thrilling
> looming over my *mother*, characterized.
> Her voice in the distance
> *unintelligible illiterate.*
>
> These are the monster's words. (63)

If dominant discourse acts as a major agent of dominant ideology, Moraga could easily become "the monster" that severs the cord to her mestiza culture simply by becoming a member of this agency. The author uses "unintelligible" and "illiterate" as proper English words in reference to those who fail to enter discourse for lack of language; Moraga portrays her mother as literally shut up and out. Gaining further ground in the English of academia ("to gain the word") increases the "distance" from her mother, her mother tongue, her *mestizaje*. That "It's the Poverty" is one of the few poems of *Loving in the War Years* written entirely in English illuminates a telling absence: her mother, who, drowned out by the expanding influence of the dominant language over her daughter, cannot be heard. With the interracial and multilingual family at "risk," Moraga illustrates that language contextualizes the home. The "loss," though Moraga does not name it, is then uttered.

Loving in the War Years records Moraga's progression from monoracial child to writer to multiracial author; naturally, the book's ending works symbolically and linguistically as the return to the home. Moraga, after illustrating the lack, addresses Spanish as the missing link: "I must return to the fact that not only has the mother been taken from me, but her tongue, her mothertongue. I want the language, feel my tongue rise to the occasion of feeling at home, in common" (141). The authorial voice grows double-tongued in recognition, transforming into the multiracial voice before the reader's eyes:

> On the surface of things I am not supposed to feel that my language has been stripped from me—I am "born American." College English educated, but what I must admit is that I have felt in my writing that the English was not cutting it. ¿Entiendes? That there is something else, deep and behind my heart and I want to hold it hot and bold in the hands of my writing and it will not come out sounding like English. Te prometo. No es inglés. (141)

Ultimately, Moraga socially "comes out" as a multiracial by overcoming her writer's block, which is symbolized by the "lack." The Spanish "promiso" seals the deal: once one realizes the cage of racial exclusivity, one cannot return behind the socially sponsored boundaries of monoracial existence/language because the transformation has already begun. Moraga requires the employment of multiple languages to fully articulate and render a more complete expression of her multiplicit being; likewise, when she is able to articulate herself, she finds her place, her home, as a mestiza.

Moraga rejects the Whitewashed identity of her youth and replaces it with a multiracial identification accessible to all. Refusing to assume a single racial/cultural expression, she articulates what Anzaldúa has dubbed "the new *mestiza* consciousness," or *la conciencia de la mestiza:*

> The new *mestiza* copes by developing a tolerance for contradictions, a tolerance for ambiguity. She learns to be an Indian in Mexican culture, to be Mexican from an Anglo point of view. She learns to juggle cultures. She has a plural personality, she operates in a pluralistic mode—

nothing is thrust out, the good, the bad and the ugly, nothing rejected, nothing abandoned. (379)

Moraga's writing via this "pluralistic mode" assembles wholeness and presence traditionally denied the historically pathologized "mixed-blood." The new mestiza usurps the role of the tragic mulatta, acting as the positively rendered multiracial role model. Her "tolerance" for ambiguity extends to the reader/onlooker, who must, in order to cope with the new refusal to be monoracially categorized, broaden the binary expectations that surround racial classification both visually and ideologically. The pluralistic consciousness is transmitted through the word from the life of the multiracial mind to the mind of the reader; there it may transform how he/she reads the human body as "raced." Moraga presents the body as the place of racial hybridity, where the newly adjusted eye may observe the convergence of multiple racial identities that are simultaneously and mutually expressed. Moraga implements *la conciencia de la mestiza* through literature and language innovation, thereby designing a new multiracial body on paper.

Language as a denied vehicle becomes the body missing in action. Currently, the body sustains a special relationship with the multiracial self, because to be perceived physically as multiracial is to participate as a member of society marked by a handicap status—or else to be misrecognized as monoracial, wherein the truth is invisible. In the poem "You Call It, *Amputation*," Moraga describes the mestiza subject as debilitated physically in metaphoric illustration of a linguistic disenablement:

You call it
am pu tation

but even after the cut
they say the toes still itch
the body remembers the knee . . .

it is a shock, Woolf says
that by putting into words
we make it whole

still, I feel the mutilated body
swimming in side stroke
pumping twice as hard
for the lack
of body, pushing

through your words
which hold no water
for me. (82)

The absence of the language the mestiza first abandons with the home increases the struggle to survive outside of it, as if the parts of the body were
missing themselves. Moraga draws the comparison between being misread visually and verbally—for the multiracial subject can hardly communicate when she must struggle to remain afloat. Communication that
"holds no water" is not truly communication; the person whom Moraga
seeks to address appears deaf and dumb to her inability to reciprocate as
meaningfully as she desires. Nonetheless, the reader is induced to em-
pathize. Aloud, he/she utters "am pu ta tion" as the sounding out of silence surrounding multiracial erasure, while visualizing the "mutilated
body" as the multiracial one splintering against the grain of dominant discourse. Moraga speaks of "the shock," not of the "cut," but of the new
phenomenon of becoming whole through language; it is shocking that she
may produce a presence by speaking (out) where others maintain an absence. "You Call It, *Amputation*" best demonstrates the necessary connection of the multiracial body with the voice that has emerged from silence,
for the "tolerance" of *la conciencia* must be applied to the visual readings
of the body or "amputation" will continue.

Moraga portrays dimensions of the body that currently have fixed social readings—here, color and skin—as metamorphic in order to envision the body as too fluid to be contained by rigid classification. In the author's description of the psychological "coming-out" of the multiracial in
an embrace of *la conciencia*, the body reads as a measure of color against
the Whiteness she once accepted. In "For the Color of My Mother," her
mestiza body has

recently taken to blushing
    as if the blood wanted
    to swallow
        the flesh.

Bleed through
    guilt by association
    complicity to the crime. (71)

Blood is not the measure of shame and harbinger of doom as it has been
for the tragic mulatto/a, and neither is having "mixed blood" a crime; in-

stead, blood acts as the flood that washes away the crime of denial after exposing it. Moraga's imagining of blood brings it to life; no longer the passive determinant of fate, blood works as an agency of acknowledgment. Personified in its "want," blood means movement and change against the eternal ignominy of the tragic mulatto/a. The poem continues:

No, she had *never*
been ashamed of her face
　　not like this
　　grabbing her own two cheeks
　　her fingers pressed together
　　as if to hold between them
　　the thin depth of color. (71)

Despite Moraga's light-skinned appearance, color surfaces ("blushing") in her reconnection to the suppressed racial and cultural Otherness. The thing that granted her passing—the whiteness of her face—betrays Moraga as it succumbs to the truth. Of course, blushing does not occur on its own; only after a mental recognition does the face (whiteness) give in to a rush of blood (multiracial acknowledgment). The way blood is imagined in *Loving in the War Years*—sustenant, fertile, uncontainable—writes against the fetishization of the so-called "purity" of blood that pervades traditional American literature.

Moraga employs her reworking of blood in the symbolic rebirth of multiracial representation. In "For the Color of My Mother," Moraga's mother gives birth to her, the mestiza daughter:

at forty-five, her mouth
bleeding into her stomach
the hole gaping growing redder
deepening with my father's pallor
finally stitched shut from hip to breastbone
　　An inverted V
　　Vera
　　Elvira

I am a white girl gone brown to the blood color of my mother
speaking for her (60)

It is her bleeding that ultimately makes the multiracial real. The mouth simulating vagina, Moraga gives textual birth to herself in the connections of blood and native brownness, mother and mothertongue, birth and (re)production. Moraga is "a white girl gone brown to the blood color of my mother / speaking for her," a clear literary and existential evolution from her previously disconnected and "unintelligible" mother/ mother culture of "It's the Poverty." Here, "Elvira" is pronounced; compare this to the dejected and isolated tone of "It's the Poverty," in which the unsaid is mourned. Moraga assumes literary authority over writing and reading the interracial reproduction of the body as well as the textual production of the multiracial.

Finally, continuing to rewrite the body as the site of racial hybridity, Moraga employs a trope that Arteaga highlights in *Chicano Poetics* as wholly mestiza in nature. Having researched her roots, Moraga unearths phrases and symbolisms of Nahuatl, a language indigenous to the area of Mexico that her maternal family called home.[7] Because Nahuatl is, needless to say, almost never used in American literature, Moraga requires this linguistic return to produce the parts of herself that have been missing. While the linguistic devices of English are incapable of forging multiple ideas at once, Arteaga defines the *difrasismo* of Nahuatl as the "means of representing something in the coupling of two elements" (6). For example, the Nahuatl phrase *in atl in tepetl*, meaning "water and hill," signifies "city," while *in xóchitl in cuicatl*, "flower and song," is "poetry." Any two things in the world can come together to assume a larger, aggregate meaning. Arteaga outlines how *difrasismo* can be manipulated in more complex ways than the English poetic staples of metaphor and simile, "so that the world is conceived by this common and multifaceted trope" (7).

I argue that *Loving in the War Years* extends the Nahuatl *difrasismo* into the reader's mind as a model for reconceptualizing "race" as multiple modes of being. Against the traditional fetishization of blood as the measure of "racial purity," Moraga uses *difrasismo* to reconfigure blood as the fundamental human connection. As "la güera," Moraga's skin has worked as "a badge of difference" from darker-skinned mestizos/as, and yet, symbolic of their underscoring sameness, it also acts as "a porous boundary through which connections can be made" (150). The blood-color rushes to her pale face in *conciencia;* deep and pale, White and Other come together at the surface while knowledge spills forth as blood. Neither symbolically nor biologically does blood mean difference, but signifies something shared through the pliable agency of skin. From brown (home/ blood) to white (academia/skin) to brown *and* white (hybridized existence), Moraga juxtaposes the multiple possibilities of *blood* and *skin* to mean *hybridity*. The chaotic crossings of this example of *difrasismo*, as well as the Nahuatl framework from which it is drawn, deconstruct "race" as a measure of purity while successfully illustrating multiracial existence.

The textual hybridity of *Loving in the War Years*, a crossing of poetry, analysis, theory, and prose rendered in English and Spanish, and contextualized within Nahuatl dialect and customary knowledge, illustrates racial hybridity as a model for change that stands accessible to peoples socially divided. Arteaga calls Moraga's work "truly a heterotext," which "actively resists simple definition" and classification, much like the multiracial body (36). Its fluid structure bears the birth of the new American multiracial body and reconceives the reader (the once monoracially identified subject) as a "raced" being. *Loving in the War Years* establishes an important presence through Moraga's articulation of the once unsaid; that is, Moraga creates what dominant discursive thought fails to identify: a site of multiracial expression.

CONCLUSION

It is clear that multiracial people, because of their current outsider status to all races, may enhance society's understanding of intra- and intergroup relations and identity formation (Root, 231–236). We must continue, as Moraga and other authors have, in the project of displacing monoraciality as the norm. Only in understanding where we draw lines in the name of "race" can we overstep them as naturalized boundaries and can the multiracial free him/herself from the marginalized spaces in between. It is tragic that our racial categorizations map themselves onto history and literature and in doing so limit these ventures as points of departure for the mind. Because the writer's mind can oftentimes support complexities where society would break into chaos, and because she is experientially ready for the task, let us borrow the lens of the multiracial writer to celebrate the possibility of racial hybridity in us all.

Moraga introduces the mestiza as a model for the American multiracial, and *la conciencia de la mestiza* as the racially hybrid consciousness; the fate of the mestizo/a as a racial being in America will determine the fate of the American multiracial. Her concern is with the phenomenon of mestizo/a concession to single-race status in exchange for the potential benefits of a monolithic American racial identity—either for the social caliber of whiteness or the homogenized poverty of an "Hispanic" status. The decisive "choice" of identity assumption reproduces the either/or limitations of the traditional "Black/White" binary. She states in the

Introducción, "I write this book because we are losing ourselves to the gavacho[/whiteness]. I mourn my brother in this" (x).[8] For the "Hispanic" mestizo/a, racial identity on paper has been largely self-determinable, since the individual may elect the race "of Hispanic Origin." However, a single race must still be specified. Campaigning from the Association of Multi-Ethnic Americans and other groups has resulted in the relaxation, with the 2000 Census, of the strict "one box only" purity code. This Census Bureau decision to allow the individual to check "multiple boxes" is the first ever to permit racial inclusivity and hybridity. We must recognize this simple step as a major relaxation of one agent of compulsory monoraciality.

Against monoracialized discursivity, Moraga's mestiza not only "sustains contradictions, she turns the ambivalence into something else," that is, the multiracial may write out a new reading of American "race" (Anzaldúa, 379). If we turn to rely on the model of racial hybridity in order to resist hierarchical division that ensues from "racial purity," White ceases to occupy its absolute superiority because it would cease to corner racial privilege. Laurie Shrage contends that racial hybridity or

> multiracialism does not lead to an invention of new human kinds but calls our attention to areas of overlap between different categories. Being multiracial and multiethnic may challenge pernicious customs of differentially valuing human kinds in the following way: if a black person can be white and a white person can be black, then black and white persons cannot have different degrees of moral worth by virtue of being black or white. (292)

"Race," in other words, would reveal its socially constructed nature, while remaining available as a meaningful context or reference set for the transmission of cultural/ethnic ancestry, knowledge, and tradition. Racial "overlap" already exists, but in naming it we can learn to read "race" differently. We may step away from reading this essay and back into the social reality that the Black person next door can also be White, that many White people who are Black live a segregated life confined to the American ghettos, that "race" has reduced historical complexity to a series of stereotypes configured by a single measure of "purity."

The mestiza is then a model for the current monoracially identified American to "come out" as a multiracial. Being "Black," for example, according to *la conciencia* requires the personal and social acknowledgment of one's complete racial inheritance. To filter out such recognition from one's daily life ultimately sustains our historical tradition of "racial amnesia." Moraga is successful even if the reader whose own racial identification has not subsequently changed will, from now on, legitimize the racial hybridity of others. Arteaga writes that

> since the new consciousness is elected by choice and since the object of production is consciousness rather than the body, the *mestiza*'s subjectivity can be widely inclusive. It is not inherited from sexual intercourse like race but is taken on in response to the ambient forces of repression. (25)

From its birth, every time *la conciencia* is embraced, the multiracial emerges into social realness.

The multiracial author must exercise whatever she needs to in order to relay this consciousness. And I do not mean, just because it is Moraga's way, to present multilingualism as the premier means to multiracial expression. Not all of us come from homes contextualized by diversity of language or culture. However, references to and infusions of specific cultural knowledge and dialects, like the highly complex tropes and multifaceted consciousness of "Black English," reshape American academic writing enough to subvert the monoracializing tendencies (or Whitewashing) of dominant discourse. Moraga's autobiographical account demonstrates a resistance to academic expectations or "standards," which are, while claiming universal appeal, highly particular. In a similar spirit, this essay seeks to reflect and continue that resistance.

As witness to Moraga's textual existence, I confirm the reality that the whole time I grew up in social isolation, I was never really "alone." Others were out there, all of us marked by the particular phenomenon of compulsory monoraciality; and this common factor is the universal element of my writing. Unlike the tragic mulatta imprisoned by what has been written of her, I am the multiracial who writes herself. I learn from Moraga, a role model for multiracial authorship, that racial hybridity is the mode in which I must (for now) move. My voice, the literary manifestation of my multiraciality, is continuously at birth.

What am I? I am an American Southerner who is "mixed." This statement will be rejected; but I defend it as I defend my life, for my existence is at stake.

Notes

1. Paul R. Spickard contrasts this tribute to the American "Columbus Day," celebrating the accidental discovery by the Spanish of a New World to call their own.

2. Note that because the population of Spanish soldiery was small, it is unlikely that mestizos are a product of the wholesale rape of Native American women, historicized by postcolonial thinking as fact.

3. This is not to allege that Mexicans and "Latin Americans" do not suffer from their own historicized racial paradigms, no less problematic; however, in this particular comparison, "Latin Americans" have no monoracializing "rule" analogous to the *hypodescent* of American history.

4. "Chicano/a," meaning "Mexican-American" (as opposed to "Mexican"), has been embraced as signifying political unification in an act of self-naming; because my concern is racial hybridity, rather than questions of nationality, I prefer "mestizo/a" for this writing.

5. "Whites" have been de-Europeanized and assimilated into a generalized racial group just as "Blacks" have. See Frankenburg.

6. Refer to Giles for a historical creation of the *tragic mulatto* formula and its pattern throughout the media.

7. Nahuatl is spoken mainly in a region of Central Mexico and is a linguistic legacy of the Aztecs.

8. "Gavacho," like "el gringo," is a Mexican-Spanish signifier for "the White man" in the recognition of a White patriarchal, postcolonial context.

Works Cited

Alarçon, Norma. "The Theoretical Subjects of *This Bridge Called My Back* and Anglo-American Feminism." In *Making Face, Making Soul*, ed. Gloria Anzaldúa, pp. 356–366. San Francisco: Aunt Lute Books, 1990.

Alcoff, Linda. "*Mestiza* Identity." In *American Mixed Race: The Culture of Microdiversity*, ed. Naomi Zack, pp. 257–278. Lanham, Md.: Rowman & Littlefield, 1995.

Anzaldúa, Gloria. "*La conciencia de la mestiza:* Towards a New Consciousness." In *Making Face, Making Soul*, ed. Gloria Anzaldúa, pp. 377–389. San Francisco: Aunt Lute Books, 1990.

Arteaga, Alfred. *Chicano Poetics.* New York: Cambridge University Press, 1997.

Davis, F. James. "The Hawaiian Alternative to the One-Drop Rule." In *American Mixed Race: The Culture of Microdiversity*, ed. Naomi Zack, pp. 115–132. Lanham, Md.: Rowman & Littlefield, 1995.

Ferber, Abby L. "Exploring the Social Construction of Race." In *American Mixed Race: The Culture of Microdiversity*, ed. Naomi Zack, pp. 155–168. Lanham, Md.: Rowman & Littlefield, 1995.

Frankenburg, Ruth. *Displacing Whiteness.* Durham, N.C.: Duke University Press, 1997.

Giles, Freda Scott. "From Melodrama to the Movies." In *American Mixed Race: The Culture of Microdiversity*, ed. Naomi Zack, pp. 63–78. Lanham, Md.: Rowman & Littlefield, 1995.

Goldberg, David Theo. "Made in the USA." In *American Mixed Race: The Culture of Microdiversity*, ed. Naomi Zack, pp. 237–256. Lanham, Md.: Rowman & Littlefield, 1995.

Moraga, Cherríe. *Loving in the War Years.* Boston: South End Press, 1983.

Morrison, Toni. *Playing in the Dark: Whiteness and the Literary Imagination.* Cambridge, Mass.: Harvard University Press, 1992.

Nakashima, Cynthia L. "An Invisible Monster: The Creation and Denial of Mixed-Race People in America." In *Racially Mixed People in America*, ed. Maria P. P. Root, pp. 162–180. Newbury Park, Calif.: Sage, 1992.

Rich, Adrienne. "Readings of History." In *Snapshots of a Daughter-in-Law*, pp. 36–40. New York: Norton, 1967.

Root, Maria P. P. "Within, Between, and Beyond Race: From Shortcuts to Solutions." In *Racially Mixed People in America*, ed. Maria P. P. Root, pp. 3–11, 342–345. Newbury Park, Calif.: Sage, 1992.

Shrage, Laurie. "Ethnic Transgressions: Confessions of an Assimilated Jew." In *American Mixed Race: The Culture of Microdiversity*, ed. Naomi Zack, pp. 287–296. Lanham, Md.: Rowman & Littlefield, 1995.

Spaulding, Carol Roh. "The Go-Between People." In *American Mixed Race: The Culture of Microdiversity*, ed. Naomi Zack, pp. 97–114. Lanham, Md.: Rowman & Littlefield, 1995.

Spickard, Paul R. "The Illogic of American Racial Categories." In *Racially Mixed People in America*, ed. Maria P. P. Root, pp. 12–23. Newbury Park, Calif.: Sage, 1992.

United States Census Bureau. United States Department of Commerce. *http://www.census.gov/prod/2001pubs/mso1-bp.pdf*

Yarbro-Bejarano, Yvonne. "De-constructing the Lesbian Body: Cherríe Moraga's *Loving in the War Years.*" In *Chicana Lesbians*, ed. Carla Trujillo, pp. 143–155. Berkeley, Calif.: Third Woman Press, 1991.

Zack, Naomi. "Introduction." In *American Mixed Race: The Culture of Microdiversity*, ed. Naomi Zack, pp. ix–xi, 297–308. Lanham, Md.: Rowman & Littlefield, 1995.

ABOUT THE CONTRIBUTORS

Evelyn Alsultany is a Ph.D. Candidate in the Program in Modern Thought and Literature at Stanford University. In addition to multiethnic identity, her work focuses on Arab-American Studies and Latino Studies.

Adrian Carton lives in Australia, where he teaches history at the University of Sydney. His mother was born in Britain of English and Dutch origin. His father was born in India of Bengali, Burmese, and French origin.

Carole DeSouza graduated summa cum laude from Duke University with a B.A. in English and Women's Studies in May 2001. She will be attending law school in New England Fall 2003. She was born abroad to an East Indian father and a French mother.

Stefanie Dunning is Assistant Professor of English at Miami University, Ohio. She received her Ph.D. from the University of California, Riverside, in 2001 and her B.A. from Spelman College in 1995. Her work, which often examines questions of miscegenation, mixed-race identity, and race theory, has been published in *Black Renaissance/Renaissance Noire*, *MELUS: Journal of the Society of Multiethnic Literature in the United States*, and *The Stanford Black Arts Quarterly*. She is an activist and a writer based in Cincinnati, Ohio.

Richard Guzman is Professor of English and chair of the department at North Central College in Naperville, Illinois, where he also directs the Master of Arts in Liberal Studies program. He is also president of the Association of Graduate Liberal Studies Programs. A musician and performance poet, he has published music, poetry, and essays; his latest book (edited with David Starkey) is *Smokestacks and Skyscrapers: An Anthology of Chicago Writing*. A speaker and consultant on diversity issues for companies and schools, he has been honored by the State of Illinois for helping to bring a comprehensive diversity plan to one of the state's largest school districts.

Cathy Irwin received her Ph.D. in English from the University of Southern California. She is a writer and teaches at Scripps College in Claremont, California.

SanSan Kwan received her Ph.D. in Performance Studies at New York University. She is an Assistant Professor of Theatre and Dance at California State University, Los Angeles. She is currently working on a book manuscript titled *Choreographing Chineseness: Global Cities and the Performance of Ethnicity*.

Sean Metzger is a Ph.D. Candidate in Theatre at the University of California, Davis. His publications include articles in *Quarterly Review of Film and Video*, *The Journal of Homosexuality*, and *Zorro and Co*. He currently works as adjunct faculty at several universities in Los Angeles, where he is also an educational consultant.

Orathai Northern is a Ph.D. Candidate in the Department of English at the University of California, Riverside. She is currently working on her dissertation, which examines the cultural and transnational politics around African American hair.

Raquel Scherr Salgado holds a Ph.D. in Comparative Literature from the University of California, Berkeley, and currently teaches in the English Department at the University of California, Davis. Her publications include *Face Value: The Politics of Beauty*, *West of the West: Imagining California*, and the translation into Spanish of *Our Bodies, Ourselves*. She is presently working on a book of personal essays that draw on her mixed-race experience during the 1950s and '60s as the daughter of Max Scherr, the radical Jewish publisher, and Juana Estela Salgado, a Mexican medical student, herself a first-generation mestiza of Indian, Dutch, Spanish, and French ancestry.

Kenneth Speirs is an Assistant Professor of English at Kingsborough Community College, Brooklyn. He is currently working on a book about autobiography and the American West.

Alice White's writing has appeared in the academic journals *The Velvet Light Trap* and *Link: A Critical Journal on the Arts in Baltimore and the World*, and in the anthologies *Generation Q* and *Seeds from a Silent Tree*. She is also an award-winning film- and videomaker whose work has screened widely in the United States and Europe. She is an American-born adoptee of Korean and German-Irish origin.

Naomi Zack (Ph.D., Columbia University) is Professor of Philosophy at the University of Oregon, Eugene. Her most recent book is *Philosophy of Science and Race*, and she is also the author of *Race and Mixed Race, Bachelors of Science: Seventeenth Century Identity, Then and Now*, and a textbook, *Thinking about Race*. She is the editor of *Women of Color and Philosophy, American Mixed Race: The Culture of Microdiversity*, and other anthologies, and has written articles on race, racism, mixed race, gender, and seventeenth-century philosophy. Zack's current projects are an existentialist theory of mind and an examination of race and immigration in the United States.